KNOWLEDGE IS POWER!

For all my colleagues
in DACE

Tom
++

Tom Steele

KNOWLEDGE IS POWER!

The Rise and Fall of European Popular Educational Movements, 1848–1939

PETER LANG

Oxford · Bern · Berlin · Bruxelles · Frankfurt am Main · New York · Wien

Bibliographic information published by Die Deutsche Bibliothek
Die Deutsche Bibliothek lists this publication in the Deutsche
Nationalbibliografie; detailed bibliographic data is available on
the Internet at ‹http://dnb.ddb.de›.

British Library and Library of Congress Cataloguing-in-Publication Data:
A catalogue record for this book is available from *The British Library,*
Great Britain, and from *The Library of Congress,* USA

ISBN 978-3-03910-563-2

© Peter Lang AG, International Academic Publishers, Bern 2007
Hochfeldstrasse 32, Postfach 746, CH-3000 Bern 9, Switzerland
info@peterlang.com, www.peterlang.com, www.peterlang.net

Printed in Germany

for

Sylvia, Joe and Elaine

Contents

Preface and Acknowledgements   ix

Chapter 1
Introduction: Popular Education and the Emergence of
    the Public Sphere   1

Chapter 2
The Bourgeois Public Sphere: Science and the Citizen   19

Chapter 3
Education from Below: the Plebeian and Proletarian Spheres   41

Chapter 4
Nicolae Grundtvig: The Danish Folk High School Movement
    and the Struggle for University Extension   67

Chapter 5
Spain and Italy: Rationalist Education and Popular Universities   93

Chapter 6
French Radical Freemasonry, Comtean Positivism and the
    Rise of the *Universités Populaires*   125

Chapter 7
German and Austrian Popular Education: Science,
    Marxism and the *Neue Richtung*   149

Chapter 8
The Nordic People's Enlightenment in Sweden,
    Finland and Norway   185

Chapter 9
Belgium and Holland: Anglo-Saxon Imperatives, the
    Rise and Fall of University Extension   209

Chapter 10
Central and Eastern Europe: New Nations, New Humanity   · 241

Chapter 11
Conclusion: The Fall and Rise of Popular
    Education Movements   279

Bibliography   293
Index   305

Preface and Acknowledgements

This study is indebted to the European Society for Research into the Education of Adults (ESREA), whose annual research seminars in Cross Cultural Adult Education from the early 1990s provided many of the papers from which much of the understanding found in this book is drawn. Colleagues who attended these seminars have been a constant source of inspiration and support. Particular thanks are due to Doctor Barry J. Hake of Leiden University who was the principal organiser of the seminars, Professor Richard Taylor now of the University of Cambridge for his unfailing support and positive criticism, and Professor Stuart Marriott, formerly of the University of Leeds, whose painstaking tracking-down and translation of sources and their elegant interpretation has offered a scholarly model which, sadly, I have inadequately followed. Professor Marriott's notes on Martin Keilhacker's (1929) *Die Universitats-Ausdehnung-Promblem*, for example, were invaluable. Amongst other colleagues from the ESREA seminars I should like to thank Professor Bastiaan van Gent of Leiden University, for his good humour and broad sympathies, Doctor Christian Stifter of the Vienna Folk High School Archives for his insights into the Viennese *Volksheims*, Doctor Kari Kantalsami of Helsinki University for his advanced theoretical understanding of Finnish popular education, Doctor Pere Solá and Doctor Ramon Flecha of Barcelona University for their contributions to the study of Catalonian radicalism and Professor Alejandro Tiana-Ferrer of Salamanca University for his careful interpretation of the Spanish popular universities. I should also like to thank Doctor Xandra de Vroom of Leiden University for her work on the *Nut* and the Dutch radical press and Doctor Michel Schärer of Geneva for conversations on Swiss popular education. Professor Wolfgang Seitter of Frankfurt University offered important insights into the German-Spanish connection, especially Krausism and Johann Dvorak of Vienna gave significant shape to the Modernist impulse in Viennese popular education. I am especially grateful to Professor Jindra Kulich of Vancouver for his written advice and for generously sending me copies of his invaluable research on Eastern European popular education.

Former colleagues at the University of Leeds have read and commented on earlier papers I have given including, Doctor Malcolm Chase, Jill Liddington, Doctor Janet Coles and Professor Tony Jowett now of Northern College. At the University of Glasgow a similar invaluable service has been contributed by Professor Mike Gonzalez, Liam Kane, Robert Turner, Keith Hammond and Professor David Jasper. Very special thanks are due to Professor Jean Barr, whose friendship and intellectual insight have been a constant support. At the University of Edinburgh I am very grateful to Ian Martin, Mae Shaw, Doctor Jim Crowther, Professor Lynn Tett and Colin Kirkwood for many rambling conversations about these issues. I am particularly grateful to my colleague Professor Reverend Jack Dyce of the Scottish United Reformed Church for his work on Nicolae Grundtvig and the Danish Folk High Schools. Other colleagues who have contributed important insights and friendly criticism include Martin Ryle at the University of Sussex, and Professor Kate Soper of North London University, Professor Andrew Prescott of the Centre for the Study of Freemasonry at the University of Sheffield, my old friends Professor Roger Fieldhouse and Rosanne Benn of Exeter University and Doctor Ahmed Gurnah, who cast many a sceptical eye. I should also like to thank Professor Peter Jarvis of Surrey University, Professor John Field of Stirling University and Professor Michael Peters for their encouragement and good counsel over the years. The loving support of my wife Lynne has been unfailing and (despite protestations to the contrary) her practical criticism has frequently made me rethink my positions on many matters.

Previous versions of Chapter 6 have appeared in the *International Journal of Lifelong Education*, Vol.21, No.5 (September–October 2002) and *Ethics, Ideals and Ideologies in the History of Adult Education* (2002) eds Balazs Nemeth and Franz Poggeler, Frankfurt: Peter Lang. Chapter 2 is based on Scientific Societies, European popular education and the public sphere' in *Adult Education and Globalisation: Past and Present* (2004) eds. Barry Hake, Bastiaan van Gent and Jozsef Katus, Frankfurt: Peter Lang. Chapter 11 draws on material published in other collections, some co-authored by Richard Taylor including 'Citizenship and Global Chaos – education, culture and revolution' in *Active Citizenship and Multiple Identities in Europe* (2005) eds Danny Wildemeersch, Veerle Stroobants and Michael Bron Jr., Frankfurt: Peter Lang, and from Chapter 3 of Richard Taylor, Jean Barr and Tom Steele (2002) *For a Radical Higher Education, After Postmodernism*, Buckingham: Open University/ SRHE Press. I am very grateful for the permission of editors and co-authors to use them.

I am afraid this study is by no means comprehensive, lacking as it does any extended commentary on Portuguese or Swiss activities or indeed any consideration of the rise of Zionism in Europe as embracing a vital educational movement, which I suspect await later scholars. I have tried to indicate what I see as the main trends in European popular educational movements from the revolutions of 1848 to the outbreak of the Second World War by which time it was clear that the Enlightenment and Romantic impulses that ignited the movements had been snuffed out by totalitarianisms of the left and right. I do not take the now familiar view that such outcomes were the inevitable consequence of the Enlightenment period and I have drawn on the work of Jurgen Habermas in trying to show how, on the contrary, the popular embrace of much enlightenment thought has informed the politics of a just, democratic and tolerant society rather than its opposite. It seems to me that the popular aspirations of most of the movements described here have been for a qualitatively better way of life, an ending of traditional class privileges, new forms of sociability and fellowship and clear-eyed understanding of social matters, free of clerical dogma and untested authority. Where nationalism has been an inspiration, it was rarely allowed to be of the blood-and-soil type pursued by the political right and had primarily been a vehicle for liberation from oppressive imperialisms and for inclusive democratic reform. It is indicative that when the regimes of Nazism and fascism took power in the 1920s and 1930s they were swift to take over and close down popular educational movements, while, in the Communist bloc, folk high schools were just as quickly incorporated into the party political propaganda machine and deprived of their self-determination. The resurgence of autonomous social movements, in which popular education plays a signal role in the later part of the twentieth century, particularly in Latin America, has demonstrated clearly that although the methods might change, the impulse for critical understanding and public enlightenment in a still savagely discriminatory system is as powerful as ever.

Chapter 1
Introduction: Popular Education and the Emergence of the Public Sphere

Wissen ist Macht – Macht ist Wissen
Willhelm Leibknecht (1872)

This study is an attempt to map the theory and practice of popular (adult) education in Europe during the long nineteenth century, beginning with the post-Enlightenment period and ending with the socialist formations of the early twentieth century. Starting with the scientific societies of the late-eighteenth centuries, and continuing through the emergence of Danish folk high schools, French *universités populaires*, Austrian *Volksheims*, German *Arbeiterkreisen*, Swedish study circles, the adoption of English university extension, women's campaigns for Higher Education, Social Democratic Party education and independent workers' education, this study describes the major popular educational formations of the modern period. The study concludes with reflections on the radical popular educational tradition and the new social movements.

Popular education belongs to the public sphere, indeed was a crucial vehicle for its formation. But the public sphere was in reality an intersecting series of spheres each with their own public, but with at least two predominant – the bourgeois and then the plebeian or proletarian spheres. The idea of a bourgeois public sphere that was historically distinct from the medieval and classical spheres was what occupied Habermas (1989) in *The Structural Transformation of the Public Sphere*. The era of capitalist economic production and the dominance of the middle class is characterised by a number of features of which the most notable are the formation of a separate political state, which was distinct from the monarchy and the aristocratic governing class and, secondly, its underpinning by a market economy unhindered by feudal obligations. Habermas drew on an original formulation by Immanuel Kant which emphasised that the bourgeois public sphere both depends on the existence of a market economy rather than a feudal medieval economy, on the one hand, and on the state which is relatively free from monarchic and religious absolutism, on the other. But both the state and the market economy also rival the public sphere, which strains to be both inclusive and democratic, because both the state and the market economy are neither wholly democratic nor universally inclusive.

A key feature of Habermas's bourgeois public sphere is that it is constituted of private individuals and that these individuals, by virtue of the emergent empiricist and rational philosophies of the Enlightenment period, assume a vulnerable but defensible private realm. Even the English philosopher Thomas Hobbes, who believed that the state should have sufficient power to arbitrate, roughly if necessary, between contesting individuals, saw it as axiomatic that individual freedom should and did exist as a right. The public sphere was thus bourgeois not by virtue of an exclusive class composition, since aristocrats frequently played leading roles in constituting it, but because 'society' was itself bourgeois and this created a distinct form of public interaction.

To be clear, this public sphere owed nothing to the feudal system that preceded it in which the estates had no separate existence from the king and his court. It came about initially through the development of salon life and the sociability that accompanied it. It also depended on the new spaces of sociability that opened up such as coffee and tea houses, where for the most part the newly emergent male professions met to make deals, discuss the news and debate politics and poetics. These spaces differed from but overlapped with the older forms of public square and tavern, which increasingly became the public spaces of the plebeian and later proletarian classes (which is the subject of Chapter 3).

Central to Habermas's account of the bourgeois public sphere is the notion of 'civil society'. While civil society could not have been brought into being without the capitalist market economy, the institutions of sociability and forms of communication that characterised it developed relatively autonomously from the economy itself. Long distance trade required news of markets which was often received in the forms of letters and 'accounts' but inevitably market trends were not the only news. As Benedict Anderson (1989) has demonstrated, this communication engendered a need for print capitalism and widespread literacy that in their turn both standardised languages and fostered the imagined linguistic communities known as 'nations'. Literacy in turn required a generalised education in the vernacular rather than clerical tuition in classical languages and hence education itself was forced to become a more systematic and widespread business.

The bourgeois public sphere was defined by the popular struggle against absolutism for constitutional monarchy and freedom of thought, as a new area for social communication. According to Eley (1992) Habermas drew to an extent on the work of the British cultural critic and adult educator, Raymond Williams, in looking at the shifts in meaning from the world of 'letters' to the structure of society through linguistic analysis. He notes for example, the emergence of the concept of a 'nation' accompanies that of the public sphere and the contiguous sense that 'nation' means a public for a 'national' discourse. Within this new space *voluntary organisations* such as literary societies, scientific societies and, as Eric Hobsbawm has noted, freemasonry are the main indicators of progress. Often crystallised into local clubs with names like 'Harmony' which are used by exclusive elites, these new autonomous associations, which are not to be confused with older forms of corporate organizations, become fundamental to *bürgerliche Gesellschaft*. In creating this new communicative space the emergent bourgeois class tries to establish itself as a universal hegemonic class, for which the lower classes become subordinated objects of philanthropic support and cultural edification.

This dynamic new civil society was both more inclusive and more generally social than previous forms of social life but also, although increasingly 'public' nevertheless excluded the large majority of the population. In short it was composed largely of male professionals and entrepreneurs. Those excluded from the public sphere included women, children, working people and in many countries, such as Scotland, non-Protestants. Significantly, the professional groups that came to constitute this public became both self-conscious of their elite role and critical of public authority. They employed a newly developed critical discourse of rationality and universality to defend the public sphere from the incursions of the state and so to ensure a realm of freedom for the private propertied individual to conduct his trade, to make his leisure-time free and to educate his family – although of course paradoxically it required the state to guarantee those freedoms, to reform the feudal laws which were preventing free trade and especially, to regulate labour.

However this *reasonability* was to have much wider con-sequences because, while the initial targets of this discourse were the follies of authority and the doctrinal obfuscation of the clergy, those same critical tools could and would be turned on themselves. The rational bourgeoisie both needed and called upon the support of the 'the masses' to rid themselves of arbitrary and superstitious authority, while limiting their access to the public sphere. But the more intelligent of the masses were themselves discovering that the universal discourse of freedom and rights should equally apply to them and, as a consequence, were decreasingly content to allow their interests to be subordinated to those of the bourgeoisie.

Thus, the deployment of rational critical discourse which defended the public sphere of the bourgeoisie, itself became the tool of a wider politics. As Calhoun notes:

> The Bourgeois public sphere institutionalised, according to Habermas, not just a set of interests and an opposition between state and civil society but a practice of rational-critical discourse on political matters [...] The very idea of the public was based on the notion of a general interest sufficiently basic that discourse about it need not be distorted by particular interests (at least in principle) and could be a matter of rational approach to an objective order (Calhoun, 1992: 9).

Hence the public sphere that opened out in the eighteenth century under the impulse of the property owning bourgeois to create a sphere of freedom for his business, family and religion, almost immediately outstripped this limited aim. The public sphere was immediately challenged by those who were excluded and wished for a much more generous conception of the 'public'. Thus the bourgeois public sphere was *ab initio* a contested space to which women, workers and other religious dissenters demanded access. As a consequence Negt and

4

Kluge (1993) argue, other countervailing spaces were created, the most significant of which was the 'plebeian' or alternatively 'proletarian' sphere.

In the Kantian construction of the bourgeois public sphere that Habermas drew on Negt and Kluge insist that the reality never matched the theoretical abstraction. According to them, the actual experience of the entrepreneur and manufacturer was too parochial and localised to become universal. The entrepreneur could not of course identify his own private interest with the common good as that would have been catastrophic for trade. He therefore relied on a whole phalanx of middle men and professional support to generate the general understanding that would complement his own partial knowledge of the world and its ways. However this *collective* effort required for world historical understanding was implicitly a threat to his own *privatised* existence since it always risked subverting the ethic of possessive individualism upon which his identity relied (Negt and Kluge, 1993: 12).

What too of the role of women? With the proud exceptions of Poland and Czechoslovakia and possibly France, women are for the most part excluded from or marginalised by most of the movements surveyed in this study. But Mill's pamphlet on the *Emancipation of Women* and Emile Littré's promotion of feminism in France, were widely influential. Harriet Martineau's translation and popularisation of Comte's positivist sociology and women's participation in university extension and the self-education of suffragism were key to opening of the pubic sphere to women.

Education and Modernity

Public education was essential to opening up the public sphere. As a systematic intervention into the life of ordinary people and as a tool of social regeneration and reform it is a corner stone of modernity, dating from the period of the seventeenth-century Scientific Revolution and eighteenth-century Enlightenment. Educational reform and the radical revaluation of sources of knowledge or epistemology really go hand in hand. The challenge made both to accepted canons of knowledge and to the power of the knowledge holders – the Church especially – accompany popular demands for systematic education and 'really useful knowledge'.

The first signs of what came to be called philosophical empiricism, or the belief that the most effective route to understanding came not from rote learning the works of traditional authorities but from first hand experiential investigation, dates from the fifteenth century. Bruno, Vico, Galileo and other embryonic scientific speculators were prepared to challenge the authority of church doctrine and occasionally paid for this with extraction of their lives or liberty. The advancement of science is classically linked to the Protestant spirit and capitalist entrepreneurialism of the Northern European states. In Britain, William Gilbert's experimentation with magnetism (*De Magnete*) to devise a form of compass for merchant ships set new standards for scientific investigation. Francis Bacon followed closely with a major treatise on what came to be seen as the foundation of philosophical empiricism, *The Advancement of Learning* (1605) and his later work *De Augmentis Scientiarum* (1623) attempted a systematic classification of all branches of knowledge. Bacon dismissed the abstract disputation of the scholastic theologians, then the dominant intellectual class, as self-serving obscurantism. Instead he proposed that knowledge was only certainly gained by a gradual ascent from the observable particularities of an event or substance to the general level of theory, otherwise known as the *inductive* method. The culmination of Bacon's project was *New Atlantis* (1627) a consciously utopian work, which described and advocated a community whose progress depended on its ability to conduct collective scientific research. Bacon was thus one of the first moderns to actively promote the view that human progress depended on the scientific approach to human affairs.

Bacon 's belief that the advancement of knowledge depended on its application and that learning must be put to social use fuelled the intellectual and political ferment then about to engulf Britain in civil war. Indeed as Hill has shown the intellectual legitimisation Bacon gave to challenge orthodox opinion and vested authority was a major

6

source of succour to the Parliamentarians in their struggle for the rule of law against the arbitrary authority of the crown (Hill, 1965: 109–10). From the earliest days, therefore, the movement for scientific inquiry and popular knowledge was to have politically radical implications and application.

Bacon's method and spirited writing had a major impact on the philosophers of the Scottish Enlightenment. Simon claims that 'what gave Scottish intellectual life its particular vigour was this interest in contemporary changes, which extended over the widest field of social activity and learning' (Simon, 1960: 31). The Scottish Enlightenment has often been reduced to a footnote in the history of the rise of British Empiricism and Utilitarianism. However, it is increasingly realised that it affected the whole tenor of the European Enlightenment from Immanuel Kant, a great admirer of Francis Hutcheson to Auguste Comte, the founder of classical sociology (Herman, 2003).

The primary context for the rise of the Scottish Enlightenment was the public sphere growing around the ancient Scottish universities, particularly those of Glasgow and Edinburgh, where Francis Hutcheson and then his pupil Adam Smith held chairs in Moral Philosophy, although, because of his religious dissent and doctrinal scepticism, the most celebrated philosopher of his time, David Hume, was denied chairs in both institutions. Unlike their prosperous English counterparts, Oxford and Cambridge, Scottish universities were relatively impoverished and not subject to the handsome collegial endowments made by the English aristocracy. They had therefore to listen more closely to the needs of the growing cities in which they were established. Glasgow, especially, was emerging as a great centre of trade with America for which finance, ships and of course slaves were urgently needed and from which tobacco and cotton was imported. The universities themselves were swift to apply the insight of 'natural philosophy' as science was then called to industrial technology. As early as 1727 the University of Glasgow opened the doors of its natural philosophy classes to artisans who might benefit from scientific instruction, one of the first examples of popular scientific education practised by a university anywhere. One beneficiary of this open practice included the university's leading technician, James Watt, the inventor of the steam engine.

7

Simon notes that Scotland's chief contribution to knowledge was made by those who were influenced and stimulated by the radical industrial and social changes, under the stern gaze of John Knox's Presbyterianism. They turned to systematic historical investigation, which in turn laid the basis for a new science of society. The most notable of this generation of 'social scientists' at Glasgow was of course Adam Smith, who became Professor of Moral Philosophy in 1752. His lectures on natural theology, ethics, jurisprudence and political economy provided the kernel of his internationally celebrated work *The Wealth of Nations* (1776), published in the same year as the American Declaration of Independence and treated with critical reverence both by Marx in *Capital* and much later by Hayek and his generation of neo-liberal economists.

However, it was Smith's predecessor, Francis Hutcheson (1694–1746), who most significantly altered the intellectual climate in Glasgow and prepared the way for this generation of social scientists. His introduction of the ideas of Bacon, Locke and Newton to his Scottish students stressed the role played by experience in acquiring moral attitudes. Morality, he insisted was not divinely inspired but arose from perceptions and subsequent reflection on them. It was Hutcheson who introduced the notion that the philosophical concept of virtue should be 'equivalent to that which pleases' (Bowen, 1981: 150). Hutcheson was one of the first therefore to attempt a rigorous application of Bacon's sense-empiricist argument to human conduct and morality and his work laid a systematic basis for a thoroughly secular examination of morality. It was Hutcheson who invented the phrase 'the greatest happiness of the greatest number' which became the catchcry for a new school of philosophy known as Utilitarianism. This strand of thought was then developed by David Hume (1711–1776), Jeremy Bentham (1748–1832), James Mill (1773–1836) and his son John Stuart Mill (1806–1873) with various inflections on the main theme. As Bowen notes, the educational consequences of such a revolution in thought were enormous in that philosophical bases were being established for an entirely new understanding of society and ideology of education:

In arguing that sense experience is the basis of humanity, that morals are dependent upon interpretation of experience, that virtue is that which pleases, and that socially responsible pleasure issues from the greatest good of the greatest number, Hutcheson was undermining the whole of seventeenth century educational thought and practice (Bowen, 1981: 150).

Following Hutcheson, Hume's major works, *Treatise on Human Nature* (1739) and *An Enquiry Concerning Human Understanding* (1748) stressed the role of sensation and experience as the sole source of ideas and hence the construction of the human mind. This emphasis turned philosophical thought away from deductive speculation towards psychological observations and inductive reasoning. Crucially, Hume shifted the emphasis of speculation on the human condition away from theology towards social history, sociology and politics. Education, as Bowen notes, then 'entered the realm of the socially controllable' (Bowen, 1981: 151). The impact of this epochal shift was registered most strongly in the social thought of post-revolutionary France where, arguably, the creation by Saint Simon and August Comte in the post revolutionary period of forms of positivist thought bent on reforming society under the leadership of scientific investigation and methods was a signal inspiration for radical popular education in the century to come. However, British liberal thought and practice in the late-nineteenth century also had a major impact when the idea of 'university extension' inspired European intellectuals to extend the benefits of university study to a wider audience.

This study, then, attempts to chart the ways in which popular educational movements became widespread over Europe in the second half of the nineteenth and early twentieth centuries by concentrating on developments in territorial regions and demonstrating the cross cultural connections. It tries to show the importance played by popular education in the rise of national democratic movements, workers' movements and to an extent women's emancipation. The new forms of national identity and the contest for political representation take place in the space of educational enlightenment and although by World War Two at the end of our period, popular educational forms frequently fell victim to totalitarian regimes, their heritage was crucial to the restoration of democratic governments and aspirations of ordinary people once those forces had been defeated.

Outline and Argument

This introduction has introduced Habermas's fruitful concept of the bourgeois public sphere and considered some of its limitations. In Chapter 2 the study focuses on the bourgeois public sphere and the expansion of science and citizenship. I argue that public education is an essential element in defining this sphere and describe the spread of European associations for popularising science in the post-Enlightenment period, in the light of Baconian empiricism and Cartesian rationalism. The correspondence of the growth of scientific understanding and programmes of social reform in popular education are exemplified throughout Europe, where the role of speculative freemasonry in promoting scientific study especially in Catholic countries emerges as a key element in the promotion of popular education.

While scientific popularisation, initially, is very much confined to bourgeois and aristocratic elites, Chapter 3 examines what is happening lower down the social scale and charts the growth of the emerging plebeian and proletarian spheres. This chapter outlines the origins of these public spaces beginning with the English Civil War of the mid-seventeenth century and the cycles of English Radicalism through Paineite republicanism, Owenite co-operation and 'Knowledge' Chartism. It then considers European developments in the wake of the French Revolution through to the beginning of the organised labour movement and the movement for political and independent working class education.

A clear exception to the urban industrial base of much popular education with its scientific and proletarian emphases was the small farmer communities that dominated most of Europe. The needs of this otherwise alienated class were met most effectively by the folk high schools envisaged by the Lutheran pastor Nicolae Grundtvig in Denmark. In Chapter 4 we therefore examine the Danish Folk High School Movement and the consequent struggle for university extension in the cities. The model of a residential education for groups of small farmers devised by Grundtvig and his disciple Christian Kold became widely influential across northern and Eastern Europe (and subsequently in India and Africa in the post-colonial period). This chapter considers the origins of this formation in the period of Danish crisis of national identity in the mid-nineteenth century under the pressure of German expansionism and the function of education in creating a modern rural economy.

In the Catholic south of Europe a different struggle was taking place and in Chapter 5 we examine the Rationalist movements and Popular Universities in Spain and Italy. While the growth of liberal, secularist and anti-clerical politics dated from the French Revolution earlier in the century, the experience of catastrophic defeat and occupation by Napoleonic forces in Spain had deeply injured national pride, even that of progressive liberals. After the Bourbon Restoration a period of inwardness and anti-European sentiment sealed Spain off from modernising influences. Eventually, however, Spanish intellectuals travelled to European, though emphatically not French intellectual centres, and began to rediscover the European Enlightenment. Educational movements were a prime attempt by the liberal middle class to modernise Spain but they met intransigent resistance from the Catholic Church. The phenomenon of Krausism, a liberal Hegelian doctrine of moderate reform, inspired a generation of anti-clerical intellectuals and Krausists, often through masonic networks, embodied the democratic revolution of 1868 and the 1874 Spanish Republic, in which republican reformers determinedly set out to Europeanise Spanish thought and institutions. The *Ateneo* and other meeting places between intellectuals and workers fed into Spanish Republicanism and established common ground. However they were not always popular with anarchists, especially in Catalonia who attempted through the Rational Schools to create an independent working class educational order. The great educational reformer, Francisco Ferrer, drew on these sources as well as European progressive educational theory for his widely influential Modern School but was eventually tried and executed for subversion. In Italy similar masonic networks were widely held to be responsible for the *Risorgimento* and the popular universities but they too did not inspire the more militant working class in the north many of whom turned instead to revolutionary socialism.

In Chapter 6 the study considers French radical freemasonry, Comtean Positivism and the rise of the *universités populaires*. One of the main, yet underreported, formations of popular education in Catholic countries was anticlerical freemasonry, which Hobsbawm describes as the true middle class International, and from Voltaire to Comte and Popper carried the ideals of Enlightenment science into the popular arena in opposition to the Church and the State. This chapter concentrates on one of the most effective of the masonic educational associations, the *Ligue de l'Enseignement* and its embrace of Comtean positivism as a vehicle for social science and political 'third way' reform. From their origins in France during the Dreyfus affair, the *universités populaires* also erupted in a radical wave across Catholic southern Europe, but just as quickly disappeared.

The rise of popular education in Germany in the mid-nineteenth century corresponded with one of the most dramatic and crisis ridden periods in the history of that or any country and Chapter 7 contrasts German and Austrian popular educational movements looking closely at the role played by Marxism, science and the *Neue Richtung*. The elitist German universities had little interest in popular education and liberal intellectuals struggled to gain a hearing for extending the benefits of higher learning beyond their walls. By the latter half of the nineteenth century this academic isolation was becoming a severe handicap to the ideals of equality and social justice nurtured by the liberal elements of civil society. Nevertheless local initiatives did bear fruit in the shape of reading societies and libraries through which popularisation of broadly scientific themes took place often again through masonic inspired networks. Some university intellectuals like Rein and Natorp managed to create a form of university extension on roughly English lines but despite some successes were frustrated by the reluctance of the universities to back them formally.

The German concept of *Bildung* meant education in the broad sense of cultivation or 'self-development' based on the individuality of 'the soul', described by Simmel as 'every kind of learning, virtuosity, refinement in man', but the very nobility of this enterprise appeared to exclude those from the lower orders. In response, another source of popular education was the workers' educational societies (*Arbeiterbildungsvereine*) in the first half of the nineteenth century that also sought emancipation through access to the scientific knowledge from which they felt excluded. Towards the end of the century, the formation of workers' and socialist parties in Germany created for the first time a 'pure' proletarian public sphere where popular education attempted to serve the interests of the workers' movement 'untainted' by bourgeois ideology – despite the intensive presence of bourgeois radical intellectuals. We consider this process and focus on the educational activities of the most highly developed of the workers' parties, the German SPD. It considers how far the Marxism of the period was capable of allowing independent thought and follows various critiques, through the Workers' Internationals and the struggle between Marxism and anarchism for the workers' movements. In yet another response, alarmed by the intensification of class struggle in the workers' organisations, a new generation of German liberal intellectuals attempted to create a more intensive form of popular education harnessed to what they called the *Neue Richtung* or New Direction.

In contrast to its close neighbour, turn of the century Vienna was one of the most creative sites of popular adult education in Europe, centring on the construction of a number of *Volksheims*, or specifically adult educational centres where, in an ideology of 'scientific neutrality', both science and the arts were taught to a very high level, even higher at times than that of the University itself. The development of this radical culture in the heart of the old Habsburg Empire was reflected in the positivism of its philosophy and in what became known as Austro-Marxism. Many SPD intellectuals saw in the *Volksheims*, especially in that of the Ottäkring, the crucible for developing the ideal socialist societies, until the *Anschluss* when they were imprisoned or forced into exile. We consider how such an intense intellectual and creative activity came to have such important popular educational resonance.

The Nordic countries by contrast have an enviable record of democratic participation, which has been maintained through gaining universal suffrage early and the rights of mass mobilization for protests and demonstration, although each of the four countries, Denmark, Sweden, Norway and Finland, differ in their historical paths taken to these rights. Chapter 8 then studies the Nordic People's Enlightenment especially in Sweden, Finland and Norway. Located in the northernmost part of Europe the Nordic countries were never subjected to the word of Rome and, following Lutheran principles, created nationally distinctive cultural institutions. Not surprisingly all the Nordic countries developed some version of the Grundtvigian folk high schools, although largely free of the atmosphere of nationalist religiosity that Kold had instilled. But perhaps their most important contribution to popular education was the 'study circle' which first emerged in Sweden and was developed initially by the masonic-like Good Templars movement in 1894. Both the folk high schools and the study circle organizations provided for the free and voluntary study of human, social, scientific and cultural studies and activities in order to strengthen democracy, community and offer specialist knowledge for adults beyond the ordinary schooling system. Sweden also developed a strong university extension movement, which, as in England, appealed mostly to the lower middle classes and especially school teachers.

In Finland the situation was somewhat more complex as popular education was initially inspired by intense nationalistic feeling against first Swedish and later Russian hegemony. Finnish popular education takes institutional root around the turn of the twentieth century but is marked by a continuation of the hegemonic enlightenment process begun earlier. The mid-nineteenth century *kansanvalistus* or 'people's enlightenment' which lasted until 1917 was followed by the more radical *kansansivistys* or 'people's education', which carried the same sense as the German *Volksbildung* in seeking the more intensive individual approach associated with the *Neue Richtung*.

The Nordic people's enlightenment was not dissimilar to the general European pattern of nation building and modernization and also exhibits a tendency to isolate and massage out class conflict. The working classes through popular education were encouraged to see themselves as part of an emergent democratic nation in the process of throwing off ancestral imperialisms. The general defeat of revolutionary socialist ambitions following World War One, however, re-

14

sulted in the success of reformist social democratic parties, which presided over the dramatic extension of the franchise to working people and women. To this extent they have become models of relatively wealthy, egalitarian, tolerant and welfarist societies with a high degree of social harmony and educational achievement, in sharp contradistinction to the Anglo-Saxon neo-liberal models of the late-twentieth century. The emphases of popular education on citizenship, general humanistic development and dialogic learning have without doubt been instrumental to this process and created a powerful social bond between individuals. The negative aspects of nationalistic xenophobia have, at the same time, been relatively successfully curtailed by a strong social democratic politics in which popular educational practices have received a high priority.

In Belgium and Holland, university extension on the English model underwent contrasting fortunes, which are examined in Chapter 9. While Belgium was a rising industrial power shaking off the shackles of Dutch hegemony and a conservative Catholic educational tradition, Holland had a long established popular education institution in the shape of the *Nut*, a well-bred schooling system and a sceptical university establishment. A three way cultural pull was exerted by Britain, France and Germany such that while British popular education was seen as a model of class rapprochement by many intellectuals, the left inclined to the more class conscious models of the French *universités populaires* while others looked to the German *Neue Richtung*. In Belgium, university extension was adapted with enthusiasm as a vital tool of Flemish national independence, whereas in Holland it was contested both by conservatives and socialists. In Belgium the socialist party of Vanderveldt and Destrée closely followed the English university extension as a model of 'scientific' education while the Walloon, French speaking, territory, where there was a lack of interest on the part of the working class, later adopted the French model. In Holland popular education was very much embedded in voluntary associations such as the *Nut*, which drew informal support from the universities. Subsequently, a form of university extension was adopted and *universités populaires* were also established in some industrial areas. The Danish folk high school model, on the other hand, was resisted as too nationalistic for the

Dutch situation, although the British religiously-inspired Woodbrooke type residential colleges were admired and to an extent emulated. Other forms of significant popular education were the Belgian masonic *Ligue de l'Enseignement*, which preceded the French *Ligue* by a year in 1864 and also the *Maison des Peuple* in Belgium and the *Volkshuisen* in Holland which were forms of working men's clubs with largely sociable and mildly educational purposes.

Although it could be argued that The Netherlands, Belgium and Holland, created no great innovations in popular education, the hybrids they produced are significant of specific national cultural developments. While in Belgium the social movements were fractured in a number of directions by for example Flemish nationalism, anti-clericalism and then socialist class struggle in the more composed atmosphere of Dutch cultural life it was the older enlightenment voluntary society, the *Nut*, which took the lead and then renewed it in the controversy over university extension. In Belgium the contrast of Ghent-based and Brussels-based university extension was a good example of opposing nationalist and socialist pressures, while both attempted to confront the 'social question' by steering a middle way between laissez faire economics and revolutionary socialism. The masonically based anticlericalism of Belgium was of course intens-ified by the educational control exercised by Catholicism and its subsequent political organisation, which did not of course exist in Holland. Although both countries succumbed to a form of pillari-zation, largely orchestrated for the benefit of the confessional groups, in Holland the role of the state as a 'neutral' arbiter and arguably its more developed civil society, proved more successful in educational terms. Holland too had a more highly developed educational system which, in the thought of its university intellectuals at least, precluded the need for university extension as a form of 'deficit' education – although there is no sense in which that was actually the case in England. The *Nut*'s frank view that it was in the end the middle class and not the masses that needed higher education was an admission few in England were prepared to concede.

Nationalist movements and popular education were more closely connected in Eastern and Central Europe than anywhere else. Chapter 10 examines how the struggle against the decaying empires of the

Habsburgs and Romanovs and the doctrinal dominance of their respective clerical allies galvanised first the middle classes and then the lower orders into demands for enlightened reform and, at length frustrated by continued repression, revolution. The baleful influence of Czarist Russia and it secret police made sure that all liberal educational activities were kept under close scrutiny and wherever possible eliminated. Although most obvious in Russia itself, the Baltic countries and the Russian controlled Poland constantly fell foul of this invasive policing. Nevertheless, in these countries forms of covert nationalist education, often under the guise of agricultural institutes as in Poland or literary societies elsewhere, flourished for brief periods. In Poland especially, it was remarkable that the most radical associations were often inspired and led by women of the intellectual class and that the movements themselves were working class rather than middle class in composition. The opposition of the Church and its collaboration with the imperialist regimes meant the rural peasantry were often sequestered from the enlightened ideas of the intelligentsia behind ideological veils of archaic mystery, nursing a gnawing xenophobia that occasionally turned into vicious anti-Semitism.

In the Habsburg regions the nationalist movements of Hungary and Czechoslovakia adopted enlightenment ideas with vigour, creating in turn varieties of 'national' science and folk traditions that galvanised popular opinion. Perhaps the most inspirational of the educational leaders was T.G. Masaryk who became Czechoslovakia's first president and who through his determined adoption of French positivistic modes of sociological thought and sympathy with the workers' movement, embraced one of the most advanced forms of university extension in Europe. In the Balkan states, so long the impoverished battlefields of continental conflict, popular educational enlightenment was more transient, gaining footholds here and there but often erased by resurgent imperialism. The absence of universities of course made any form of extension impossible but frequently groups of idealistic students returning from study in Paris and Heidelberg might begin courses of popular education or attach themselves to older institutions. The irony is that in many of these states the arrival of post-World War Two Communist regimes (with the possible exception of Yugoslavia) rapidly turned whatever popular educational movements existed into vehicles for party propaganda and erased their autonomous progressive character.

The study concludes by considering the fall and rise of popular educational movements in the late-twentieth century. The fate of much popular education was to be absorbed into state regulated provision such as the Responsible Body status in Britain and the various state funded provisions in Europe, or captured by political movements such as Communism and Nazism. It has been argued that the expansion of education at all levels, primary, secondary and now higher, has made popular educational movements redundant. However the emergence of new social movements over the last three decades involved in issues such as feminism, ecology, peace, disability and currently Third World debt, anti-globalisation and anti-war have questioned this. Equally the functionalist and vocationalist spin put on much formal adult education has evacuated it of meaningful personal cultural development and radical social purpose. The conclusion reflects on how far the radical traditions of popular education between the revolutions of 1848 and the World War Two might inform the new social movements and contain potential for a renewed radical, critical and above all popular adult education.

Chapter 2
The Bourgeois Public Sphere: Science and the Citizen

The emergence of a bourgeois liberal public sphere briefly outlined in Chapter 1 assumed a central role for education, in such things as scientific understanding, reasoned debate, moral autonomy and, especially, citizenship. Initially a project of the liberal bourgeois and aristocratic patrons to disseminate scientific understanding and the values of reason to the middle classes and artisans, popular education became at once a space of contestation. Following this sketch of the contested bourgeois public sphere of the eighteenth and nineteenth centuries in terms of popular educational movements, it is possible to see at least two kinds of activity. But they are not as clearly separated as the model suggests. The first is centred in the Scientific Societies founded and frequented largely by middle class professional groups but relatively porous to artisans and others. The second is the sphere of mutual aid and co-operative self-help groups created by artisans and skilled workers that were to lay the basis for the national labour movements which is the subject of Chapter 3.

As we have seen, the new scientific and rational philosophies generated during the period of the early Enlightenment were frequently allied to arguments for social reform and in general this seems to be the case throughout Europe. Despite the aristocratic patronage of the earliest scientific societies in Italy, such as the *Academia dei Lincei*, of which Galileo was the leading member in 1601, and its successor, the *Academia del Cimento*, Jesuitical persecution meant that their potential for popular enlightenment was never realised. Consequently the struggle for science moved westward from the Papal heartland and became inseparable from political and religious reform (Bowen, 1981: 50).

A survey of European popular educational movements reveals a number of stages related to the socio-economic development and political circumstances of the various regions. It is clear that a widespread move to popularise science beginning in the seventeenth century saw by the mid-nineteenth century the founding of scientific societies in almost all European metropolitan centres. It also marked the beginning of a movement for universities to secularise their activities and become research based institutions centred in rational and empirical investigation. Following the French Revolution, demands for constitutional change and democratic citizenship or what Perry Anderson calls a 'Rational Patriotism' are made by radical groups across Europe (Anderson, P., 2002). Towards the mid-nineteenth century these turn into Romantic nationalist movements, which are less interested in the mathematical and physical application of scientific methods than in reconstructing versions of 'nation' based in idealisations of the folk and reinventing folk traditions and customs. This is particularly the case in those central and eastern European nations, struggling for independence from Habsburg and Romanov domination.

The Popularising of Science and Social Reform

Popular educational movements in Europe have a long history that could be extended almost indefinitely back into the middle ages to traditions of religious dissent on the one hand and marginalised cultural groups on the other. While the former reacted against doctrinal dogmatism and clerical corruption by creating radical interpretations of the bible and identified themselves with the landless poor, the latter used more traditional oral forms of communication. Through folk song and epic they strove to create a historical continuity with a distant heroic age and the image, as in Celtic and related folklore, of the 'Return of the King' that would deliver them from the Saxon, Norman, Muslim or Mongol yoke. They also used the carnival and feast days to 'turn the world upside down' when the village idiot might become king for a day and all forms of authority were ritually mocked.

Perhaps the most significant break from the medieval period into modern times can be traced to the heretical movements that led to new dissenting, or proto-Protestant formations, such as the Hussites in Bohemia, the Cathars in Southern France and the Wyclif-led Peasant Revolts in England. These demands for religious tolerance and democratic priest-free forms of worship pre-figured the Protestant Reformation and, significantly for our purposes, were stimulated new forms of learning and understanding. The print revolution of the fourteenth century made the bible and other religious and classical humanist texts available to a much wider public than the traditional monastic scholars and the few literate members of the royal court (Anderson, B., 1989). It created new publics for communication, information and learning, most crucially in the expanding mercantile cities of Europe where a new urban class of merchants, small scale producers and service professions was rapidly developing. It was this class, so graphically drawn in Boccaccio's *Decameron* and Chaucer's *Canterbury Tales* during the middle- and late-fourteenth century that heralded the eclipsing of monarchical and clerical authority and foreshadowed the emergence of 'the People' onto the historical stage. Until this time the concept of the People was foreign to political discourse in which there were only 'estates' or 'orders' that rose in pyramidal form from the brute earth to God in his heaven.

The demands of the new capitalist economy for profitable technological invention spurred on scientific inquiry, the break from scholastic Aristotelian philosophy and the development of empirical and rational forms of investigation. The consequent formation of new groups of secular intellectuals, who although formally dedicating their investigations to the glory of God, frequently, like Galileo and Kepler, found themselves in conflict with Papal authority, often forfeiting their freedom and lives for the privilege. Science and dissent therefore found themselves closely linked despite the fact the former aimed for 'objectivity' and neutrality. Science and reform also became closely tied and the English tradition, in particular, attempted to yoke scientific progress to social betterment.

In Britain, Francis Bacon established a significant strand of this tradition with a major treatise on what came to be seen as the foundation of philosophical empiricism, *The Advancement of Learning* (1605). Bacon dismissed the abstract disputation of the scholastic

philosophers, then the dominant traditional intellectuals, as arid speculation and had little time for the humanists and occultists. Instead he
proposed that knowledge could only positively obtained by a gradual
ascent from the observable particularities of an event or substance to
the general level of theory, otherwise known as the *inductive* method.
Bacon's subsequent work, *New Atlantis* (1627), was a project of
utopian speculation in which he described and advocated a community
whose progress depended on its ability to conduct collective scientific
research. Bacon was thus one of the first 'moderns' to promote the
view that human progress depended on the scientific approach to
human affairs. Bruno and Vico in continental Europe developed
rationalist and humanist approaches but suffered the Papal consequences and although progress in Catholic countries was erratically
blessed by authority, in general it was the emerging Protestant
countries that pushed forward the scientific spirit and social reform.

The consequent development of British empiricist, materialist
and sceptical philosophies under Locke, Newton, Hobbes and Hume
and the emergence of the French *philosophes* is well known. The three
revolutions of the eighteenth century, American, French and Industrial, it is argued would not have taken the form they took without
these new currents of learning and critical understanding.

Descartes and French Rationalism

Between the Vatican's apostatising of scientific learning in the early
seventeenth century and the British empiricist but increasingly fract-
ious civil tendencies, Catholic France allowed a limited public sphere
for scientific learning. Here amateur scientific groups achieved a
fragile degree of public space but not so much so that Renée Descartes
(1596–1650), a leader of Enlightenment rationalist thought, did not
find it safer to remove to Holland in 1628. After the Huguenot Wars
and Henri IV's conversion to Catholicism, the Catholic ascendancy in
France permitted a Jesuit resurgence in education. As a consequence
the University of Paris restricted entry to Catholics, suppressed

vernacular instruction and censored printing. The founding of the *Académie Française* as a counterweight by Cardinal Richelieu in 1635 was a mixed blessing, though. While it encouraged a more secular and tolerant culture of learning, even a cultural renaissance in France, the 'protection' that Richelieu extended to amateur scientific groups, brought their activities under uncomfortably close official scrutiny.

An example of this was a circle organised by the journalist Theophraste Renaudot, who published its proceedings as the *Conferences du Bureau d'Adresse* which had a wide following. Less ambitious than the British scientific societies, it discussed topics such as whether the French language was sufficient for 'learning all the sciences'. Richelieu, according to Bowen, 'recognised the opportunity to use the informal society as a means of creating a *national* consciousness through the purification, enrichment and elevation of the French language' (Bowen, 1985: 54). Thus by letters patent this amateur group was transformed into the *Académie Française*. Five other academies were founded within the next forty years including the *Académie des Sciences* in 1666.

Amongst the amateur groups that preceded the *Académie Française* was the circle of the Dupuy brothers, the *Cabinet des Freres Dupuy* which dated from 1616 and was in part dedicated to the work of Francis Bacon (whose portrait hung in their meeting place). There was frequent correspondence and exchange with English scientific groups. Another was the group around Marin Mersenne, a friend and colleague of Descartes who, after the trial of Galileo in 1633, counselled extreme caution in pushing forward scientific enquiry. Nevertheless the Convent of the Annunciation in Paris was the centre of scientific activity in France until his death.

Even in exile, Descartes was to have a major influence on French intellectual life and his *Discourse on Method* became a major text of the unfolding European Enlightenment. Always contrasted to Baconian empiricism, the Cartesian rationalism advanced by Descartes was less contentious in Catholic Europe because it admitted of *a priori* knowledge, usually in the eye of God (whereas British empiricists denied the existence of any knowledge that could not be verified by the senses and experience). Descartes was nevertheless scabrous of his own Jesuit education at La Fleche and committed himself to abandon the study of letters 'and seek no other science than the knowledge of myself, or the great book of the world' (quoted in Bowen, 1985: 58). He was sympathetic to empiricism and the realist and materialist vision of Bacon and Galileo but gave more weight than they did to the intellectual constructions of perception and the use of reason.

Amongst the followers of Descartes, Habert de Montmor's private academy became increasingly scientific in orientation. Although a member of the *Académie Française*, Montmor was extremely dissatisfied with what he called 'a stupid rabble' because of its tame subservience to state policy. His own academy unsurprisingly failed to win official support and only when it expired in 1664 were moves to establish the *Académie des Sciences* begun. Despite the hostility of the Jesuits of the University of Paris, Colbert established the new Academy because of the perceived threat from the progress being made by the British Royal Society, which had been founded a few years earlier. Although the Academy could not be said to have thrived, because of political control and clerical opposition, it made a major contribution to popularising science through the publication of its proceedings in its journal the *Journal des Sçavans*. This became widely read despite Jesuit censorship and in turn stimulated the foundation of other learned journals. Thus a wider public for scientific understanding was established in France (and fostered by masonic groups).

By the end of the seventeenth century therefore, the public sphere suggested by Habermas was haltingly apparent in Europe's most wealthy and influential country. Though clearly not as popular, vigorous or as radical as the British scene, it added a distinctively *rationalist* position to dialogue with that of British empiricism. But as a consequence of dogmatic intolerance and the suppression of free thinking activities, the head of steam for civil unrest already apparent in Britain, was within the next century to create Europe's most decisive political and social rupture.

In Britain scientific rationality spread rapidly beyond the relative conservatism of the lodges to the broader population. An interesting example of the way this fusion of science and social reform took hold of the imagination of individuals is that of Tom Paine (1737–1809) himself. Paine, who wrote the *Rights of Man* (1791 and 1792) as a defence of the French Revolution and *The Age of Reason* (1793) as a deist attack on the Christian Church was also a leading light in the

24

American Revolution. His pamphlet *Common Sense* (1776) was written 'in a language as plain as the alphabet' for popular consumption and was widely influential among the artisan class. He himself was an example of the 'new man' from the lower orders prepared to promote the rational reform of society for the good of all.

As a young man in the 1760s Tom Paine spent much time browsing London bookshops for books on science and the new circulating libraries. He also attended lectures on philosophy including those given by Benjamin Martin and James Ferguson. This self-educational activity was, according to Tom Paine's biographer John Keane, 'undoubtedly significant, for it brought him inside the circle of two of England's most reputable itinerant lecturers, whose energies were poured into bringing Newtonian science to captivated audiences otherwise excluded by prejudice from advanced education' (Keane, 1995: 42). Martin was a highly skilled spectacle maker, globemaker and editor of *The General Magazine of Arts and Sciences*, which published articles on philosophy, mathematical instruments, natural history and philology and was author of *The Philosophical Grammar* (1735) which Paine probably read. Paine also bought a globe from him. Ferguson was a renowned Scottish astronomer and author of *Astronomy explained upon Sir Isaac Newton's Principles*, and made easy to those who have not studied mathematics. He was also a friend of Benjamin Franklin. Paine liked his 'amiable simple character' and 'superb clarity of thought and speech'. Ferguson offered lessons for two guineas per person on using globes but for Paine this contact did not just arouse his passion for science but, despite little explicit politics, 'introduced him to a new culture of political radicalism that rejected throne and altar' (Keane, 1995: 43).

While Newton was the overriding spiritual presence in this circle, Martin and Ferguson took intellectual leadership from the scientist, radical and educator, Joseph Priestley and corresponded steadily with other men of science. 'They often referred to Bacon's phrase "Knowledge is power", as though it were their watchword in further education, and they certainly regarded the whole field of scientific knowledge as common ground fit for cultivation by the united labors of individuals for the common benefit' (Ibid.). The audience, Keane argues, were men and women 'mainly self-educated shopkeepers and artisans, many of whom leaned toward unorthodox religious views, and religious Dissenters, with strong leanings toward political radicalism' (Ibid.). They were 'decidedly modern in outlook'. For all of them the key problem was 'to reconcile the Christian doctrines of faith in God and spiritual conversion with the coolheaded empiricism of scientific reason' (Ibid.: 44). But there was clearly a tension in this task, reinforced by the uneasy regard of the clergy and political authorities. The solution for these devoutly religious men, who discovered that the 'Word' of the Bible could not be reconciled with their own scientific discoveries, was to remove divine intervention from their calculations. God was depersonalised and reduced to the status of primum *mobile* (a fore-runner of contemporary creationism).

According to the Newtonian faith that Paine adopted there was a 'natural order' designed by the 'Omnipotent Architect' for the guidance and benefit of humanity. Moreover, the laws of the natural order could be discovered by human reason, without the intervention of the clergy or revelation, and used as standards for evaluating the ideas, conduct and institutions of any given political order. Newtonians criticised the gloomy Puritan view of the 'Day of Doom' and dwelt on what became characterised as the Whig view of progress, the infinite 'Goodness and Wisdom' of the world. Many of those who were attracted to their scientific lectures believed that the natural laws could be applied to a science of government driven by the spirit of inquiry, criticism and human improvement: 'Just as there was a universal law of gravitation, binding together the physical world so there was a universal law of benevolence, binding together human beings for the sake of their happiness and freedom' (Ibid.: 45). The Georgian political establishment both feared Newtonianism (despite George III's own passion for science) and pilloried its followers. Consequently, the Newtonian circles became breeding grounds for a new radical politics where Paine became convinced that the sciences were friends of liberty.

As the example of Tom Paine reveals, without the formation of a public or publics for the new philosophy and scientific investigation, it too would have been confined to the cloisters and the alchemical workshops of the privileged few. In effect *society* itself was being born during this period, where the idea of individual ethical autonomy and collective contract challenged the old corporate idea of medieval Christendom with its seamless robe of religious authority and monarchic absolutism. The new public defined by these individuals and social beings, Habermas and others argue, can be seen as both constituting and constituted by a bourgeois 'public sphere'.

By the later eighteenth century in Britain it is clear the Baconian desire for a new rationally and scientifically based society was widespread among the newly established urban professional classes. This was especially so in the dissenting groups that found themselves excluded from participation in government or from freedom to worship. These groups were often at the centre of movements to popularise science among non-aristocratic groups. As Simon notes, they were often 'profoundly at variance with many aspects of the social order' and debarred from attending English universities or holding public office (Simon, 1960: 23). They could and did attend Scottish universities and established their own Dissenting Academies in the northern industrial towns, as famously did Joseph Priestley in Warrington (Uglow, 2002: 72–5). They also established the leading scientific societies of the period such as the Lunar Society in Birmingham and supported movements for the abolition of slavery and the American war of independence. Many enthusiastically acclaimed the work of Rousseau (whose *Emile* was translated into English in 1762) and, like Paine, welcomed the French Revolution as the beginning of a new era. These republican sympathies, however, attracted penalising legislation and dissenters were debarred from teaching in schools and colleges. The same repressive atmosphere encouraged Oxford and Cambridge universities to steer a course away from scientific studies and they became little more than seminaries for the clergy and the classical education of gentlemen until the late-nineteenth century reforms.

Local experimental societies therefore in the late eighteenth and early nineteenth centuries were almost the only means of educating a wider public in science. However because of the increasingly repressive climate induced by the fear of Jacobinism, they lost their earlier utopian spirit and became rather narrow in outlook. One figure of the earlier period who stands out as linking the ambitions of science with radical social reform and education was Joseph Priestley (1733–1804), whose tenure at the Warrington Academy for dissenters promoted scientific enquiry and the freedom of students to 'follow the dictates of their own judgements, in their enquiries after truth' (quoted in Simon 1960: 29). In 1791 he published a radical tract on education *The Proper Object of Education in the Present State of the World* which urged freedom in education from religious doctrine and the requirements of the state. Priestley was to become the victim of Tory mobs and forced to emigrate, however, and his direct influence was increasingly confined to radical groups.

With the early radical promise of the British scientific societies increasingly marginalised, two new forms of voluntary organisation came into being, the Literary and Philosophical Societies and the Mechanics Institutes. The 'Lit and Phil' Societies begun in Manchester in 1781, followed by Liverpool, Leeds (which had a 'Phil and Lit') and Sheffield were the preserves of the local liberal elite of industrial manufacturers and professionals. They characteristically viewed themselves as the cultural 'guardians' of the new industrial municipalities. In Leeds the society comprised the most prestigious of the local industrialists who earnestly discussed the latest scientific findings, industrial techniques, and theoretical material. This group, many of whose families had only a generation ago emerged from the class of skilled workers, shortly founded the Leeds Mechanics Institute for the skilled education of artisans, as an adjunct to the Phil and Lit. As such it was very much under their patronage with the consequence that religious and political matters were forbidden from discussion. Bowen estimates that in the mid-nineteenth century Britain had about 600 mechanics institutes and scientific societies with about 100,000 members. The mechanics institutes with their technological and functional emphasis were, however, the direction into which scientific societies in Britain turned in the mid-nineteenth century and were widely influential, if hotly contested, spaces, as we shall see.

In The Netherlands there was a similar if more moralistic pattern. The first large voluntary organisation for education and information was established by leading liberal businessmen in 1784 under the title of the Society for Arts and Sciences with the motto, 'For the Common Benefit' (SBF) or *Nut* as it was known. This society was the culmination of previous efforts during the eighteenth century by liberal sections of the middle class in establishing Rational Improvement Societies on Enlightenment principles. Many of these, such as the Economic Branch and the Society for the Improvement of Agriculture met with little success. According to van Gent, in 1778 five types of voluntary society were named (van Gent, 1987) including: general scientific societies, specialist societies such as the Society of Letters, societies with charitable or educational purpose, societies concerned with advance and practice of the sciences and the arts, and miscellaneous less formally organised societies. Significantly, all the societies were engaged in some kind of *educational* activity like popularising science and cultural development. However, the primary aim was as much moralistic as enlightening, to correct the behaviour of the lower orders. Under the motto of 'improvement not social promotion' they intended to encourage virtues and discourage insurrectionary behaviour, or what van Gent lyrically calls a 'civilizing offensive' by 'the forces of organised virtue' (Ibid.: 283).

As in Britain, the SBF drew its support from religious dissenters, many of whom were members of the 'Patriots', republican, middle class democrats stimulated by the success of the American Revolution. While the short-lived Batavian Republic of 1795–1806 promoted SBF educational reformist views energetically, van Gent notes Schama's rather sober take on these reforms that: 'quite apart from its independent importance as a disseminator of new educational and philanthropic ideas, the Society was instrumental in supplying exactly those squadrons of dedicated enthusiasts needed by the state to staff its agencies' (Schama, 1977: 533; quoted in van Gent, 1987: 283). Such societies therefore may well have begun the process of educating new professional functionaries for the modern state. Support for the SBF was maintained by William I after the counter-revolutionary restoration of 1815. Van Gent claims that 'in addition to lectures to its own members on topics such as science, health and the upbringing of children, popular lectures were held in the optimistic hope that this would diffuse useful knowledge among a very broad audience from the lower orders and in this way put an end to the prevalence of massive poverty' (van Gent, 1987: 284). If so, this is an indicator of the kind of unrealistic expectations the liberal middle classes had of popular education, when it might be argued that what was really required were radical economic reforms. This turn from Enlightenment radicalism of the earlier utopian period to moralistic persuasion marks a significant shift in attitude as reaction to the French Revolution and the defeat of Napoleon in Europe takes root.

In Germany and Scandinavia similar societies existed which shared the same general aims but differed in emphasis. The highly prestigious Berlin Society of Sciences was founded in 1700 in the spirit of Gottfried Liebniz and modelled on the elite societies of France and Britain. Like them, its ideal of popularising science was restricted to a privileged and largely aristocratic circle. However Germany reformed its educational institutions in the wake of this scientific activity much more swiftly and by the 1850s had taken the lead in founding scientific societies and research institutes. But, as Bowen remarks, the ideological shift we have noted was even more evident:

> In an age of political repression after the revolutions of 1848, neither industries nor governments wanted holistic, socially responsible science: industrialists wanted profits, government wanted conformity: scientists, mechanics and technologists accepted these conditions in return for employment and research facilities, and this was reinforced by a system of rewards and honours (Bowen, 1981: 345).

Freemasonry and the Enlightenment

A puzzlingly neglected theme, from the point of view of popular education, is the role played by speculative freemasonry. In his book *The Age of Capital* (1985) Hobsbawm wrote:

> Bourgeois Europe was or grew full of more or less informal systems of mutual advancement, old boy networks or mafias [...] One among these types of network, freemasonry, served an even more important purpose in certain countries, notably Roman Catholic Latin ones, for it could actually serve as the ideological cement for the liberal bourgeois in its political dimension, or indeed, as in Italy, as virtually the only permanent and national organisation of the class. (Hobsbawm, 1985: 286–7).

Habermas's theory of the Public Sphere, as a significant force for modernity, defines it as the struggle against absolutism for constitutional monarchy and as a new area for social communication. The formation of voluntary organisations such as literary societies and particularly freemasonry is one of the main indicators of progress. These were crystallised into local clubs with names like 'harmony' and were composed of exclusive elites, fundamental to *bürgerliche Gesellschaft* and hostile to older forms of corporate organization. In this creation of a new communicative space the bourgeoisie, according to Habermas, tries to establish itself as a universal class where it commands knowledge and the lower classes become object of philanthropic support and cultural edification. What we see developing here is a self conscious middle class sphere exemplified by a reading public, commercialised leisure, public entertainment and expanded education (Eley, 1992).

Stevenson (1988) argues that modern freemasonry emerges in Scotland in about 1600 when traditional masonic craft rites were modernised and a new structure was formed by William Schaw, who traced freemasonry's roots to the Egyptian builders and the Jewish Temple. Masons were different from other medieval crafts because they were itinerant and hence needed temporary lodges. The older type of craft lodges had declined by 1560 and the growth of Protestantism. The new lodges emerged later but used the legacy of the mythical history of the craft, identification of masonry with mathematics, lodge organisation, secret signs and words and rituals of initiation. They shared the Renaissance belief in superiority of ancient civilisation over the medieval and held that 'Scottish stonemasons had a part to play in recovering ancient wisdom essential to the future of mankind' (Stevenson, 1988: 6). They organised new style permanent lodges in which, after 1630, outsiders begin increasingly to appear so that by end of the seventeenth century some lodges are dominated by 'gentleman, non-operative members of high social status' then equated with 'speculative' masons (Ibid.: 8). Many lodges had humble members who were neither masons nor gentlemen but often fellow craftsmen. The ideal of brotherhood was central and the metaphors of architecture and masonry were unique in binding together highest and lowest in society. They also believed in morality without religion, although this was not necessarily drawn from tolerance but its opposite, possibly because of a deal with the Scottish Church, which had no problem with masonry so long as it steered clear of religion: 'Perhaps it even saw freemasonry as channelling a yearning for ritual which might otherwise have led to popery in to a harmless activity' (Ibid.: 10). This new masonry adapted successfully to the Enlightenment which had achieved significant progress in Scotland by the mid-eighteenth century as we have seen. The centre of gravity of the new masonry, however, rapidly shifted to England where it was developed further, while Scottish Enlightenment philosophy had a marked influence on the growth of European enlightenment thought.

The Speculative Freemasonry that emerged around 1717 in London was swiftly adapted in Europe largely by virtue of links with Holland and the Orange family which had been transplanted by the Whigs into Britain as its first constitutional monarchy (Ibid.). Here an interesting divides begins to take shape. While the English lodges espoused Newtonian and Whig deism in a political conservatism that reflected the new polity, radicals and republicans looked towards Europe. Their adoption of pantheism and materialist doctrines was regarded as dangerous and subversive increasingly by those who led Anglo-Saxon masonry. Under the energetic activism of the Huguenot refugee, Desaguliers English masonry held fast against atheism and radicalism and remained strongly committed to the Whiggery and royalty that would enhance the stability of free trade and the personal freedoms enjoyed by the burgeoning middle class.

Nevertheless lodges were powerfully infected by the spirit of scientific progress and political liberty and some scientific societies, especially those newly formed on the continental Europe, were synonymous with masonic lodges and played a vital role in the diffusion of scientific knowledge (Ibid.: 125). In England and Holland it was Newtonian mechanistic science that predominated, while the masonic Chambers *Cyclopaedia* was an important vehicle for its further spread across Europe. European masonry was distinctly more educationally disposed than its British parentage and it became a leading force in mathematics and egalitarianism, which were seen as closely related.

Although Dutch masonry was content to adopt the relative conservatism of the British, because of the historic Orange link, the first lodges in France were seen as a potential threat and strongly opposed by Desaguliers and the British Protestant establishment. The French lodges appear to have been established in 1720 by Scottish Jacobites and it was rumoured that James II had in fact wanted to establish masonry as no less than a *defence* of Catholicism. This mistrust of French intentions, on both religious (although there was no basis for the anti-Catholic panic) and political grounds was never dispelled and by the mid-nineteenth century members of the 'atheistic' Grande Orient were not permitted entry to British lodges at all. European masonry nevertheless offered an umbrella for liberal free-thinkers, which even in its British constitutionalist form, was popularly adopted as inspirational challenge to political and religious absolutism.

Two of the most important bases for enlightenment speculation in the early-eighteenth century were in Paris and Vienna. French freemasonry, in its modern form, took the 'Scottish Rites' and, swiftly embracing Enlightenment principles, became an intellectual precursor to the French Revolution, although it did not embrace its political methods. The Lodge of the Nine Sisters, established by the Grand Orient in 1776 as a learned society dedicated to fostering the arts and sciences was at the heart of the French Enlightenment (Weisberger, 1993: 80). The lodge was notable for its contribution to chemistry and physics and the 'materialist' side of Enlightenment thought. Its members included Voltaire, Benjamin Franklin and a Dr Guillotin, shortly to become notorious for one of his more sanguine inventions. Others contributed to the public success of the Montgolfier brothers' hot air balloon ascents during the 1780s. The lodge was strongly associated with promoting the aesthetic ideal of neo-classicism, which arose from their masonic belief in the value of ancient ideologies and paradigms on the theme of nature. They were also active in state reform proposing that France should be a nation in which 'the inalienable rights of man could be respected' (Ibid.: 103). Jacob believes that the lodge's most significant organizational function was its promotion of surrogate institutions especially for educational purposes such as its funded lycées and public lectures (Jacob, 1981). Nevertheless the lodge itself fell victim to the Revolution whose birth it nurtured and in 1790 its activities were much constricted. By 1792 the craft was perceived as threat to the Revolution by the Jacobins and, like the Enlightenment principles that had energised it, the lodge was dissolved.

In the Habsburg and Romanov empires of central and Eastern Europe, the leading vehicle for scientific societies was also Speculative Freemasonry. One of the earliest and most interesting of these masonic scientific societies was in Vienna. Speculative Freemasonry 'became openly identified with the Enlightenment in Josephinian Vienna' (Weisberger, 1986: 129). As a result of the 1781 Masonic Patent of Joseph II, True Harmony Lodge was established to serve as the first learned society in Vienna. Like the Parisian Lodge of the Nine Sisters, the Viennese True Harmony Lodge became a political centre for advocates of state reform, stimulated the study of literature and philosophy, served as locus for scientific research, and enlisted the support of aristocratic and middle class enlighteners. The lodge published two journals: a science journal edited by lodge master Ignatz von Born and a literary one edited by prominent writer Alois Blumauer.

Masonic science however was always complicated by the search for mystical origins and Speculative Masons still hungered for what they regarded as the mystical secrets of the original Egyptian pyramid builders. They held that the mathematical secrets of the Egyptian masons were subsequently passed to the Jews who used them in the construction of the Temple in Jerusalem. If they could be recovered they believed that scientific reasoning could understand the laws of nature as divinely harmonised and that, of necessity, man was benevolent and virtuous. Consequently they tried to establish a correspondence between enlightenment theories of science and masonic theories through an understanding of the natural and occult science in which the scientific outcomes were almost accidental. Nevertheless, the outcomes included major breakthroughs in sciences such as geology which were disseminated by means of their journal. True Harmony Lodge rapidly became an international centre for study of geology.

Science was not the only object of study in the lodge. The *Journal für Freymaurer* published articles and poems by lodge members illustrating importance of ancient ideologies to masonic thought and they held that modern concepts of masonry constituted the basis of civil morality and universal ethical system. Evidence of their widespread network within the Habsburg Empire comes also from articles in the journal where, for example, Blumauer praised philanthropic Prague masons and encouraged the Viennese to do the same. They perceived masonry as a 'cosmopolitan institution devoted to the diffusion of Enlightenment tenets throughout the world' (Weisberger, 1986: 138). After a brief but brilliant career True Harmony however was closed in 1788 by an imperial patent that restricted activities during revolutionary threats.[1]

1   The following is a curious tale, from the web, of social mobility through education in masonic circles: 'The story of Saint Angelo Soliman – a Moorish slave & a master mason'. Viennese freemasons took great pride in their egalitarianism, sometimes demonstrating it by initiating members whose company bourgeois society might otherwise have rejected. A celebrated example of masonic broad-mindedness involved a one-time slave named Angelo Soliman. Born in North Africa in the early 1700s, Soliman was sold into slavery as a child. He was educated by a succession of wealthy European owners, wound up as a tutor in an aristocratic household in Vienna, and became a popular figure in court circles. Eventually he was freed and he married a widowed baroness. In 1781, he was initiated into the prestigious True Harmony Lodge, whose members included many of Vienna's social elite.

Soliman even became Grand Master of that lodge and helped change its ritual to include the reading of serious academic and scientific papers, a practice that eventually spread to lodges throughout Europe and enhanced Freemasonry's reputation for intellectual rigour. Similarly, Soliman's membership the secret brotherhood became a famous example of masonic progressive thought.

Still, the former slave met with a most peculiar fate. When he died in 1796, his body was claimed by the Holy Roman Emperor Francis II, who ordered it flayed and stuffed. (The monarch had a bizarre habit of collecting stuffed human corpses.) Francis then put the dreadful piece of taxidermy on display in his private museum, despite the pleas of Soliman's daughter and the outraged protests of his masonic brothers. The grisly relic remained in the imperial collection until the Austrian Revolution of 1848, when a grenade pitched into the Palace library sent the remains of Angelo Soliman up in a merciful burst of flames (http://www.geocities.com/poitoujoi/The1stBlkMason.html).

From Rational Patriotism to Romantic Nationalism: Czech and Polish Science

However, with the defeat of Napoleon and the restoration of the older imperial dynasties in its wake, Enlightenment ideas gave way to more parochial concerns. In the Austro-Hungarian province of Bohemia (in the former republic of Czechoslovakia), the scientific societies that followed in the wake of the masonic centres in Vienna and Prague became increasingly a vehicle for the oppositional nationalist movement. Herman (1988) notes that the emergence of the 'new science' was closely bound up with national identity and opposition to the Austro-Hungarian government. The first scientific society to be founded, the Royal Bohemian Society of Sciences, in 1790 was intended to serve the imperial state. But its members leaned increasingly toward a Czech provincial patriotism and following the end of the Napoleonic Wars, Herman notes the 'decline of Enlightenment classicism and the rise of the pre-romantic tendencies which stressed emotionality, glorified nature and national individuality' (Herman, 1988: 324). From the earlier preoccupation with science as the key to the mind of God and the harmony of nature, a popular concern with national identity became increasingly apparent. Alarmed by this tendency, the Austro-Hungarian government suppressed an allied attempt to form a society for Czech culture and literature. But in response the first scientific journal in Czech, *Krok*, emerged as an instrument of Czech nationalism asserting that a nation could not exist without its own science. Allied institutions included the Patriotic Museum of Bohemia, founded in the 1820s, which drew a wider social group into a scientific forum. Subsequently, *Matice ceska* a scientific/cultural association, formed in 1831, became the most popular development of mass organisation of middle class support for Czech nationalism.

A further development in the formation of scientific societies began in the 1870s with Jan Purkynê's programme for the constitution of scientific societies to form an Academy. Herman again notes:

> The general trend of the scientific based development in the Czech lands towards a national Czech science – that is, the sciences accomplished and

written about by people who supported the Czech national movement – expanded more or less gradually and after the '60s was considerably intensified. The broad masses of the Czech educated class were successfully attracted to it. The rise of 'Czech science' and its scientific base represented an objective process which steadily continued despite various obstacles imposed (Herman, 1988: 327).

The widespread desire for such an Academy was demonstrated by the fact that funding was raised on co-operative basis through popular mobilisation. Science here thus broke through to a concern for social life and perhaps its most impressive attainment lay in the formation of a theory and practice of *social* science under the general leadership of a leading mason, later to become the first president of independent Czechoslovakia and who was then editor of the journal, *Athenaeum*, T.G. Masaryk.

A similar fusing of scientific societies with nationalist aspirations took place in Poland, then divided under the tri-partite rule of Austria, Russia and Prussia. Trzeciakowski (1988) notes the emergence of new forms of society drawn from all groups interested in science and art and like Bohemia, not just the aristocracy. The first of these new forms of association was the Society of Friends of Science of Warsaw (1800–1831). He argues that the specific circumstances of the Polish situation were determined by the partition, the suppression of the political independence movement and, crucially, the elimination of the Polish language from government following the abortive uprising of 1848. These new societies, as might be expected, were based in university towns and in non-violent nationalist groups where 'Scholars and writers who had previously been sucked into the turmoil of political life returned to the serenity of their studies, where they considered how best to concentrate their energies' (Trzeciakowski, 1988: 293). The Society of Friends had little alternative except to be officially non-political and religious with the declared aim of 'the expansion of science and arts in the Polish language'.

As in Bohemia, efforts were made to popularise science with political connotations to awaken national pride. But despite the official non-political front, the studies in Polish language were regarded as a subversive expression national identity and the Society was closed by the Russian authorities. However, other associations were shortly founded in smaller centres by 'amateur lovers of science motivated by the noble passion of researching regional history' that carried on the work of raising the national consciousness (Ibid.: 295).

The most important of these was the Poznan Society of the Friends of Science, founded in 1857 to cultivate the sciences and competence in Polish language by August Cieszkowski a wealthy but philosophically inclined landowner. Again, as in Bohemia, testifying to the popular nature of this initiative, even the poorest appear to have contributed to the new building to house the society in the 1880s. Honorary membership was offered to foreign scholars including Joseph Lister of Glasgow and, significantly, medical science was the biggest beneficiary of the scientific effort. After period of stagnation the SFS becomes incorporated into the newly formed Academy of Arts in 1871, which was modelled on *Academie Francaise*. According to a contemporary, Marcel Handelsmann:

> It was Polish. Not only was it living, creative scientific organisation, but it was also a symbol of our presence, our national existence. It was the sole internationally recognised representative of our nation, divided and suffering (quoted in ibid.: 298).

Subsequently the Warsaw Scientific Society was founded in 1907 after the revolutionary events of 1905 but by then it had lost the popular character of the earlier scientific associations and appealed only to professional scholars.

Polish scientific and allied societies thus contributed to the creation of a 'national' public sphere in a number of ways through specialist publications, awakening interest among non-professionals, popularising science through publications and lectures that raised the general intellectual level, and 'economic progress'. The societies popularised a course of action designed to maintain national identity and encourage social development through intellectual and economic activity. The cultivation of the Polish language and national tradition through scientific works, collections of national treasures and conferences, strengthened internal national unity and awakened national pride.

Arguably, in the nineteenth century, all scientific associations of central and Eastern Europe under the dominance of the Russian and Austro-Hungarian empires shared proto- or covert nationalist aspirations despite the avowed neutrality of their dedication to sciences. Kantasalmi (1996), as we shall see later (in Chapter 8), argues that same case for Finland in its more complex nationalist aspirations to throw off both Russian and Swedish dominance.

Conclusion

The scientific societies and the popularisation of science that spread over Europe during the seventeenth and eighteenth centuries add substance to the argument for the formation of a bourgeois public sphere based on freedom of thought, discussion and rational enquiry during this period. However, as we have seen, this public sphere is patchy and insecure. It is threatened both by archaic political forces and religious intolerance on the one hand but by subaltern forces on the other that generate their own oppositional public spheres. More-over, the bourgeois sphere changes quite dramatically as the nine-teenth century progresses and countries under imperialist dominance generate a new cultural nationalism. Thus science, which we have argued, was always associated with social and political reform, becomes increasingly hitched to concerns for national identity.

Anderson, as we have noted, asserts that the Congress of Vienna in 1815 reinstates a counter-revolutionary world from which emerges a *cultural nationalism* as opposed to *rational patriotism* of the Enlightenment period (Anderson, 2002). This may be to underestimate the radical power of the appeal to 'the folk' in achieving national independence, since it is clear that such movements found that a rational, empirical science alone was not going to overthrow their imperial masters. Similarly in Britain and France, the older public spheres are incapable of containing the crystallising class antagonisms of rapidly industrialising countries by rational argument alone. Sig-nificantly, as we shall see, by mid-nineteenth century, while the European bourgeois cultural elite is turning away from science as a rational solution to social ills, the hopes for its explanatory and liberating power are taken up by the emergent proletarian class forces as 'scientific socialism' and the space of the bourgeois sphere of class reconciliation is almost fatally damaged.

Chapter 3
Education from Below: the Plebeian and Proletarian Spheres

While coffee house culture and dramatically improved communications characterise the bourgeois public sphere described by Habermas, at the same time a related but separate sphere of activism and self-education based on the 'public square' the public house and the workplace is emerging. After an initial pre-industrial utopian phase during the English Revolution of the 1640s, a 'plebeian' sphere begins takes shape around popular agitation for political and social reform. Despite official repression of this sphere and its publications by the nineteenth century an ideology of co-operation and mutual self-help generates a considerably autonomous sphere of industrial working class association and learning. Owenism and Chartism in Britain openly contest bourgeois private property rights and restricted democratic representation. The whole period is characterised by cycles of defeat and regeneration but also by the gradual emergence of an independent politics of labour contested by reformist and revolutionary wings. The reformist wings make compromises with their national bourgeoisies on the bases of an enlarged franchise and state welfare legislation. But by the end of the century the Workers' Internationals have created an international proletarian sphere of campaigning activism and self-education under the direction of social democratic and socialist parties that marks the first truly proletarian sphere.

Negt and Kluge, while generally sympathetic to Habermas's theory of the public sphere, attempt to expand what they see as an underdeveloped area of the original thesis. This is the area that Habermas describes as the 'plebeian public sphere' and which they prefer to call the 'proletarian public sphere' (Negt and Kluge, 1993). This sphere they say acted as a counter-concept to the bourgeois public sphere of critical rationality, although it shares some of its characteristics. They claim that the working classes, in Britain especially, developed educational, protective and activist organisations that were clearly distinct from the bourgeois sphere. However, because of repressive emergency legislation between 1792 and 1818, passed in the wake of the French Revolution, the workers' movement could only develop in cycles. There followed a steady growth of a 'workers' intelligentsia' drawn from 'a group of urban and in part rural tradesmen and industrial specialists, either from their own resources or as interpreters of theoreticians who originated from other classes' (Ibid.: 188). The cycles moved from the demands of small producers for autonomy against the old oligarchy, to an industrialised workforce wanting to overcome capitalist relations of production and distribution through co-operative decision making structures. The emergent workers' movement from about 1820–1832 was divided between those demanding a restorative anti-capitalism and those who allied themselves with bourgeois electoral reformism. Nevertheless, both consolidated the view that the situation of the working classes could not be improved by reliance on the good will of the middle and upper classes alone but by autonomous action and mutual solidarity. The 'masses' so called, gradually transformed themselves through their journals, mutual improvement societies and mass actions into a political force or what a troubled government militia commander, General Byng, in 1819, called 'the transformation of a rabble into a disciplined class' (quoted in ibid.: 189).

In the same vein Eley (1992) maintains that Habermas's initial public sphere thesis excluded too much of relevance. It was too bourgeois-orientated and ignored the Jacobin, Chartist and anarchist strains in continental labour movements. Eley notes three areas where revision could be fruitfully made to Habermas's original thesis. Firstly, subaltern groups also wanted the idea of reasoned exchange, either derived from the middle class sphere or from their own internal dynamic. Habermas's oppositions of 'educated and uneducated' and 'literate and illiterate' do not adequately describe the historical reality, as there is not only a conventional disabled plebeian sphere but also one that is both literate and radical. Secondly, the widespread impact of French Revolution in South, East and Central Europe leads to further nationalist movements and intelligentsias with a shared political vocabulary despite different socio-economic conditions. These groups well-understood the causes of their own economic and social

42

backwardness, frequently ascribed to imperial domination. They understood the urgent need for new *national* public sphere, as we have seen in the previous chapter, albeit stimulated externally (because of the international character of the Revolution) rather than from indigenous pressure and oriented to the otherwise excluded 'People'.

Finally, Eley argues, Habermas misunderstood the nature of the competing public spheres in peasant, working class and nationalist movements by idealising the bourgeois element and ignoring other radical traditions such as the radical *dissenting* movements described by E.P. Thompson in *The Making of the English Working Class* (1968) and Christopher Hill in The *World Turned upside down* (1975). These show that Habermas's classical model is already subverted in its origins and they redefine 'citizenry' to include what is ignored in Habermas's model. The bourgeois struggle, they suggest, is not just against authority and absolutism but against the plebeian element at its heels. The radical plebeian London Corresponding Society, for example, is no less rational than the bourgeois Birmingham Lunar Society. Eley concludes therefore that the bourgeois public sphere is really structured as a setting 'where cultural and ideological contest and negotiation among a variety of groups takes place rather than [...] the spontaneous and class specific achievement of the bourgeoisie in some sufficient sense' (Eley, 1992: 306).

By its very nature the countervailing public sphere to that of the bourgeois is harder to define. Its continuities with the folk life of the Middle Ages were undoubtedly strong and the traditions of carnivals and feast days in which the feudal and clerical authorities were mocked ragged were obvious. As Bakhtin lyrically demonstrated, the notion of the public sphere of 'the people' or the 'folk' can be traced to the *public square* in which markets and feasts marked the virtually unassailable occupation of public space by the lower orders with their own folk and popular traditions, customary rights and modes of communication (Hirschkop, 1999).

But there is also a significant break from this medieval cultural form to the modernity of the English Revolution where instead of the *symbolic* deposing of the king and the institution of the local 'idiot' as 'king for the day', the parliamentary forces, not only legally tried the king but also executed him. This was not simply the cultural letting-off of steam that reduced the tension in the medieval boiling pot but the violent rupture to the modern democratic period and an end to the 'great chain of being'. A republican *Commonwealth* for the first time in modern history replaced an absolutist monarchy.

The intellectual origins of this new polity have been traced to the emergence of Christian humanism in Europe during the Italian Renaissance when, as we have seen, the Church's teaching on the nature of the cosmos and human life came under intense scrutiny and doubt. Elsdon claims that this scepticism and celebration of a new understanding of humanity 'was quickly naturalised and impressively developed in the England of the Sixteenth Century' (Elsdon, 2003: 42). He sees a continuity in educational thought running through the *Enchiridion* (1503) of the Dutch humanist philosopher Desiderius Erasmus (1467–1536) of Rotterdam, the *Utopia* (1516) of Thomas More (?1477–1535) and Thomas Elyot's *Gouernour* (1531) which all lay emphasis on the importance of extending education to adults in the new life. While More, however, recoiled from the consequences of the vernacular translation of Tyndale's Bible (1525), the power of the English language in poetry and tracts was not lost on other humanists like Walter Raleigh and Philip Sidney whose *History of the World* (1614) and *Defence of Poetry* (1579–1580) respectively were passionately educational. The immediate heirs of this tradition were the Puritan poets and above all the radical heretic John Milton (1608–1674), whose *Paradise Lost* (1667) and *Paradise Regained* (1671) suggested an all too human heaven and hell (Hill, 1977).

While Christian humanism was most dramatically felt in the seminars of the governing classes, the crucial difference in the cultural make-up of 'the People' was arguably made by the coming of 'the new experimental philosophy' that boldly advanced individualistic and autonomous forms of learning.[1] Radical Roundhead soldiers took this to heart when Cromwell became intolerably dictatorial, and as 'Diggers and Levellers', they became 'the revolution within the revolution'.

---

1   Another was the Elizabethan and Jacobean theatre that staged new forms of class conflict. As Moretti has suggested, due to Shakespeare's history plays that portrayed a mostly violent and weak lineage of Norman English kings, who were incapable of establishing a just rule of law and were frequently and justifiably deposed (Morretti, 1983: 42).

The English Revolution

The radical implications of this democratic approach to knowledge were always to the fore and in his book *The Law of Freedom* (1652) the Leveller leader, Gerrard Winstanley insisted that education of the elite alone would create only a class of idlers and promoters of their own privileges:

> One sort of children shall not be trained up only to book learning and no other employment, called scholars, as they are in the government of monarchy; for then through idleness and exercised wit therein they use their time to find out policies to advance themselves to be lords and masters above their labouring brethren (quoted in Hill, 1975: 287).

Winstanley (1609–1676) himself was one of the first of the literate lower orders to express their own interests, politically. His powerful and lucid prose was addressed to the ordinary man and eschewed 'the traditional parrot-like speaking' of the universities, creating a model for successive writers and agitators. His writing and speeches graphically demonstrated the levelling influence of Baconian science on the English Revolution of the mid-seventeenth century, before it was eventually thwarted by Cromwell's turn to dictatorship and the subsequent restoration of the monarchy later in the century. For a short period the dream of a radical section of Cromwell's soldiers to make the term 'masterless men' one of celebration rather than rebuke, announced the origins of a separate public sphere of the plebeian classes. As Hill noted, the radicals of the English Revolution wanted a thorough-going *cultural* revolution as well as political reform (Hill, 1975). They aimed to end the distinction between specialists and laymen and drive the scholastic theologians out of the universities. Nor did they want the democratic prospects of the new science to founder on the rocks of a reefed-in sphere of academics. Winstanley in particular wanted science to be taught in every parish by an elected non-specialist teacher and applied to the problems of life. Science and its emancipatory prospects, he insisted, should be accessible to all intelligent enquirers.

The English radicals were also well aware of the utopian educational ideas emanating from the continent of Europe, such as the ideal for a reformed educational system of the Moravian Protestant, Jan Comenius (1592–1670). His *Gate of Tongues Unlocked* (1633) had been translated into English in 1636 and Comenius, a devotee of Francis Bacon, had visited London in 1641 at the invitation of the German educational reformer, now settled in England, Samuel Hartlib (d.1662). Following Comenius, the radicals proposed universal education in the vernacular for boys and girls to the age of eighteen and then six years at university for the best pupils. William Petty, another radical, advocated subsidised colleges for mechanical artisans and 'literary workhouses' for the poor. Not surprisingly, literacy rates during the Revolution rose substantially. Winstanley also wanted learning to be combined with manual work 'to ensure that no privileged class of idle scholars should arise' (quoted in Hill, 1975: 301).

In a compelling theorisation of the period, Benchimol argues that an oppositional public sphere of the plebeian classes opened up during the English Revolution, which was not merely a form of cultural compensation but a direct political struggle. He suggests that Habermas's failure to include the period of the English Revolution in his formulation of the 'public sphere' was a significant omission (Benchimol, 2001). The reason for this is that the period of the English Revolution, especially the 1640s, redeems the latent progressivism in Habermas's model because of its inclusive tendency and its contingent and provisional character that forces innovation.[2]

One of the primary means of communication was the *political pamphlet* of which many thousands were published and directed largely at the Parliamentary troops and their supporters during the English Revolution. The existence of these pamphlets suggests both a dramatically wider reading public and new kind of popular political

2   It could be argued that the existence of this sphere gave increased urgency to the need for the Bourgeois public sphere, since the British middle classes immediately found that their struggle for economic and political freedom had to be conducted not only against the aristocratic elite but also against the demands for equal treatment by the immediately subaltern classes of the artisan and small tradesman.

writer capable of writing a plain prose for the Everyman audience educated by the Revolution. This popular constituency had traditionally got its news and marked its celebrations orally, rather than in writing, and the new style of pamphleteering had to reflect the spoken quality of words. The language of the dissenting pulpit, the radical assembly and the tavern had to find a popular written form, a vernacular form that was distinctly from the Latinate obfuscations of the clerics and the tortured complexities of the university wits. As Benchimol notes 'the Leveller critic John Lilburne's prose style (comes) to life out of a cultural atmosphere where self-education and political polemic mixed freely with clear-headed social observation and sweeping passionate denunciation' (Ibid.: 116).

A defining document of Leveller politics and a founding document of British radical politics was the *Remonstrance of Many Thousand Citizens*, a pamphlet written by leading radicals on the imprisonment of Lilburne in 1646 which 'articulated a radical alternative political vision that exemplifies some of the best aspects of an oppositional plebeian cultural discourse' (Ibid.: 117). The *Remonstrance* was a plain speaking denunciation of the political fixes of the ruling classes, written in the name, for virtually the first time, of 'us' the popular classes that supported the Revolution. Tragically, it was peremptorily suppressed by Cromwell who either executed or transported the Leveller leaders but although the double defeat of the Levellers (first by Cromwell and then by the Restoration of the monarchy) ended utopian aspirations for several generations, their arguments remained to trouble successive political establishments until the present day. It was the part of the Puritan poet John Milton to allegorise this revolt and suppression of popular aspirations in some of the finest verse in the English language, in *Paradise Lost, Paradise Regained* and *Samson Agonistes* (1660) which Hill calls 'a poem about the people of God in defeat anywhere' (Hill, 1979: 362). All three poems, Hill claims, are deeply political 'wrestling with the problems of the failed revolution, the millennium that did not come' (Ibid.).

A century later, a natural successor to the populist demands and pamphleteering of the Levellers was John Wilkes (1727–1797), whose pamphlets were even more widely read and discussed; his *English Liberty Established*, Benchimol believes, was 'the most popular single piece of propaganda of the period' of the 1760s (Benchimol, 2001: 124). One political outcome of much of this radicalism was the Supporters of the Bill of Rights movement (which also included a radical section of the wealthy commercial class) that gave a significant institutional form to the plebeian agitation. Possibly for the first time it advanced the 'rights talk' of the Lockean philosophers into a political programme. The 'mob', in one of its phases, now begins to take on the aspect of the 'radical crowd'. The already radical character of the plebeian sphere was then fundamentally marked by the French Revolution of 1789, which, in the execution of the monarch and establishment of a representative republicanism, many saw as an echo of the English Revolution of the 1640s. In leading industrial and commercial towns of Britain, Francophile Jacobin movements rapidly gained ground.

Jacobin Education

The most articulate expression of this vernacular political culture was the work of Thomas Paine (see previous chapter). Though he was personally absent for most of this period in America or France, it was the widespread dissemination of Paine's writings through the educational activities of the Jacobin groups that raised his prominence. Despite his being outlawed by the authorities, his *Rights of Man* (1791, 1792) and *The Age of Reason* (1793) were copied many thousands of times in cheap paper pamphlets for widespread distribution and urgently discussed in reading circles in all the industrialising and commercial towns of Britain. Paine's writings mark the coming to maturity of the plebeian public sphere in many respects. He creates a prose style of outstanding transparency for the popular reader that utilises a critical vocabulary of natural rights and social justice and establishes these philosophical concepts as the legitimate discourse of the 'inferior classes'.

We now reach the truly educational moment of the plebeian sphere in Britain, which differs significantly from the occasional learning in political agitation that took place earlier. Largely because of Paine's influence, this is no longer the proto-Murdoch-style popularism of Wilkes but the serious deliberation of political causes that characterised the radicalism of the Levellers carried on in a transformed language of human rights and justice. What Paine does is to appropriate the somewhat arid language of constitutionalism and give it a popular resonance that reflects the dynamism of the Jacobin sphere itself.

The two most characteristic popular educational formations of this period are the Sheffield Constitutional Society and the London Corresponding Society (1792). Both of these societies could be called mutual-improvement or self-help groups in the sense that they were the organisations of working people and small traders themselves for their own betterment. They were radical political organisations for which education was a central function and not, as in the bourgeois sphere, merely educational organisations that were socially concerned. They largely lacked any middle class involvement, except for occasional meetings with radicals such as Thomas Carlyle, and they emphasised pragmatic political education aimed at collective action rather than the aesthetic cultivation, which was now increasingly characterised the bourgeois public sphere.

The extent of artisan involvement in these societies was considerable. The Sheffield Corresponding Society alone had around 2000 members and printed and distributed around 1400 copies of Paine's *Rights of Man*, implying a readership of some thousands more. The younger London society was dedicated to a social, economic and political agenda of reform through the informed participation of its members. They were animated by both intellectual earnestness and moral purpose, 'to enlighten the people, to show the people the reason, ground of all their sufferings' as one witness at the trial of Thomas Hardy, the secretary of the London society, asserted (Thompson, 1968: 165).

One of the leading 'popular educators' of this period, although it is probably not a title he would have recognised, was John Thelwall (1764–1834), whose revision of Paine's natural law arguments was brought to a very popular audience in the taverns as well as in the London Corresponding Society. His twice weekly lectures were published in his journal *The Tribune* until it was suppressed by the authorities. Thelwall who, according to Thompson, 'straddled the world of Wordsworth and Coleridge and the world of the Spitalfields weavers' synthesised the complex and often disparate ideologies of the various radical agitations into a something resembling a coherent political programme, and in that respect, 'took Jacobinism to the borders of Socialism' (Ibid.: 172, 175).

The suppression of the Corresponding Societies by special legislation in 1799 – a fateful forerunner of contemporary anti-terrorist legislation – effectively curtailed the British Jacobin sphere and, once more, most its leaders were jailed or exiled. The Romantic poets Wordsworth and Coleridge, who were on the edge of these circles, described political apostasy and retreated from the fray, while Shelley and Byron, who still maintained their Radical principles, largely sought their battle lines in Europe, although Shelley's *Mask of Anarchy* (1832) was a coruscating indictment of the Peterloo Massacre in Manchester in 1819. In Scotland, Robbie Burns hitched his radical star to a more wary masonic humanism, 'a man's a man for a' that'. Indeed it was Scotland where another stage of the educational development of the plebeian sphere had already begun to emerge, a stage that was forced to abandon its more radical political ambitions, that of 'mutual improvement'.

Mutual Improvement

The opportunities for plebeian and working class education in Scotland were considerably widened by the activity (if not necessarily the vision) of the Presbyterian reformer, John Knox, who demanded a school in every parish and the right of the 'lad o' pairts' to a good education regardless of background. Compared with their English counterparts, the poorer Scottish universities already fostered a greater access that encouraged both intelligent artisans, such as James Watt, the inventor of the steam engine and English dissenters, such as Joseph Priestley, to study within. They also nurtured an intellectual enlightenment in which as we have seen, the likes of Adam Smith,

Adam Ferguson, Francis Hutcheson and above all Thomas Reid were quietly creating a 'philosophy of common sense' for an educated public (MacIntyre, 1987). Literacy rates were also much higher due to the schools reforms and a culture of high-mindedness was widespread. The celebration of the 'democratic intellect' was to underpin the ideal of Scottish education for the next century or so (Davie, 1964).

A fascinating account by Jonathan Rose of working class self-help has revealed much about the independent learning of skilled workers in the nineteenth century (Rose, 2001). In Scotland and to a great extent in the industrial areas of northern England, working class, voluntary collectives were often associated with the non-conformist chapels in which Methodists, Wesleyans, Presbyterians, Quakers and others sought complete freedom of expression in politics, literature, religion and ethics. The movement grew so tenaciously over the nineteenth century that possibly twenty-five per cent of all workers were involved in mutual improvement by the 1880s.

The Scottish origins of mutual improvement were largely in the weavers' libraries of the early eighteenth century in the lowlands and the south-west, where skilled men had an astonishing literacy rate of seventy-four per cent. Subsequently the movement grew in the central belt and north-east where, associated with the Free Church, it became the backbone of radical liberalism. Reflecting the outlook of mutual improvement, in 1858, *The Peoples Journal* was founded which, by 1914, sold around quarter of a million copies weekly. The reading rooms and adults schools of mutual improvement were often an alternative to the Mechanics Institutes, which were founded and governed (as we noted in Chapter 2) by paternalistic middle class reformers during the mid-nineteenth century. The first mutual improvement societies had been founded a century earlier, such as the Spittalfields Mathematical Society (1717), which was made up mostly of weavers. In common with the European scientific societies, this society was dedicated to the practical understanding of science, the important difference being that it had no aristocratic or bourgeois patronage and was entirely composed of artisans and small tradesmen.

The scientific impulse was maintained in the great expansion of the societies in the early-nineteenth century but it was turned, as far as the repressive political climate allowed, towards social and political reform. (The London Corresponding Society had itself been organised loosely on the mutual improvement society model, which centred on loaning books and weekly discussions but its constitutional radicalism was a different matter.) Rose notes that a society in Salford and Hulme (Manchester) using scientific lectures as propaganda for Tom Paine's 'materialism' was organised around 1817 by Rowland Detrosier, a fustian cutter. This society became the first of a radical network that flourished in northern industrial cities thereafter.

By 1840 the Mutual Improvement movement had become established throughout the south of England also where Alan Davenport, estimated that there were fifty societies around London alone. In his autobiographical account, Davenport, a follower of Robert Owen, maintained, men and women studied science including the science of government 'with all the gravity, deliberation, and confidence of old and experienced professors' (quoted in Rose, 2001: 72). Again, this was not a politically neutral activity and Davenport issued grave warnings to the government about the revolution that was coming as result of the working classes linking science and technology to social justice:

> Will they (governments) be the last in the race of improvement, and cling to the old worn-out laws and institutions? while inventive genius with steam and mechanical powers, is revolutionising every nation and changing the political, the commercial and the manufacturing systems of the world! Are they so blind, or so infatuated, that they neither see, nor will be persuaded of the approaching storm – the moral earthquake, which will shake the world and convulse Europe from its centre to its circumference [...] unless an universal change in the political and social systems of nations takes place, and a more equal distribution of human subsistence shall be conceded (Davenport, 1997: 26–8, quoted in Rose, 2001: 72).

By the late-nineteenth and early-twentieth centuries the working class was saturated by the spirit of mutual improvement. But although it had a radical leading edge, it was by no means revolutionary and in some ways culturally quite conservative. This was the reformist political culture that produced many of the leaders of the nascent Labour Party and in particular, Ramsay Macdonald, the first Labour Prime Minister. The Radical politician, Francis Place, however, noted the moral improvement of society members, especially the dramatic improvement of working class manners by 1851 (he also noted, ironically, that by 1822 many had improved so much that they had become prosperous businessmen). Samuel Smiles, the ideologist of self-help and talisman of Mrs Thatcher, was also indebted to the movement.

Working Class Movements: Owenism and Chartism

Despite the cycles of suppression of the radical movements from the Levellers onwards, the underlying causes of distress continued to harm working people and, under industrialisation, intensified. While many serious working people became involved in mutual improvement societies, a flourishing radical press was also developing apace that appealed to the more politically inclined. During the nineteenth century the plebeian sphere gives way to a more distinctly *proletarian* sphere based on the industrial working class. New agitational newspapers such as Wooller's *Black Dwarf* and O'Connor's *Northern Star* were addressed precisely to this class and took radicalism into the factory. Plebeian radicalism, nevertheless, is active in a variety of ways as in William Cobbett's *Political Register*, (1802–) which, in a style which Hazlitt called 'plain, broad, downright English', while vehemently critical of laissez-faire capitalism, nevertheless failed to envision a future for an industrial working class and advocated instead a return to rural values.

The factory owner, Robert Owen who later coined the term 'Socialism' to describe his vision, attempted practical utopian experiments that both improved the conditions and wages of his workers, and housed and educated them to an unprecedented degree. His advocacy of 'co-operation' stimulated the co-operative movement of working people to make commodities affordable by collectively eliminating the marketeer's profit. The national and then international growth of this movement, which was echoed in the schemes of Fourier, Saint-Simon and Proudhon in France, created the potential for a semi-autonomous working class or proletarian social sphere in the industrial towns of Europe.

His 'utopian' writings on the other hand created a stimulus for an alternative and oppositional political programme to the liberalism of the bourgeois sphere. In many respects Owen's experiments in harmonious living were not concerned with a critique of capitalism but as an attempt to adapt religious and philosophical thinking to practical circumstances (Silver, 1965: 95). As such they were profoundly educational, relying as they did, on the learned understanding of natural and divine harmony in proto-masonic fashion. But it was the relative failure of Owen's American utopian experiment at New Harmony that turned him towards the incipient labour movement. Owen then inspired the creation of the first genuinely working class organisation, the short lived Grand National Consolidated Union in 1834.

Owen's contribution to popular education was not necessarily original, since it relied to a great extent on pre-existing enlightenment theories. However it was his insistence that human character and class differences were not immutably fixed but were the product of circumstance that altered opinion. As such, he believed, character was malleable and would respond to a programme of rational education which in turn could lead to a more rationally ordered and just society (Ibid.: 97). In the four essays that constituted his A *New View of Society* (1816) 'Owen, in fact, spelled out more fully and urgently the case for a basic revolution in thinking about education anyone else since Locke' (IIbid.). The educational aspect of Owen's vision continued into the 'Owenite Halls of Science', paid for by public subscription, that mushroomed over industrial England and Owenism was to remain a radical tendency long after his death.

Another significant development was the founding of the London Working Men's Association in 1836 as a 'political and educational' association, which intended to attract the 'intelligent and influential portion of the working classes' (quoted in Morton, 1976: 431). Morton believes this primarily educational association might have led a quiet and useful life had not the crisis of 1837 revived the demand for parliamentary reform, Chartism. The Association drew up a petition to parliament which embodied the six demands that became known as the People's Charter: equal electoral districts, abolition of property qualifications for MPs, universal male suffrage, annual parliaments, vote by ballot and the payment of MPs. None of these demands seem controversial now and the gendered aspect that excluded women from the vote (and signalled the ideological limits of the movement) has been long surpassed but they were enough to bring down the wrath of the government. Despite mass popular support and collecting over a million signatures not only was the petition refused but the leaders were arrested.

Chartism was, according to Eley, 'the first mass political movement of the industrial working class, transcending the divisions between "artisanal" and "proletarian" workers to a remarkable extent' (Eley, 2002: 19). Its forms of organisation and educational core laid the basis for the more fully developed proletarian public sphere that characterised the second half of the nineteenth century and challenged the bourgeois sphere for the cultivation of working class consciousness. This is not to deny that in some respects the spheres did not overlap, as exemplified in the figure of Thomas Carlyle. Better known as a cultural critic for the *Edinburgh Review*, Carlyle for a while embraced the fledgling working class movement and denounced the atrocities of Peterloo. William Cobbett's *Political Register* and other writings were also sympathetically received. Paine, it has to be said, also found in Adam Smith's political economy a rational model to be applied to the constitution. In this respect, although oppositional, the proletarian sphere shared that of the middle class.

One aspect of this was the priority given to science. Of the subsequent period, Hobsbawm noted:

> The major intellectual development of the years from 1875 to 1914 was the massive advance of popular education and of self-education and of a popular reading public. In fact self-education and self improvement was one of the major functions of the new working-class movements and one of the main attractions for its militants. And what the masses of newly educated lay persons absorbed, and welcomed, if they were on the democratic or socialist left, was the rational certainties of nineteenth-century science, enemy of superstition and privilege, presiding spirit of education and enlightenment, proof and guarantee of progress and emancipation of the lowly. One of the crucial attractions of Marxism over other brands of socialism was precisely that it was 'scientific socialism' [...] Galileo's 'And still it moves' was persistently quoted in socialist rhetoric to indicate the inevitable triumph of the worker's cause' (Hobsbawm, 1989: 263).

In fact this tendency was already well advanced among an elite of working men a half century earlier as we have seen. Increasingly, however, it advanced a radical separation of political interest from the liberal bodies that had fostered the movement into a demand for its own class-based political party and socialist programmes of reform.

European Anarchism and Education

In France and a number of other continental European countries a more distinctive educational ideology and practice was emerging in the wake of the French Enlightenment, the conception of *education intégrale*. Inspired by Condorcet's speech to the General Assembly in 1892, French libertarian theory relies much more closely on the bourgeois public sphere of the revolutionary phase (and uncannily foreshadows the language of 'lifelong learning'):

> To offer to all people within the human race the means to provide for their needs, to assure them of their well-being, to provide opportunity for them to exercise their rights and to know and to perform their duty. To ensure that everyone has the facility to perfect his occupation, to enable him to perform the social functions that he endeavours to exercise, to have the opportunity to develop the whole range of his natural gifts, and to establish thereby in actuality the equality of all citizens [...] should be the first objective of the national education [...] Finally, we have observed that education should not abandon people at the very moment they leave school; but it should seek to respond to the needs of all ages, for there is nobody who cannot learn something useful; this second education is more necessary than the first one since, during childhood it has been more limited [...] Thus education must be general, and include all citizens [...] it should include the whole range of human knowledge and ensure that people at every stage of their life have the facilities to preserve and extend their own knowledge (Condorcet, 1804).

The conception of *education intégrale* was central to educational theory linking the co-operative autonomous morality of the child with a particular social output incorporating the *mentalité* of fraternal community. It assumes a certain authority and art or technique of cultivation that anticipates Durkheim's belief in pedagogy as the systematic scientific process of reflection on the existing activity of education. It foregrounds *fraternité*, the anarchist programme resting on the spontaneous creation of a new communal life and life and social order. Idea of *education intégrale*, originally developed in the work of Fourier and Proudhon but can be traced back to Rabelais, envisaged a new educational order that would be inaugurated in three ways: by techniques of moral, social and intellectual teaching; by example and practice of communal life and labour and educational campaigns notably in the writings of Peter Kropotkin and Elisée Reclus and also the Scot, Patrick Geddes (Steele, 1998). Its focus is on the rational workshop or *atelier* in the commune as the pivot of new economic relations.

The characteristic thrust of French anarchism was towards 'communal individuality', as opposed to individualistic nihilism of the Germans Stirner and Nietzsche, espousing both freedom and censure. In this respect it was a practical application of the theory of the Enlightenment philosophes especially Diderot, who embraced a naturalist morality of propagation of species, coupled with the conservation and liberation of the individual. Yet the individual is anchored firmly in the social world where *l'homme complet* should have recourse to rules, a taste for order and happiness linked to others. Kropotkin later redefined authority in the moral teaching of 'mutual aid' but still harboured reservations about how far it could become susceptible to coercion and persuasion without conviction.

Suggestive of Rousseau, anarchist educational theory treated humanity as a species with distinct capabilities that could be developed and shaped through education but it was nevertheless suspicious of the coercive implications of the social contract. The concept of *education intégrale* 'from the complete worker to the complete man' offered the basis for the discussions of the First Working Men's International Congress (1866) and all later major educational speculation. The anarchist theorist Proudhon proposed workers' associations as centres of production and education to resolve the conflict of freedom and authority, liberty and regulation through what he called 'social individualism'. Considered puritanical and reactionary by the more spontaneist wing of the anarchist movement, he took a pessimistic view of human nature. He insisted that generosity and altruism were not instinctual and as a consequence *fraternité* or 'solidarity' had to develop from moral responsibility, 'which in turn forms the object of teaching and formation' (Fidler, 1989: 33). Proudhon places a much greater stress on adult education. He envisaged two educational stages: a primary factual stage for children which is completed by a secondary formal stage as adults 'where this initiation into rudimentary theory and the world of work is transformed into a more complete merger of theory and practice', which combined dependence on logical theory in philosophy and encyclopaedic approach to social and pure sciences (Ibid.: 34). Through this surprisingly rigorous approach Proudhon's aim was to instil same the confidence in the common man as was found in the ruling elite: 'Man henceforth placed in an organised milieu, sure of himself, sure of society, sure of acting, possessing, and savouring life in fullest measure' (quoted in Ibid.: 35). Proudhon's ideas had considerable impact on the nascent socialist and anarchist movements of the First International (1864–1889) and the anarchist communism of Reclus and Kropotkin. Despite the Congress of Berlin's decision to prioritise the economic and political emancipation of the working class, the International stimulated educational awareness and activities such as the Jura Federation and other forms of workers' education.

The reason for the rapid dispersion of anarchist educational ideas throughout Europe in the later-nineteenth century was partly because of the exile of many of the French participants in the Paris Commune of 1871–1872 but also due to the relative lack of interest by socialists in educational theory and practice. It may also have been because it extended the proletarian sphere beyond the arena of immediate political struggle and offered a meaningful and long-term engagement with the moral and spiritual life of the workers neglected by more 'scientific' approaches. Reclus for example has a great influence on the Dutch educator Henri Roorda van Eysinga, whom he exhorts to live a life of constant teaching in order gradually to change the world by a new morality. Eysinga was in turn a member of the Spanish educator Francisco Ferrer's *Ligue Internationale pour l'education Rationale de l'Enface* and drafted pedagogical principles for the *Ecole Ferrer de Lausanne*.

Other anarchist educational theorists included Jean Marie Guyau who wrote about the conjunction of morality without sanction and natural urges and impressed Reclus and Kropotkin by his appeals to 'fecundity of will'. Reclus believed also in the need for intellectual education and that the dignity of study would engender its own sense of solidarity. He insisted on the need to teach the *grands faits*, a mastery of fundamentals upon which subsequent self-directed autonomous learning depended. An important female educator, Madeleine Vernet, opened a school, *L'Avenir Social* (1906–1910), which made a virtue of poverty and the simple life with minimal financial outlay and attempted to promote a thoughtful minority of conscious militants in the proletariat. However the most developed example of *education intégrale* as serving the organised working class is the *Ecole Ferrer de Lausanne* (1910–1918) under the French-Swiss militant, Jean Wintsch (1880–1943). He involved the local syndicats in seeking a people's school as the specific reflection of *fraternité civique* engendered by collective work and aspiration, which he recorded in his 'Essay in working class education' (1911). Wintsch wrote:

> The end of all truly emancipatory effort is to render man conscious and active, incapable of tyrannizing or being tyrannized. In such a fashion education must develop man's awareness of his rights and obligations [...] Education thus makes a man a true cell, whose exchanges with other cells in the body social become perfectly natural and spontaneous (quoted in Fidler, 1989: 46).

Anarchist inspired popular educational movements made headway mostly in the Catholic south of Europe. The Catalonian Rationalist Schools and workers' *Ateneo* in many of Spain's larger cities (as we shall see in Chapter 5) were fiercely autonomous and highly suspicious of socialist reformism and state orientation (Solá, 1996). They also refused the liberal paternalism of the university extension initiatives, although many of the university intellectuals were sympathetic to them. Ferrer's Modern School in Barcelona became the model for anarchist schools and stimulated developments in many other parts of Europe and America, including Geneva, Liverpool and New York.

The most spectacular eruption of anarchist inspired popular education were the *universités populaires* in France dating from the mid–1890s (discussed at length in Chapter 6). Although workers' co-operatives Nimes and Montpellier provided the original models, the first was established by an anarchist printer Georges Deherme in Paris in 1893. They spread like wildfire in the wake of the Dreyfus affair so that by World War One there were over 200 in France. However they just as rapidly expired and within a few years only a few sociability clubs existed. Both the French and Spanish examples cannot however be separated entirely from the anticlerical masonic educational initiatives of the mid-century such as the French *Ligue de l'Enseignement*. In Spain the masonic modernising movement of Krausism had galvanised many university intellectuals into a relationship with the rebellious lower classes although in Solá's view many of the Spanish popular universities, so called, catered mainly for lower middle class masons (Solá, 1996: 70).

Working Class Political Autonomy

Clearly the movement towards working class political and educational autonomy was extremely complex. Levy has noted how those who identified with socialism and anarchism as political philosophies were drawn from a variety of social backgrounds and for a plurality of reasons. As we have seen scientific and technocratic argument gained strength by the late-nineteenth century, especially in the 1880s and the Second International where 'older types of popular radicalism are criticised and overturned by self-defined "scientific socialists"' both Marxist, and non-Marxist (Levy, 1987: 6). These included successful bourgeois professionals who declared for socialism because they saw it as a movement requiring their technical/managerial skills. Moreover most socialist workers were not 'disciplined factory workers' but artisans and labourers in small workshops. There was also an influential, often Bohemian, group that embraced dissident anti-industrial and romantic traditions such as that epitomised by William Morris and his craft circle in Britain.[3] The many divisions within

3   This theme of 'reactionary radicalism' or a return to a pre-industrial idyll
    continues to haunt the working class movement throughout the century and into
    the next. It should be noted that English Levellers movement was still primarily
    agrarian and craft-based rather than industrial and that this form of radicalism
    survived well into the industrial period. It continued to support an alternative

socialism reflected broader cleavages of broader civil society particularly the romantic/bucolic versus technocratic/modernising split.

Despite the complex social background of those who identified with the new working class movement and particularly the intellectuals who were attracted to it, all agreed that a clean break had to be made from the political liberalism of the bourgeois sphere. Thus the proletarian sphere was constructed on the bases of three pillars of agreement: trade unionism, co-operation and socialism. Although it rapidly developed both reformist and revolutionary wings the workers' movement was characterised by some form of scientific socialism. Educationally, they now drew heavily on their own internally produced 'organic' intellectuals as well as the radical journalists, teachers and economists who were attracted to the movement.

In some senses the most completely achieved proletarian sphere was that of the German workers' movement organised through the Social Democratic Party (SPD) in the late-nineteenth century (discussed in Chapter 7). Its main period of activity was 1890–1914 but its autonomy from liberal circles had been achieved much earlier than other European workers' parties as a result of legislation in 1860, which allowed it parliamentary representation. Lidtke notes that: '[T]he German socialist labor movement began within the framework of workers' educational societies that had been founded by liberals as early as the 1840s' and then detached themselves to form independent workers' education (Lidtke, 1987: 160). Educational activity was at the core of the SDP's attempt to create 'ideological clarity' among organised workers, through educational programmes to disseminate the principles of the SDP and the free trade unions. Though this differed substantially from the open-ended scientific enquiry of the earlier scientific societies, it reflected the desire to think scientifically about social reform that had begun with the Levellers.[4] Moreover, it

anti-industrial politics that clearly informs William Morris's utopian novel *News from Nowhere* and the 'New Life' socialism of Edward Carpenter. Modern ecological movements pay it more than a nod and the more extreme end of the movement may be seen in contemporary New Ageism.

4   This open-ended enquiry was rarely as free as it sounded since political and religious pressures were always present in the form of funding, orthodoxy or worse. Masons and others wanted to prove a divine harmonious order that excluded class struggle, while industrialists wanted inventions that would

drew, according to Lidtke, on the inheritance of Humboldtian *Bildung*, namely learning and cultivation as means for the development of the complete individual. This was serious study not entertainment to which they gave the name *Arbeiterbildung*. Whether the twin aims of ideological clarity and development of the complete individual were compatible is of course debatable but it was the pattern that Marxist workers' parties subsequently followed.

The Rural Problem and the Folk High Schools

The proletarian sphere opened up by the industrial workers' movement was not of course comprehensive or even inclusive of all non-bourgeois social groups and there was a serious failure in many cases to extend this sphere to the small farmers, peasants and rural workers that still comprised the majority of the lower classes. Eley argues that this failure compromised the ability of the workers' movement to attain majority support for a programme of socialist reform.

During the mid-nineteenth century various rural and religious associations that were not allied to the workers' movement created schemes of education for themselves. The most important of these was of course the Danish folk high schools under their founder the Lutheran preacher and writer Nicolai Grundtvig (discussed in Chapter 4). The movement was founded in the heat of the Danish struggle with German territorial ambitions in Schleswig-Holstein. In effect it was a project of national identity formation in the face of imperialist aggression. Educationally, it diverged from the pattern of rationalist enlightenment common to the movements so far described and firmly rooted itself in folk experience and customs. Grundtvig believed implicitly in Herder's assertion that individuals were rooted in a *Volk* and could not be understood other than as an instinctive part of a larger national, rather than class-based, collective, which has a cultural particularity. Though a learned man himself, he was suspicious of

generate higher profits. Some scientists simply wanted Faustian power over all things.

62

book learning for his rural constituency and saw many enlightenment and scientific ideas as breaking up organic communities. The folk high schools therefore encouraged collectivism and mutual self-sufficiency on the land.

Although Grundtvig was the inspiration behind the folk high school movement, in reality it was Kristen Kold who materially founded the movement and there were significant differences between his approach and Grundtvig's that Kulich describes:

> The touchstone of the difference between Grundtvig's and Kold's ideas is their view of man's place in the universe [...] Grundtvig wanted to awaken them to their potential as human beings; religion had no place in his conception of the school. To Kold, awakening was first of all a religious awakening, awakening to a Christian life, while enlightenment was only secondary. Grundtvig's aim was an enlightened citizen; Kold's was a practising Christian. (Kulich, 1997: 445).

To say that the folk high schools were enormously successful is to understate their effect. There can hardly be one peasant-based or small farmer society in northern and central Europe and subsequently throughout India and Africa, where Grundtvig's ideas have not been debated and put into practice. They appealed essentially to small farming communities, especially those that were also involved in 'nation-building' on scanty resources. But equally important was that they placed a much higher value on traditional collective experience and practices than the modernist procedures of scientific socialism. Clearly rural folk saw much in scientific socialism that offended their customary practices and religions and found collective strength in a more practically-based and sociable forms of education based on song, movement and story-telling. While this made the folk high school movement in many countries vulnerable to the subsequent 'blood and soil' ideology of National Socialism, that unfortunately has confirmed many socialists in their suspicion of the movement, it nevertheless suggested a critical aporia in the socialist movement that returned to haunt it in the mid-twentieth century.

Women's Movements and Feminism

If the proletarian sphere was deficient in dealing with the agrarian question, then it was almost criminally negligent in its attitude to women. Despite the rhetoric of women's emancipation to be found in most socialist parties, their actual practice was profoundly lacking. In Germany Bebel's pamphlet *Women under Socialism* published in 1878 was one of the most widely read in the SPD's output, yet the characteristic attitude of German socialists was that women should be prevented from entering skilled trades and that their true place was in the home cooking and child-rearing. The issue of women's suffrage was made secondary to male suffrage and the major issues of work; domesticity and sexual freedom were reserved until after the socialist revolution. As a consequence, women's issues in Germany made little headway.

In the centralised mass socialist parties of Europe there was a general tendency to marginalise women's issues and restrict women's participation in what Eley calls a 'masculinist culture of labour movements and family centred ideology' (Eley, 2002: 103) hence there was little room for democratic feminism. There were relative exceptions to the rule in the Scandinavian countries where feminist issues became relatively incorporated into national self-determination. In Czechoslovakia the independent women's movement broke from the Austrian socialists to campaign on their own programme and in other parts of the Habsburg Empire, like Hungary, there were significant feminist movements. However, in most Catholic countries there was no significant mobilization of women.

In Britain the women's movement was much more visible. The various movements for women's suffrage had developed under the wing of liberalism, led by John Stuart Mill's advocacy in parliament. Mill's pamphlet on the *Subjection of Wome*n (1869) was widely read and the women's suffrage groups were sites of intensive self-education. In some respects they fostered yet another partial public sphere, which drew both on radical middle class reformers and working class socialism. Especially in the industrial north, the culture of pluralistic socialist, theosophist, vegetarian and avant garde cultural groups fed a powerful movement for women's domestic and cultural liberation (Liddington and Norris, 2000). The culture of the 'New Woman' was firmly embraced by many young women schoolteachers like Mary Gawthorpe who were to find a voice in the clubs and associations that bordered the trade union movement and on occasion were to make a significant impact on the movement itself (Rowbotham, 1997; Liddington, 2006). Significantly, campaigners for women's suffrage were in the lead in demanding university extension classes from the universities of Oxford and Cambridge and may have benefited most from them, although not always receiving the specific education they desired (Swindells, 1995).

Conclusion

If the concepts of plebeian and proletarian spheres are modified from Habermas's original thesis, the foregoing argument has attempted to show that they are useful ways of thinking through the problematic of 'popular education'. I have tried to show here that effectively there have been many forms of popular education, which will be explored further in subsequent chapters. They share many characteristics including the enlightenment belief in the power of rationality and scientific enquiry. Even Kold's folk high school taught methodical farming theory and encouraged a shift into more rational practices. The general tendency of the nineteenth century though, appears as opening a division between a bourgeois sphere that pursues popular education for class harmony and cultural perfection and a proletarian sphere that views popular education as a tool for self-help and radical political change. This increases as the century matures and culminates in the revolutionary periods of 1905 and 1917 when social democratic and evolutionary socialist parties attempt to define and corral the educational provision of the intellectually active working class.

However, where the models are less helpful is in thinking about the rural spheres of education and self-help and the place of the women's movements. Both of these were either excluded or marginalised from the proletarian sphere and had an ambiguous relation with the bourgeois public sphere. They both tended to be idealised by the liberal middle class in ways that were not helpful. The more romantic nationalist movements saw the peasantry as the source of folk wisdom (so not in need of 'education') while many liberal reformers saw women as the ideal of purity, 'angels of the hearth' whom education might corrupt. Both were a source of anxiety for socialist and labour movements who tended to ignore their specific needs.

Chapter 4
Nicolae Grundtvig: The Danish Folk High School Movement and the Struggle for University Extension

Denmark in the mid-nineteenth century was in a period of significant transition from the small but notable empire of the eighteenth century to the modernised national state of the twentieth century. Because of her disastrous support for France during the Napoleonic wars of the early nineteenth century, Denmark suffered a number of indignities that severely affected her national self confidence. Amongst these were the bombardment of Copenhagen by the British fleet under Nelson in 1807 and the subsequent loss of Norway to Sweden, which severely curtailed the idea of a Greater Denmark in the popular imagination. The conflict with Germany over Schleswig-Holstein in the mid-century and the consequent loss of the province were further blows to Danish self-esteem, which fostered intense discussions about the nature of Danishness itself. It was in this context that the founding and flourishing of the Danish folk high school movement is best understood.

Constitutionally, Denmark was a monarchy in which the king had almost absolute powers of patronage and enjoyed substantial loyalty from the Danish population. An identifiable Danish public sphere operated from the late eighteenth century when, so long as Danish subjects did not criticise the regime in principle but remained at the level of the local and particular, free speech and publications were permitted. Clubs and periodicals were quite widespread and a strong cultural identity was provided in literature and philosophy most notably by Hans Christian Andersen and Søren Kierkegaard respectively (Wahlin, 1993: 248). Denmark's rich literary history stretching back to the sagas and heroic myths of the seafarers of the Viking period and beyond became a cultural source for a renewed identity and the revival of these works became the passionate pursuit of a number of scholars including Grundtvig himself.

The gathering crisis of empire compelled the Danish monarchy to undertake widespread constitutional reform and various cycles of social and political modernization took place from the 1830s, which resulted in system of local government and elected parish and town councils. The population was overwhelmingly rural with only small centres of urbanisation, most notably Copenhagen itself. As a result of reforms in the late-eighteenth century most of the land (seventy-five per cent) was owned by small farmers. At the national level, the first democratically elected advisory assembly (estates) was introduced by the government in the 1830s but with a very restricted franchise. The franchise was gradually extended throughout the nineteenth century, finally including women only in 1915. Although the system functioned relatively well and the king himself was a popular figure, demand for liberal reforms grew. Eventually the crisis turned into the 'national' question, or the future and identity of the whole state of Denmark.

Education and Enlightenment

Arguably, the 'Enlightenment of the Folk' (*Livoplysning*) through education has played a much greater role in Denmark than in any comparable state. It has the much stronger sense of being driven by a movement which has its origins in civil society rather than as the product of government policy. This popular character has given it a dynamic which has had considerable effect beyond the national borders and has as a consequence been influential in the formation of popular educational institutions throughout Scandinavia and beyond. In many respects the movement associated with Grundtvig and the folk high schools was the most important rural educational movement of the nineteenth and twentieth centuries.

One consequence of the special nature of Danish popular education and the legacy of Grundtvig personally has been a strong tradition of scholarship. One of the most interesting recent analyses has come from the stimulating educational theorist Ove Korsgaard (2000). Korsgaard identified five distinct but overlapping traditions of 'enlightenment' in Denmark, and in turn suggested three dimensions of description and analysis. The traditions he has identified are as follows: 1. Christian enlightenment, 2. civic enlightenment, 3. popular-national enlightenment, 4. workers' enlightenment and 5. personal enlightenment. Each of these traditions of enlightenment in turn can be illuminated through descriptions and analysis of their internal relations. Each is located within a moment in the *history of ideas* which are embraced, initiated or developed. Each also gives rise to certain *institutions* in which these ideas and practices are embodied and finally, he argues, it is possible to identify distinct curricula or *subject matter* taught or learned in each tradition.

The Christian Enlightenment, firstly, was a product of the Reformation of the sixteenth century when the Lutheran Church became the dominant institutional form of Christianity in Denmark. In common with the Protestant Reformation generally its spirit was fiercely critical of practices that might interfere between the individual believer and his God, which included Roman idolatry and the role of the priesthood. One of the principal doctrines of Lutheranism, personal revelation, meant that people had to learn to read in order to be able to study for themselves the word of God as revealed in the Bible. Hence the desire for nationwide literacy was the main driving force for the foundation for a popular adult education in the nineteenth century, the period during which modern adult education began to emerge throughout the Nordic countries.

In concert with this move towards popular literacy, Lutheranism initiated a symbolic shift in perspective from 'action' to 'faith' and from 'body' to 'spirit'. As a consequence Lutherans had little time for older communal practices, which they saw as superstitious and spiritually unhealthy. They systematically suppressed medieval, and in effect pre-Christian, rites of fertility, health and vital energy and consequently many of the forms of local 'spiritual' support offered by traditional folk practitioners.

The effect of the Reformation in Denmark was ultimately to change the Church into a 'state' church under a more formal national organisation and doctrinal control. The Church in fact changes its nature significantly from being the medieval space of ceremonial and display, hierarchy and dogma (as well as the commercial centre for relics and indulgences) and becomes instead a space of *education*, a classroom within which the printed book features as the engine of enlightenment. The invention of the printing press had in many respects made Luther's original protest against the corruption of the medieval Church more than just a localised rebellion. The mass printing of and distribution of pamphlets, especially Luther's *Catechism*, rapidly spread his rebellious ideas over Northern Europe. The Lutheran ecclesiastical rebellion also became closely identified with the growing national movement towards independent secular states subsequently recognised in the Treaty of Württemberg of 1534. In Denmark, the identity of religion and state was further strengthened when Lutheran pietism subsequently generated two decisive reforms: compulsory confirmation in 1736 and the Education Act of 1739 a consequence of which was that the state, in concert with the Church, became the driving force in education.

The second major period of enlightenment begins with the increasing secularisation of education that was an institutional by-product of the Lutheran Reformation: civic enlightenment. In common with other Northern European Protestant states, Denmark was lifted on the tide of the European Enlightenment of the eighteenth century. While the *Encyclopaedia* of Diderot and the French *philosophes* challenged the authority of the Bible, a new breed of rationalist atheists like Voltaire and sceptical scientists struck at the Church itself. Educational ideas drew on the new humanist spirit, as artic-ulated in the work of Erasmus, which challenged commonly accepted hereditary rights of blood and predestined personality. This new escape from theological determinism was further supported by the English philosopher, John Locke, who (until Rousseau) was the most influential early Enlightenment theorist of education. Locke's as-sumption that man's character was not already predetermined but a kind of a *tabula rasa*, which could be formed by instruction and learning, was moreover a challenge to Protestant doctrines of pre-destination.

This gradual secularisation and individualisation of society also had the effect of diluting Christianity as a social glue and the school gradually replaced the church as the place of communal enlightenment. Denmark adopted Locke's and Rousseau's ideas through the activities of educational reformers, like the Reventlow brothers, who with the government's approval set up an education committee in 1789. The government eventually passed a bill in 1814 stipulating that children should have seven years compulsory education and that following the compulsory period *voluntary adult education* should be made available. While Denmark was not unique in adopting enlightened educational views in Northern Europe, its legislation for compulsory schooling is clearly amongst the earliest. Moreover and no other states legislated for post-compulsory education in this way.

A challenge to this form of rational patriotism came with what Korsgaard describes as the third period of enlightenment that of 'Popular-National Enlightenment'. The characteristic of this challenge was the dramatic emergence of a *cultural nationalism* in the early nineteenth century and reaching its height in the 1840s. Here as in many other parts of Europe a new concept of the 'People' or 'Folk' as a cultural and ethnic entity informed a new political discourse that sharply differed from the former discourse of rational patriotism, as have seen (Anderson, 2001). This discourse stressed enlightenment from below rather than above and the Folk (in capitals) now came to be seen as the origin of enlightenment and power. Although the sources for this new discourse are widespread amongst Romantic writers, it was the Germanic form of the *Volk* that was most affective (*Volk* having a greater emotional resonance among the traditional peasantry than the French *peuple*, which became more closely connected with urban radicalism) and in Denmark the (almost mystical) concept of *Folkelighed* came to prominence.

One of the greatest influences on Danish intellectual life at this time was the German philosopher Johann Gottfried von Herder (1744–1803). Herder's Romantic belief in folk songs or *Volkslieder* as true expressions of the people's spirit and creative powers was welcomed by many Danish scholars as a corrective to the Enlightenment's stress on rationality and intellect. Rural folk were no longer seen merely as simpletons but as the repository of deep folk wisdom. For many radical idealists collecting folklore and folk song, by actual contact with the peasantry, signified a move towards national processes of integration. This understanding of the 'folk' contributes decisively to Danish education. Consequently, in contrast to Locke's vision of the child as a *tabula rasa*, educational reformers now took support from Rousseau's recently popularised ideas concerning the naturally self-developing subject. Herder also believed that children had innate potential that could develop in congenial surroundings and he develops the idea of '*Bildung*' in which through a sympathetic education, man realises his humanity. Herder was at pains to stress however, as against more ethnicist theories that *national* character was not similarly innate but could only be learnt through a study of language and history.

Hence the Danes achieved a middle way that reflected both the individual's innate capacities for becoming human through a sympathetic education and his or her part in a collective identity achieved through close learning of his *nation*'s literature and history. The concept of *Bildung* which differs markedly from Anglo-American 'liberal education', precisely because it includes this *national* orientation, becomes widespread in Scandinavia and Slavic areas.

However, a significant consequence was that his concept of the *Volk* sat uneasily with the Enlightenment idea of 'civil society'. Korsgaard argues that in the German cultural sphere Herder's concept of the folk replaces the idea of civil society as envisaged (particularly by the influential Scottish philosopher Adam Ferguson) in the Scottish Enlightenment as independent of the power of the State (and later under Adam Smith that the market should be independent of the state). British liberals believed the State's role in relation to civil society and the market should be limited constitutionally. While Ferguson emphasises the trilogy of the individual, civil society and the 'invisible hand' of the market, Herder can be said to emphasise the people, the nation and – a concept foreign to Scottish Presbyterians – 'the invisible spirit'. Whereas civil society was developed by British liberals in the context of a rapidly industrialising and constitutionally stable state, the '*folkelige*' (popular) society was developed by German nationalists who had yet to achieve constitutionality and industrialisation. Crucially, quite unlike British liberal thought they believed that 'the folk' was a supra-individual concept and not merely individuals tied together by a social contract – strong on organicism, it could be said, but difficult for democracy.

The Voice of Grundtvig

The name Grundtvig is very much a *leitmotif* of this narrative. It's impossible to avoid his influence or ignore the concerns he put at the heart of the national question in Denmark. Grundtvig's influence on Denmark's social and political life is almost unique in scale but it is a very complex inheritance. He clearly belongs to the period of Romantic reaction against the ultra-rationalist aspects eighteenth century Enlightenment yet he is by no means simply anti-enlightenment. Indeed his concept of *folkeoplysning* is a form of enlightenment. However, it is characterised as enlightenment from below rather than above, from the folk rather than the intellectuals and from body and feelings rather than mind and rationality. Grundtvig reacts strongly against certain strands that he believes are contrary to the life of the spirit, foremost of which was the role of 'book learning', which for him was a highly impoverished alternative to 'the living word' (*det levende ord*).

He was critical of rationalists who 'divided light from life' and what he experienced as the cold intellectualism and individualism of the French Revolution. Although he could not be considered a simple irrationalist, according to Henningsen he nevertheless disagrees with rationalists on three main counts (all of which later notably find echoes in feminist and postmodernist theory). Firstly, he holds that there are contradictions in life that can't be resolved through rationality but can only find expression in poetry and myth. Secondly, that the autonomous subject of reason or science is problematic because it leads to egotism whereas in reality (and in another tradition of philosophy) man is a social animal and exists only through his relations with others. Thirdly, Grundtvig believes that the dichotomy rationalists make between reason and feeling is disabling since true knowledge about life is 'nothing other than a feeling within us that comes to light' (quoted in Henningsen, 1993: 285). As a consequence – in a sentiment later repeated by Gandhi in his theory of basic education – true education can only take place in the mother tongue: 'only within it does the heart move freely' (Ibid.).

But Grundtvig's reaction against French Enlightenment rationalism is not to be taken as anti-modernity *tout court*. On the contrary he was profoundly interested in British industrialism and social relations and during a visit to England between 1829–1831 he was so impressed by its industrial vigour and public spirit that he underwent a kind of conversion. Here the former scholar of Nordic sagas discovered the present and began to moderate his former love of the past, and he also forms an admiration for English pragmatic realism that takes life as it is, before religious or philosophical interpretation. He is also forced to reconsider his religious and nationalist particularism and realises that love and truth are universal phenomena and not linked to particular religions. 'First a *man* then a Christian' now becomes his theme and he turns against his previous bible-based Christian zealotry. Over the next few years he completely rewrites his early scholarly works *World History* and *Norse Mythology* in the light of his new understanding of modern life.

Grundtvig's Educational Project

His contact with English liberalism concentrated Grundtvig's energies in a new direction. Although he was still concerned with the national question and the individuality of nations like the Danes, he became more focused on the needs of the *citizen* as a human being in a social context with determinate relations with others. The constitutional reforms that had advanced democratic interests and extended the franchise required knowledgeable and responsible citizens who were prepared to govern in the interests of all. Grundtvig's project then shifted to one of formulating an advanced educational system appropriate to these new needs but embedded in a rejuvenated commitment to Danishness.

Grundtvig originally planned a two-pillar educational system, one of which, the folk high schools, was to be culturally 'national' in orientation, and the other, the new university, which was to be 'universal'. The folk high schools were aimed at creating a historically embedded national consciousness that would celebrate the 'folk' or more particularly the small farmers and peasantry of Denmark. Less well remembered, however, was Grundtvig's ambition to create a Nordic university at Gothenburg 'for a new historical, universal science, encompassing the whole of life' (quoted in ibid.: 290). In contrast to the Danish folk high school, the university was to be an elite institution dedicated to the pursuit of pure science. This casts an interesting light on Grundtvig, who is often characterised as wholly opposed to scientific rationalism. In fact it is now clear that he saw something of a symbiosis between an education of the sentiments and an education of the intellect. While emphasis on the former was necessary for the people *as a whole*, distinct intellectual development was required for those who would become the specialists within the social system. After his visit to England, Grundtvig had come to realise there was an undeniable need for a 'universal' scientific approach conducted on strictly rational and empirical lines. But consistent with his earlier beliefs he still held that, without a countervailing *popular* education, such science would not be embedded within the needs of the people and may even be used against them. It was through popular education, he believed, that the new scientific ideas, generated in the universities, should be put to the test in debate and discussion. This collaboration between the people and the specialist, he hoped, would create an organic relationship between different strata and dimensions of knowledge that would tie 'scientific' intellectuals to the people as a whole. But, inevitably, his hopes were frustrated, since funding for the university was never forthcoming and the ideal unity of folk and specialists was stillborn.

Rather one-sidedly therefore, the folk element in Grundtvig's work was what he became most associated with. Although a number of folk high schools, mostly catering for agricultural education, predated Grundtvig's own project, the Folk High School at Sorø was the first to be conceived on his principles. The crucial difference lay in the social and human core of the education. Here Grundtvig advocated setting up a school for members of the state council with two related functions. Firstly, the education they received should enable them to serve as authentic representatives of the people but, secondly, should also enable them to express their deeper feelings in the mother tongue, through immersion in its poetry and myth. Thus they would understand the folk from their 'deep heart's core' (as Yeats might have put it) rather than from the cold reason of book learning.

Central to this form of popular education was his concept of *Folkelighed* (of the people), which although never defined, for him meant sociability, conversation, mother tongue and 'enlightenment for life'. In this it is possible to see the pervasive influence of Herder but Grundtvig was wary of the German use of the term *Volksgeist*. This could often degenerate into 'blood and soil' mysticism in the hands of racial purists and it is important to say that Grundtvig strenuously avoided these conclusions. On the contrary for him the life of the 'spirit' was intimately bound up with *language* rather than blood. Hence his concept of a Nordic or Danish identity was tied to its 'distinctive feature or cultural stamp' (quoted in ibid.: 289). He was not simply a nationalist, therefore, but embraced important aspects of a common humanity. His reading of Herder suggested to him a kind of differentiated universalism in the sense that 'mankind' is composed of specific peoples who share common aspects but are culturally different. His 'nationalism' thus lies in the belief that the determined protection of country and mother tongue is beneficial to everyone. This in turn is yoked to his Anglo-Saxon-inspired liberal belief in the enlightened pursuit of self-interest for the common good. In this way it could be seen that Grundtvig finds a middle way between Germanic conceptions of *Geist* and *Volk* on the one hand and the atomised possessive individualism of English liberalism. He both rejects the supra-historical reason and spirit associated with German idealism and embraces the cultural diversity associated with liberalism.

Like the Nordic University, the High School at Sorø was never founded because, although it had royal blessing, the war broke out and the National Liberal party came to power with different educational ideas. In the absence of government policy therefore, a movement of private individuals and groups set up their own folk high schools around the country, initially in 1844 at Rødding in North Schleswig. Although he supported the movement that took his name, Grundtvig was very concerned about the exclusive sectarianism of the revivalist groups, since he wanted the schools to embrace all classes and types of people. He was to some extent unhappy that the folk high schools became almost wholly associated with the political emancipation and agricultural revolution of the small farmers as a specific group and as

76

a consequence remained somewhat aloof. The folk high schools initially grew only slowly in numbers, depending largely on private individuals to fund and lead them. It was only after the loss of Schleswig Holstein to German expansionism in 1864 that the movement really flourished. However, it is possible to argue that, because of Grundtvig's project, when the national revival did eventually take place, it was not just romantically folkloric but a movement for a modern conscious nation. Reflecting the British pattern, village halls were built, societies and clubs were founded and a burgeoning cooperative movement arose, radically expanding the public sphere.

Grundtvig's Educational Ideas

As we have seen Grundtvig developed his ideas on popular education in the context the emergence of Danish nationalism and the modernisation of the Danish state in the face of a militant German expansionism and at a time when Danish cultural life was dominated by German ideas and manners.[1] Although his theology is Lutheran in origin, as was all educational change in Denmark, so his ideas gradually moved away from a religion-centred approach towards finding the common ground between Christians and others who have 'a glimmer of spirit and a spark of truthfulness' (quoted in Bugge, 1983). Grundtvig's own experience as a teacher was limited to three years in a grammar school in Copenhagen but he was very impressed on his visit to England by the tutorial system he found at Trinity College, Oxford (an inspiration, too some years later, for Albert Mansbridge when he founded the WEA in Britain).

A defining element of his thought was, as against the prevailing individualism of the rationalist Enlightenment, his emphasis on the context played by the wider community at both a local and national level. For him education was primarily social – for the good of the whole society rather than the progress of the individual alone. Equally,

1   I am indebted to my colleague John Dyce of the Scottish Congregational College for this summary of Grundtvig's educational ideas.

he was clear that education should be quite independent of church influence – just as the church should be free of state interference. Despite his identification with folk high schools normally seen as adult, his actual emphasis was on the education of young people which he regarded as the age of imagination and emotional arousal (in contrast to adulthood, which for him was the time when 'feeling' predominated, and old age which the moment of intellect).

But the living word, vital too to Luther, was always central to his ideas. Although not always transparently clear what he meant by this phrase (*det levende ord*) it was not just the sermon from the pulpit. Though he believed the animated lecture (*foredrag*) was important in broadcasting the enthusiasm of the lecturer to the students in a way no book could, he did not see this as a one way transmission. In fact quite opposite because learning was contextualised for him by interaction with others (*vekselvirkning*); learners should not sit and listen passively but actively converse, relate their experiences, express their emotions and so on. Not quite Socratic dialogue probably, because Grundtvig still envisaged a more persuasive role for the teacher but neither was it the Mosaic 'sit-stillery' so derided by a later educationist, John Dewey. Nevertheless, the kind of dialogic encounter Grundtvig had in mind was a genuine meeting of minds in a lively conversation such that those engaged would be changed by the encounter.

A further element of the living word was the importance of myth and poetry which Grundtvig elevates to a quasi-mystical level. Grundtvig's own dedication to hymn writing and singing demonstrated how much he believed that a culture's vitality was expressed in its folk songs and epics. His poem 'Tidings in the High North' (1864) runs:

> Only words that pass in story and song
> From mouth to mouth where people throng
> Sustain the life of the people;
> Only in their own and ancient words
> Is education to be found
> Given by the spirit of the people.[2]

2   Compare this with a stanza from Book XII of Wordsworth's *The Prelude* (1805):

78

How far Grundtvig actually participated in this life of the folk is questionable since as an academic writer, even when translating the Nordic sagas, his time was spent largely among books. Indeed there are times when he complains (like so many Romantic writers) that the actual voice of the people had become so corrupted, it could no longer maintain the line of the song. What his concern seems to represent is more that the folk should regain that voice before it was lost forever in the march to modernity.

For Grundtvig it was this body of lore and epic narrative that marked the distinctive nature of a people within world history, which would otherwise pass it by. But there was an ambiguity of course about how far the domain of that particular 'folk' extended. Clearly for Grundtvig it swelled way beyond the Danish peninsula and into a rather more undefined territory of the 'Nordic' people. While the modern Scandinavian countries of Norway and Sweden were obvious (if unwitting) partners to the Danes, he seems to imagine an ancient ur time of Northern seafaring folk which extended to Iceland and may also have included the Anglo-Saxons. Indeed the Anglo-Saxon poem *Beowulf* was for him a luminous addition to the Nordic pantheon. But at the heart of this was a concern for a poetic imagery that would stir the heart and move one to understanding and, eventually, action. As against this he posited the 'dead' knowledge of books which operated simply at an intellectual level and was incapable of moving the spirit.

Needless to say Grundtvig, as a voluminous producer of the written word, is at other times more generously disposed to book learning. Books are 'good friends in reserve' but only if the words they contain enable passage through to the life within. What he was

> When I began to enquire,
> To watch and question those I met, and held
> Familiar talk with them, the lonely roads
> Were Schools to me in which I daily read
> With most delight the passions of mankind,
> There saw into the depths of human souls,
> Souls that appear to have no depths at all
> To vulgar eyes. And now convinced at heart
> How little that to which alone we give the
> The name of education hath to do
> With real feeling and just sense.

often getting at was the use in schools of Latin as the medium of instruction but also the dry academic language of scholarly specialisms especially in science. Unfortunately too often what the scientific revolution had produced was not the popular enlightenment (*Folkeoplysning*) intended by its more idealistic practitioners such as Bacon and Priestley in England but yet a new priestly caste of specialists, that had no interest in disseminating their knowledge.

What he required from popular education was a transfiguration of life. This rendered the role of books redundant for the general populace – though not of course for the higher educated, which was the role of universities. But as we have seen, the test of the value of knowledge generated at this level was whether it could be interrogated and utilised at the popular level. If a folk context and understanding could not be found for the knowledge generated in universities, then it was valueless. Grundtvig was similarly scornful of 'the learned' who would not engage with the popular culture but continued to affect French or German manners and style. Indeed it was the populism of this approach that won him many followers among the lower and middling classes, even if he was dismissed, like his English contemporary John Ruskin, as a showman by his academic peers. In terms that could have been echoed by British WEA stalwarts of half a century later Grundtvig insisted that the true value of education was not to enable the individual to rise out of the lower class, as liberal ideology intended, but in raising the whole people to a higher level of culture (Steele, 1987).

While still a true believer in the confessional power of religion, Grundtvig nevertheless marks an important transitional stage to a secular humanism in education, encapsulated in his phrase 'first a man, then a Christian'. Equally concerned to see the church protected from the power of the state and the state from that of the church, he viewed education as a fundamentally human activity that built the social capacity of human beings to become a purposeful community and enriched them spiritually. This was not of course how his followers always understood him as we shall in what follows.

Kold and the Danish Folk High Schools

As we have seen the folk high schools in Denmark movement both pre-dated Grundtvig's involvement and in certain respects escaped him. As Kulich has noted, Grundtvig was not even the prime mover in those folk high schools that followed his ideas (Kulich, 1997). Much of the responsibility for this has to go to his pupil Christen Kold (1816–1870). Although Kold took inspiration from and, crucially, the blessing of Grundtvig, his practice differed in certain crucial respects. He wrote little and was very much a practitioner who lived the simple life with his students. His most significant divergence from his master's model was that his schools were Christian revivalist rather than secular, which was contrary (at least) to Grundtvig's expressed wishes. Kold's practical methods were widely influential and he appears to have maintained a myth about himself of the 'man of the people' who heroically resisted the authorities to maintain the tradition of the living word, although it appears in practice he was more pragmatic.

Kold came from humble artisan origins. His father was a shoemaker who wanted him to follow him in the trade. But his mother (reminiscent of Mrs Morel in D.H. Lawrence's *Sons and Lovers*) characterised him as having 'two left hands' and turned him towards teaching as an occupation. His moment of vocational revelation however seems to have come from listening to the revivalist preacher Skraeppenborg in the 1830s who, contrary to the prevailing climate of penitential gloom, taught that God *loves* mankind: 'I have never known anything like the life, the joy, the strength and the energy that rose up in me' Kold wrote (quoted in Kulich, 1997: 442). Kold also claims to have been inspired by Kierkegaard's *Deeds of Love* which, he claimed, was even more important than Grundtvig to him.

Pedagogically, Kold followed Grundtvig's assertion that all education centred on the act of narration, the 'living word', inspiring talk that awakened the people to their most deeply held beliefs. This subtle shift, to spiritual *awakening* rather than *enlightenment* was the goal of the schools. But larger differences were concealed; Kulich notes that:

> The touchstone of the difference between Grundtvig's and Kold's ideas is their view of man's place in the universe [...] Grundtvig wanted to awaken them to their potential as human beings; religion had no place in his conception of the school. To Kold, awakening was first of all a religious awakening, awakening to a Christian life, while enlightenment was only secondary. Grundtvig's aim was an enlightened citizen; Kold's was a practising Christian (Ibid.: 445).

While Grundtvig was very much an academic and scholar, Kold was man of the people who dressed like them and lived like them with an almost simple faith. He soon abandoned Grundtvig's own books claiming his students did not understand them anyway and moved to the oral style without books at all. Kulich believes that Kold never really understood Grundtvig's separation of the human from the Christian and never broke out of the Christian revivalist circle. Gradually he withdrew from Grundtvig's historical-poetic approach, which he abandoned in favour of an exhortation to follow Jesus' example in frugality and brotherly love, emphasising thrift, self-sacrifice and hard work. He also shifted towards a more functionalist curriculum due in part to the necessities of (the now all too familiar) compromise with local and state grant aiding authorities about curriculum and assessment, and his school began teaching chemistry, physics and surveying, for example. It is unclear how much he conceded in order to retain grant aiding but eventually his school did become near self-sufficient.

In a further pragmatic change in response to the demands of the farm hands who attended the school, Kold's school began in 1863 to accept women students. This seems to have come from a genuine desire of the men for the women to learn what they had learned so they could talk together on the same level which Kold accepted. Women were invited to participate in the schools, but at different times to the men, of course, and their curriculum was the same as that for agriculture, except for handicrafts and housework, taught by Kold's sister (who until then had been confined to the kitchen).

Although Kold's own school did not survive him, his impact was broad and despite differences, the school received Grundtvig's blessing. He nevertheless held that the folk high schools that other groups had founded during the period were inferior to his own because they pursued more secular and political aims such as Danish national life and the rights of peasants, rather than the religious struggle of life against death. Despite his own personal myth building, he and Grundtvig were spiritual and pragmatic founders of the folk high school movement, united in rejecting cramming and examinations and allowing teaching unfold as lectures and conversations about universal human topics.

The Danish folk high schools were in effect a Grundtvigian-influenced spiritual movement developed in practice by Kristen Kold after 1851, according to a later report to the World Association for Adult Education in 1929 (Hegermann-Lindencrone, 1929). While the founding generation believed in oral transmission of inspiration influenced by personality, especially that of the school's Principal, increasingly the pupils' own work became more important. The subjects of instruction included bible stories, world historical figures, the great movements of human development, problems of culture and Danish history, although there were also topics from literature, economics, sociology and natural science.

Practically, the folk high schools terms included five months residential instruction for men from November to March and three months for women May to August. The personality of the Principal was central the school's effectiveness and often the schools were his private property. Although most were based on educational principles primarily drawn from Grundtvig, they also reflected, probably not entirely in accordance with his wishes, the 'Home Mission' and the Pietistic branch of the Danish Church. More materialistically, however, key to their success was of course the movement's gradual ability to generate public funding from the state and local sources. By 1929 the folk high schools received a very substantial state subvention of fifty per cent of the teacher's salaries, twenty per cent of the principal's salary, thirty-five per cent of teaching material and ten per cent of buildings costs, in return for which the state had the right of inspection.[3]

3   According to Hegermann-Lindencrone's figures at the time of his report the folk high schools and Agricultural Schools received an annual subvention of 1,100,000 kroner for around 9,500 students (including student subventions). At 114.70 kroner per head this was a far higher unit of resource than that received by any other adult educational body; the Continuation schools for example received 160,000 kroner for 12,000 students i.e. 13.3 kroner per head, evening schools 244,000 kroner for 19,000 students i.e. 12.8 kroner per head and

The Challenge to the Folk High Schools

Central as they were to the Danish revival, the folk high schools were gradually challenged by other often urban educational forms. By the early twentieth century adult education in Denmark fielded a range of adult educational provision, the most important of which was that of the folk high schools. The other principal branch was the programme of evening classes, or Continuation Schools, which were an extension of the elementary school for adolescents and adults. These classes had in fact been allowed for in legislation as early as 1814, primarily to give instruction to post-school adolescents who attended voluntarily but they quickly recruited adults also. Subjects taught were mostly the same as those found in primary school including Danish, writing, drawing, religion, history geography, natural science, maths, foreign languages, bookkeeping, sociology hygiene, elementary agriculture and horticulture, housewifery, needlework manual work, '*slojd*', gymnastics and singing. These classes were in effect a kind of extended secondary provision and in other respects resembled what came to be called in the British system, Further Education. Other forms of provision for adults included lecture work in the villages and rural districts in meeting houses associated with folk high schools but provided by the universities in the cities under the auspices of the Popular University Union. Popular libraries remodelled on Anglo-American lines, also functioned as educational centres with many librarians taking a proactive educational role.

The pressures identified by Habermas as fragmenting early civil society such as the specialisation of knowledge, industrialisation and particularly the dominance of class formations over the original idea of a bourgeois public became more marked in late nineteenth century Denmark. Hence the fourth phase of enlightenment identified by Korsgaard was a significant break from the nationalist vision, the

workers' (trade union) education received 12,000 kroner for around 7,5000 students or 0.16 kroner per head. Thus the folk high schools unit of resource was more than ten times higher than the next best resourced group the Continuation Schools and ten thousand times more generous than the subvention for workers' education.

84

'Workers' Enlightenment'. An independent Danish labour movement emerged rapidly with industrialisation and in 1871 Louis Pio established the Danish division of the First Workers' International. But the movement was split on the crucial question of whether to establish its own independent workers' education or instead to demand greater access to that provided by the state. Further dissension was introduced by the growth of a cultural leftism, led particularly by Georg Brandes 'the Voltaire of the Nordic countries', and inspired by J.S. Mill and Comtean positivism. Workers' education – as opposed to folk education – became widespread and included a new development, study circles. The Workers' Educational Union was a student democracy like the British WEA whose provision included lectures, study circles with topics drawn from social legislation, history of trade unions, social democracy and co-operation and evening classes in mostly the same subjects as in other adult education provision. The Union also ran special courses for officials, trade union and co-operative leaders and residential and day schools for the unemployed in mostly social sciences and hygiene. It has also been argued that the success of workers' education in Denmark and Sweden was because of effective liberal/socialist alliances forged before World War One (Levy, 1987: 4). By the 1920s a General Council for Adult Education with representation from all groups became the basis for a degree of co-operation between all movements.

The leftist edge of the workers' movement was blunted by the onset of war in 1914. The failure by international social democracy to prevent World War One led to a conservative return to a more nationalistic spirit in Denmark. The Danish SDP steered away from revolutionary aims and concentrated instead on developing a welfare state for the workers. Julius Bomholt, the SDP leader, nevertheless continued to develop an independent workers' culture. After the Nazis came to power in Germany in 1933 class struggle in Denmark gave way to popularism and the workers' movement swiftly accommodated to the Grundtvigians' ideal of national popular cultural enlightenment. However, the Nazis were equally adept at converting popular concepts to their own racist ideology. In the struggle between democratic and national aspirations Korsgaard notes 'some of the Grundtvigian core concepts were part of the Nazi vocabulary, such as: folk, popular, the spirit of the people, popular revival, people's enlightenment etc'

(Korsgaard, 2000: 21). In liberal circles Grundtvig has never entirely escaped this unwelcome taint.

University Extension, Women and the City

Another current however, had also been flowing through Danish life and at the end of the nineteenth century a new cultural radicalism was also marked in the campaigns of the freshly emergent women's movement. The Swedish feminist Ellen Key became leading advocate of new educational vision *'folkbildning'* which opposed authoritarian teaching methods and instead emphasised the importance of aesthetic knowledge and personal development (Rowbotham, 1997: 37). Her very popular lectures based in the Workers' Institute in Stockholm were a source of inspiration to Denmark's progressive women. It was in large part because of their pressure for higher education, coming especially from those who wanted to become teachers, that by 1900 university extension was so eagerly embraced in Denmark. Perhaps more radical in tone than in Britain, it was based on socialist and leftist ideas involving a close co-operation of university teachers of the cultural left and workers' leaders who were inspired more by Marxism than liberalism. It was, however, strongly opposed by Grundtvigians who were highly suspicious of this form of 'scientific' enlightenment and class politics.

The folk high school model clearly did not have universal appeal and the hitherto neglected development of an extensive university based education was especially welcomed in the cities and among middle class women. And it was in Denmark's only metropolitan town, Copenhagen, that the idea of a 'scientific' education that held out a seductive charm. Froken Henni Forchhammer, who was a member of the Committee of the University Extension Association of Copenhagen, noted in 1900 that during recent years increasing numbers of men and women in Denmark had been studying university extension in England in order to be able to establish such a system in Denmark (Forchhammer, 1900: 84).

Significantly, the impetus had come from the workers rather than intellectuals claiming in Copenhagen the 'longing for closer contact with scientific methods' had spread to the working classes with the result that eight working men's associations had united to promote extension. They had in turn invited twenty other associations for cultural and educational purpose to collaborate and formed the *Folkeuniversitetsforeningen* (University Extension Association) for Copenhagen in April 1898. The University of Copenhagen readily responded by appointing a Delegacy with Dr Drachmann, a university lecturer, as secretary. The movement spread out rapidly from the capital to the provincial towns and between February and March 1899 there were nineteen courses of six lectures each, which were taught by seven lecturers (most of whom were graduates but they included one professor, one university lecturer and one lecture from a folk high school). Classes were held in the evenings between 8pm and 10pm following the English pattern of an hour's lecture and discussion. Forchhammer noted the enthusiasm among working people especially for courses on Social Economy given in Copenhagen, where most of those attending were artisans. No written work was done, though she thought it might be attempted in the current session and exams were most unlikely to be introduced.[4]

The extension committee adopted the name *Folke-Universitetsudvalg* that organised the entire system of courses centrally, recruiting and sending out lecturers to local groups, the FUF (*Folkuniversitetsforeninger*), printing syllabuses, dealing with income

---

4   The Copenhagen delegates' first report, issued in May 1899, maintained that the attendance at courses for the year was 4,648 of whom 1,537 were women and 3,111 were men, the biggest category of the men being workers (1,400) (c. twenty-eight per cent) and of the women, teachers (360) (c. eight per cent) with an average attendance of about 200. In some of the provincial towns it was much larger, in one case over 800 had attended a course. The delegates recruited a further twenty-one lecturers to the staff. During the Autumn term of 1899 thirty-three six-lecture courses were delivered, mostly one in each centre, but seven in the Copenhagen centre and the same was expected for Spring term 1900, to be delivered by eighteen lecturers. Not all of the forty centres could be accommodated, half of which were in villages and small towns. The initial small state subsidy of 5,000 kroner (£275) was mostly for use in small centres further from Copenhagen and involved no inspection from the government.

and expenditure and publishing annual reports. The 1900–1901 report numbers forty-three FUF groups, one in Copenhagen, twenty-nine in provincial towns and thirteen in the country. The groups varied considerably, some being founded for the specific purpose of extension and others based on previous associations. the standard six-lecture courses were each followed by an hour's questions and discussion, on the English model and small circulating libraries were provided (Ibid.: 44).

A flavour of a Danish student's feelings about university extension comes from the 1890s when the *University Extension Journal* contained a wry commentary on his visit to the Cambridge summer school (Trier, 1896). This was one Gerson Trier of Copenhagen who was concerned to say how much he appreciated and enjoyed the event but it appeared to fall short his two key categories of 'modernity' and 'internationalism'. He was initially surprised that the English lecturers wore gowns unlike on the continent where lecturers are dressed 'like any other mortal' and he could not help thinking of Goethe's *Faust* (Ibid.). Though he found the lectures 'were instinct with the spirit of modern times' three things exercised him. The first was the lecturers' insistence generally that modern culture rested entirely on the work of the classical period – an idea being progressively abandoned on the continent. Europeans recognised a break in the culture of modernity in that it was based on science and fostered a concern for brotherhood whereas the Greeks and Romans held all foreigners to be barbarians and slavery a necessary and natural institution. Trier was surprised therefore, about the 'renaissance' standpoint adopted in the General Course 'the more so as University Extension must needs be a democratic movement and modern in every fibre'. He was surprised that Greek and Latin had not been dropped from the curriculum of so modern a movement (Ibid.).

His second concern was the amount of time devoted to the subject of Education and that most of the members of the summer school were teachers, when he had expected to meet all sorts and conditions of person especially workers: 'So far the smaller number of busy people and especially of working men, was a disappointment to those who had expected to find a representative gathering of the great work of the Extension movement' (this observation however reveals just how important teachers were as vehicles for cultural transmission, Trier himself was one) (Ibid.).

Thirdly, he noted with evident relief the importance of the lectures on Evolution, which were a marked peculiarity of the meeting. He found this 'entirely modern' and imbued with the spirit of Charles Darwin. Here England appeared in advance of the continent in that what was emphasised was not merely the partial explanatory capability of the theory but its totality as an idea. The meeting, in the end he concedes, happily combined the 'most glorious traditions of the olden times with the modern ideas of democracy and internationalism'. Trier's obvious amusement with some of the medieval apparatus of the Cambridge school is matched by his admiration for its homeliness. He implies however that it is somewhat lagging behind the continent in its cultural ideas and hints at the 'cosiness' of the summer school (Ibid.)

Some interesting comparisons were drawn by contemporaries with the English university extension movement in its journals. The *Gazette* in 1894 carried two lengthy descriptions of the Folk High School, (March 1894, Vol.IV, pp.72–4 and September 1894, pp.146–9). The first was by Miss E. Healy and adapted from her 1892 report of the 'The Educational Systems of Sweden, Norway and Denmark' and the second by Alfred Povlsen, the Director of the Danish Association for Folk High Schools, who had been invited to give a lecture to the Oxford summer meeting. Both indicated the early origins of the movement in 1864 and the importance of religion and nationalism following the disastrous war with Germany. As a movement it was found to be highly democratic and peasant based and relied on residential courses of three or six months rather than weekly classes. The schools were also privately owned, entirely open and refused examinations, quite a different model from English extension. Povlsen went as far as to say that the Folk High Schools had taken up part of the work which was done by extension in England:

> But they take no part in the gratuitous instruction given to artisans and workmen in the towns. It is the students of Copenhagen who have here set the example and taken up a work, which undoubtedly has much more in common with the English undertaking (Ibid.: 149).

Extension in Scandinavia was then characterised by a number of elements. The first was the existence of the folk high school movement which had originated in Denmark and spread to other Scandinavian countries. This Protestant and nationalist movement had responded to the needs of a largely rural population in political and economic crisis and was both radical and rationalist. It raised the general level of folk education to a high level of self-reliance and as such itself became the model adopted many third world countries for their own populations. This movement to an extent already fulfilled some of the educational needs which in other countries demanded university extension and this may have delayed its entrance into Denmark. While in Sweden especially university extension was directly introduced by academics like Harald Hjarne, who had closely studied the English model, to a largely school teacher fraternity or rather sorority (as we shall see in Chapter 8) in Denmark it appeared to be the result of a spontaneous demand by the organised working class and women's movements. In both cases, however, it was a largely urban movement, but in Denmark it was almost certainly inscribed into a broader socialist and radical political movement. It was perceived as a modernising movement which contained the by now familiar rhetoric of 'scientific' and objective knowledge, which for some was linked with a secular belief in Darwinism and the notion of social evolution.

State support, although modest, was early in evidence and political change towards a 'modern' social democracy was associated with its introduction. There is some feeling that although it consciously modelled itself on its English mentor it differed in substantial ways. In Sweden for example, it was much more closely tied to teachers' professional needs, while in Denmark it foreshadowed the emergence of the WEA, in Britain, in its close collaboration with workers' associations. There was less attention to the detail of written work and assessment procedures and more to the question of social and political relevance. Indeed the British original seemed to at least one observer as rather quaint and old-fashioned. It seems that here, too, 'University Extension' was the name for modernising and radical aspirations of emergent social groups rather than a specific set of procedures and protocols. Without Grundtvig and the folk high schools movement, however, such modernisation might not have been so successfully achieved.

Chapter 5
Spain and Italy: Rationalist Education and Popular Universities

Modern Spanish history has been deeply complexed by its relationship to Revolutionary France. After a brief campaign of conquest, Napoleon installed his brother Joseph as king, who immediately set about trying to create a centralised administration on the French model. He created a Ministry of Education, brought universities and schools under government control and attempted to create a secular educational system. But in the face of the intransigent opposition of the Spanish Church he made little headway and the restoration of Ferdinand VII in 1813 shortly undid what had been done. Ferdinand recalled the monarchy's traditional allies and, in a decree of 1824: 'ushered in an era of severe intellectual repression, dominated by the Catholic Church, which claiming the sole possession of the truth, promulgated the doctrine that 'error has no rights' (Bowen, 1981: 465).

Since Catholic educators saw their traditional monopoly over education as an inalienable right, modernity was postponed for over half a century. Education as such should be the responsibility of the Church and the family while state education, if allowed at all, should be restricted to certain kinds of instruction. According to Boyd (1997) illiteracy and ignorance were preferable to any instruction 'that could not be reconciled with the basic tenets of faith, an argument that was recapitulated by Pius XI in 1929 in his papal encyclical *Divinis Illius Magistri*' (Boyd, 1997: 23). Catholic schools taught class harmony and Christian resignation in the face of social inequality and the backbone of the curriculum was a rote learning catechism that was 'inherently dogmatic and authoritarian' and 'explicitly anti-liberal' (Ibid.). Catholic education was aimed at overcoming an irredeemably corrupt human nature and the reality of original sin which was the 'sacred mission' of the teacher, who was supposed to be charismatic and, accordingly, lacked any formal training. Nevertheless, in the face of increasing demands for secular involvement in education, orders like the Piarists, Le Salleans, Salesians, and Marists began to offer vocational training in accounting and drafting and the manual arts while the Jesuits opened the first university for Catholic laymen in 1886 in Deusto.

Because of sporadic bouts of repression that saw liberal educators imprisoned, driven into exile, and occasionally as in the case of Francisco Ferrer, executed, opposition to Catholic hegemony in education frequently had to be clandestine. Liberal, modernising forces inevitably grew during the century and, as in other Catholic countries, one important network for liberal and progressive thought was freemasonry. According to Iris Zavala, in Spain 'The Free-masonry of that period was nothing but the universal conspiracy of the revolutionary middle class against the feudal, monarchical and divine tyranny, It was the International of that class' (Zavala, 1971: 192, quoted in Hobsbawm, 1985: 384). As we shall see, European free-masonry proved a significant channel for progressive educational theory in mid-nineteenth century Spain. Surprisingly, perhaps, only a moderate anti-clerical feeling guided the Liberal approach to state education and the *Ley Moyano* of 1857 was designed to prevent education from falling under the complete control of the Church while allowing it the right of moral supervision. But the government was not helped by the fact that municipal schools were poorly equipped, dilapidated and overcrowded, frequently lacking qualified teachers. This allowed the Church to step in, sponsoring nearly eighty per cent of private education but, while it was alarmed by the spread of secularisation of European culture and rapid growth of anticlericalism among the Spanish masses, it seemed to have no alternative programme. Boyd comments that: 'the political and moral orientation of provided by the Catholic schools seemed the most serious obstacle to modernisation and the creation of a national and civic con-sciousness' (Boyd, 1997: 137). While the history of the nineteenth century in Spain is one of increasing secularisation, it was not achieved evenly or uniformly, the oscillation between Liberal and Conservative governments often wiping out each other's reforms. The battles between Liberals and Catholics for control of education even led at times to curious alliances of anarchists with the Church over school accreditation, to insist on freedom to teach freedom from state regulation.

The Spanish Church eventually took an interest in popular education in the late-nineteenth century, primarily to combat the growing influence of socialism among workers. The bishopric in Salamanca in 1892 wrote:

> The task of the instruction and moralisation of the disinherited proletarian class is today of great importance, if the Satanic efforts of socialism to fall as a formidable avalanche on society are taken into account (quoted in Hernandez Diaz, 1996: 84).

The high point of ideological contestation came with Leo XIII's *Rerum Novarum* in 1891, which pragmatically accepted the coexistence of fundamentalist and liberal positions. In what was a dramatic reversal of fortune for the Liberals in 1876 following the restoration of the Conservative government, the Church's role was incorporated constitutionally. But the Church, in return accepted the necessity for the existence of the state and socialisation while showing great concern over the threat of socialism and the 'social question'. It also attempted to emulate existing popular educational movements in Spain and more widely in Europe, by 1900, in setting up about 300 Catholic Workers' Circles, which became the fore-runner of 'yellow unionism' and the Catholic Action movement of the 1920s.

Krausism and the Masonic Network

While the growth of liberal, secularist and anti-clerical politics dated from the French Revolution earlier in the century, the experience of catastrophic defeat and occupation by Napoleonic forces deeply injured national pride, even that of Spanish progressives. After the Bourbon Restoration a period of inwardness and anti-European sentiment sealed Spain off from modernising influences. Eventually however Spanish intellectuals travelled to European, though emphatically not French intellectual centres, and began to rediscover the Enlightenment. However it was now the epigone of that movement that dominated the university lecture halls. Eric Hobsbawm, in one of his more magisterial moments, wrote that 'backward countries' seeking to break through to modernity were often unoriginal and undiscriminating in their borrowing of ideas: 'Brazilian and Mexican intellectuals took uncritically to Auguste Comte, Spanish ones at this very early period to an obscure and second-rate German philosopher, one Karl Krause, whom they made into a battering ram of anti-clerical enlightenment' (Hobsbawm, 1985: 199).

Spanish intellectual life of the mid-nineteenth century certainly owed a great deal to the imported teachings of Karl Christian Friedrich Krause (1781–1832), an enlightenment freemason and follower of Hegel and Fichte. Never having set foot in Spain, his impact on the emergent Spanish middle class was entirely channelled through disciples like the educationalist Sanz del Río (1814–1869), who studied under him in Heidelberg. Subsequently self-taught intellectuals who gained university prominence like Giner de los Rios and the poet Machado took the humanist ideals of Krause to a wider public. Although anti-clerical in form Krausism took a relatively moderate line that sought a degree of accommodation with traditional Christianity. Boyd's view was that:

> The Spanish Krausists defined man as a rational and moral being whose evolving nature was shaped by ongoing processes of self-discovery and self-creation. Although the author of the universe and immanent within it, God did not actively intervene in the world: man's progress toward knowledge of the divine presence (in the world and himself) was an autonomous activity with its origins in man's nature. Discovery of the moral law and the moral basis of ethical conduct was thus a purely human undertaking, dependent on individual experience and rational reflection, just as the religious sense was reasoned response to the unity of God's creation, rather than a formalistic adherence to an authoritarian dogma (Boyd, 1997: 31).

Krausism was a humanist ideal of protest and renewal for the modernisation of the nation whose moral and intellectual idealism persisted long after its originators had died. Krausists embodied the democratic revolution of 1868 and the 1874 Spanish Republic, in which republican reformers determinedly set out to Europeanise Spanish thought and institutions. Not only had the Napoleonic occupation been

96

a problem for Spanish intellectuals but also French classicism whose universalism failed, for them, to recognise the importance of national cultures and literatures. As a consequence this was undoubtedly a highly significant period for the ideological influence of German thought in Spain, comparable in its scope with Coleridge's and Carlyle's adoption of currents of German idealism in Britain and de Staël in France (Lopez-Morillas, 1981).

From his professorial chair in Madrid University, Sanz's lectures attempted to show that Krause overcame contradictions in French thought through his more congenial metaphysical approach and he encouraged his students to read widely in German. Although it shared this respect for scientific thought, Krausism differed somewhat from the increasingly popular positivist approach emanating from French sources by identifying epistemology with metaphysics. Sanz dwelt on the significance of the German word *Wissenschaft* which, he argued, differed from both Spanish and French meanings of science that included moral and political 'sciences' but also from the narrow definition of quantitative or experimental science. *Wissenschaft* he maintained centred on philosophy and the idea of a single total structure of knowledge that included jurisprudence, medicine and theology for example. Sanz and his followers thus used the Spanish word *ciencia* to embrace this more metaphysical interpretation. Although the origins of this totalising can be traced to Liebniz, it was Krause's mentor Fichte, whose lectures Krause attended in Jena 1797–1799, who insisted that science was not just quantitative and empirical methodology but concerned with articulation and system.

Sanz's approach, which was calculated to appeal to Catholic doubters who did not want to throw off 'religious' modes of thought entirely, was followed by his pupil who subsequently became the most influential figure in Spanish educational reform, Giner de los Ríos. Giner described science pragmatically as 'reflective and systematic elaboration differing only from common knowledge in its quality' (Lopez-Morillas, 1981: 53). Whereas French-inspired positivism was agnostic about divine causation, science was for these Krausists, the *full* knowledge of reality of which the underlying reality was God. Thus, his idea of science was of a delicately articulated system in which each part has its own proper place in the whole in a dialectical principle of diversity in unity. For Krause the divine order could and must be grasped rationally and moral potential could only be developed to the full by the application of reason. In the Hegelian fashion, Krause held that the world is nothing but a given moment determined by and in God. Sanz's book *Ideal de la Humanidad*, a deeply humanist text that opposed dogma and revelation and proposed understanding through the means of science and rational morality was, nevertheless, placed on the Index of proscribed works by the Catholic authorities and Krausism made a heresy. But it did not prevent, and possibly even contributed to, Krausism becoming the leading educational movement and Krausists, though demonised, became the educators of modern Spain.

This conception of a 'metaphysical' science also had important consequences for the idea of the university, since it offered an ideological unity for Spain's diverse universities. Attempting to negotiate the politically delicate situation of the church's dominance of Spanish universities, which still laboured under the Index, Sanz promoted university autonomy but co-partnered with church and state. In this he was supported by Giner although the latter, suspicious of a state dominated by the church, emphasised closer integration with *civil society*. The principle of university autonomy was supported by the September Revolution of 1866 in which the Liberals rose briefly to power. They added the principle of freedom of instruction and inviolability of the teaching profession to their programme of reform. Under the provisional government, Fernando de Castro, who became the Rector of Madrid University, sent out a circular stating that science must show its own free character and a life of its own 'in harmony with the order of the world and with history' (quoted in ibid., 1981: 56). He also adapted Germany's *Privatdocent* system of teaching by a non-university professoriat. But it was a flash in the pan and German-style reform of universities was never completed and while Krausist educational theory became the basis for the later liberal reforms of 1881, they were in their turn swept away in the first years of the subsequent restoration. Krausism itself remained centred in University of Madrid and, importantly was taken up by the emergent Athenaeums (*Ateneo*) which liberal intellectuals established in co-operation with workers' movements.

As a consequence of the conservative politics of the Restoration, a shift in the liberal approach took place and Krause's ideas themselves came under criticism. The Cuban Jose del Perojo y Figueras introduced a change in the intellectual climate which promoted the anti-metaphysical shift towards the vital and the concrete characterised by the new generation of German theorists (closer in spirit to French positivism, to be discussed more fully in Chapter 6). Jose regarded Krausists as outdated and established a new journal, the *Revista Contemporánea* to introduce latest German thought. Krausists were no longer regarded as the leading progressives whereas positivists, neo-Kantians and Spencerians gained ascendancy. Again the move was inspired by direct contact with German rather than French thought since Figueras had studied under Kuano Fischer in Heidelberg. Fischer had attempted to reconcile philosophy with science by excluding the paraphernalia of metaphysics and essences and interpreting Kant's philosophy by frankly positivist standards. Hence 'Neo-Kantians and positivists formed a tacit alliance against Krausism' and, after 1874 recruited avid followers from the younger members of the Athenaeum (ibid., 1981: 59). By their assertion that the idealist schools of Hegelianism, Fichteanism and Krausism were out of date, they argued that Spain needed not yet another system or orthodoxy (like Catholicism) but openness to all contrasting streams of thought. In this, Lopez-Morillas thinks, they clearly anticipate Ortega y Gasset in insisting on Spain's necessary incorporation of European and especially German thought.[1]

---

1   In a recent aside on Krausism, Hennessy has noted its remarkably persistent and widespread influence: Krause's religion of humanity which became the philosophical substitute for any dissenting religion in Spain from the 1850s was a dominant force in the universities and an inspiration to reformers as the source of cultural and moral regeneration. *Krausismo* was a powerful influence on Martí, as a student in Spain in the 1870s; and through him, on the young law graduate Fidel Castro eighty years later, inspiring him to defend the superiority of moral over material incentives. Equally important was Krause's emphasis on the primacy of educational reform – he had been a close associate of Froebel' (Hennessy, 2005: 146).

Hennessy mentions as a more developed article, Gott's 'Karl Krause and the Ideological Origins of the Cuban Revolution' (2002) in *Institute of Latin American Studies.*

Giner de los Rios and Modernisation

The struggle for new forms of thought was continued by Sanz's celebrated successor Giner de los Rios who was born in Andalusia 1839. Giner studied law and philosophy at Barcelona where the influence of Francisco Javier Llorens, a positivist philosopher, led him to break with Catholicism. Giner's intellectual affiliations were genuinely catholic and not only German-inspired. He was attracted to British philosophical approaches and especially interested in the Glaswegian psychological school of 'common sense' of Thomas Reid, Adam Ferguson and Francis Hutcheson (see Chapter 2) which, curiously, had become strongly entrenched in Catalonia. He was also deeply moved by a visit to Benjamin Jowett, the Master of Balliol College at Oxford University and the character-forming notion of education and sport he found there. In terms of pedagogy, Giner was influenced also by Froebellian progressive ideas of the role of games, music, art and field trips and very much opposed rote distanced learning. Despite an affinity with anarchist hostility to conformity, he much admired English public schools and Herbert Spencer's concept of 'integral education' (derived second hand from the French *education intégrale*). He viewed England as a country with a conception of 'the People' that was tragically lacking in Spain, while regarding official Spanish education as producing only more worthless members of the 'pessimistic, restless and disastrous mob of "proletarians in frock coats"' (Boyd, 1997: 33). According to Lipp his ideal was a fusion of the classical Greek citizen and the English gentleman in a confluence of English and German thought (Lipp, 1962).

Nevertheless, like Sanz, Giner held Krausism supreme as an 'expression of the critical, non-conformist "Europeanizing" spirit' (Ibid., 1962: 170) that represented moral rectitude and freedom as against the hypocrisy, corruption and absolutism of the Spanish Church. Giner was impressed by what he saw in Krausism as the merger of socio-political improvement with the idea of 'religious' perfection and he was not unhappy with its incorporation of French elements such as those of Fourierist and Saint-Simonian utopian socialism. For Giner, like many humanist intellectuals, the government imposed loyalty oaths of 1867 of support for the monarchy and adherence to Catholic dogma were simply too much and he immediately resigned his post.

The *Institución Libre de Enseñanza*

It was when he was imprisoned for protesting against the Conservative government in 1875, that Giner thought up what was to be the most inspirational organ of educational reform the *Institución Libre de Enseñanza* (ILE or Free Educational Institute). The ILE was originally conceived in 1878 as an independent university to propagate the principles of modern science and philosophy and to form the new elite for the modernisation of Spain. Under such an oppressive climate, however, its university ambitions quickly foundered and instead its efforts were concentrated on founding progressive secondary schools. These were to be characterised 'not by the usual brutality, rote learning and traditionalism but personal encouragement, modern teaching methods and a modern syllabus' (Esdaille, 2000: 166). It was connived at by the notorious Conservative minister Cánovas but after 1885 was patronised by Liberal governments.

Giner's immediate concern was to counter the aggressive expansion of Catholic *collegios* in 1868–1874 during the revolutionary period and its statutes were to be independent of all political, religious or philosophical dogma. After 1881 it was exclusively dedicated to political reform through application and dissemination of the principles of modern pedagogy and exercised a profound influence during the 50 years up to the Civil War (attracting support from intellectuals like Unanumo, in the early days, and Ortega y Gasset, whose later writing on university reform attracted widespread admiration in the 1930s in Britain). Giner and colleagues developed an intensely personal method of teaching inspired by Krausism and Romantic pedagogy using the intuitive or active method with a diametrically opposed conception of human nature to that of Catholicism. In the ILE:

Classrooms were equipped with maps, laboratories, animal and mineral specimens, and artistic reproductions to permit children to see and do, rather than merely read. Students observed and took notes, read original sources, visited museums, monuments, offices and factories, sketched and drafted from life, and worked with their hands. For the lecture *ex cathedra* the teachers in the ILE substituted the Socratic method and the dialogue. Examinations, prizes, and competition were eliminated altogether and replaced by a system of continuous evaluation and feedback by the professors and of cooperative learning by the pupils (Boyd, 1997: 33).

While the Church unsurprisingly criticised the ILE's foreignness, atheism and secularisation, the ILE in fact produced a profoundly effective generation of liberal intellectuals. This network of *'Institutionalistas'* was served by the *Boletin de la ILE* fortnightly between 1877 and 1937 when it was suppressed. The ILE promoted a number of educational associations and interventions that were crucial to the modern emergence of Spain. These included especially the Association for Women's Education (1870) and university extension. Giner was eventually awarded the Chair of Philosophy and Law at Madrid after initially being denied it in 1881 by Church intervention but continued to support his brainchild the ILE and insisted that students should study abroad to gain new ideas and experiences.

University Extension, Popular Universities and the *Ateneos*

Although the main thrust of the ILE was in elementary schooling, its adherents were deeply committed to wider public education and promoted various means of achieving it. University extension, Popular Universities and the *Ateneo* in Spain were born, flourished and died within twenty years around the turn of the twentieth century (a recurring cycle that echoed changes in France). According to Seitter the influence of university extension and Popular Universities in Spain was limited to first two decades of the twentieth century (Seitter, 1994). Emerging during a period of social reform the three kinds of institution were often interconnected, not always separately identifiable and shared similar aims. Liberal sentiment wished to integrate the working class into the emergent national polity, correct social injustices and prevent social unrest, while at the same time diminishing the influence of the Church and the revolutionary left. Driving forces in the ILE included Posada, Altamira, Azcarate, Buylla, de Labra, Vincente and others. Educational provision also included education conferences, cultural meetings, workers' associations and vocational training centres.

While *Institutionistas* were very active in founding University Extension and Popular Universities in Spain, Ramon Flecha (1992) notes three distinct trends in popular educational organisations and although they were often in competition they also shared some characteristics. The oldest were probably the Scientific and Literary *Ateneos* set up by liberal and radical republican intellectuals like those associated with ILE especially in the larger towns like Madrid, Seville and Barcelona. These in some respects were related to the lay schools set up by anti-clerical, often masonic groups which supported the liberal state and encouraged civic and national consciousness. Opposed to the support of the state and what they saw as the suppression of instinctual development of children and individualistic alternatives to workers' cooperation in the lay schools, a second stream were the Anarchist 'Rational Schools', mainly in Catalonia but having a wider influence. Thirdly, alarmed by the growth of secular popular education encouraged by the Liberal governments following 1868 the Church was also stimulated into founding its own 'popular' schools under various teaching orders. While the first two forms celebrated scientific and rational approaches to education, the Church favoured traditional submission to religious authority and a conservative pedagogy that relied on rote learning and obedience. In response to the liberal engagement with workers' aspirations the Church gradually evolved a strategy of what became know as 'Social Catholicism', which made a slow transition from a traditional charity role to modern social assistance and created a number of groupings such as Catholic workers' circles, Young Craftsmen Associations and parochial schools with the purpose of educating and moralising the lower orders (Tiana-Ferrer, 1996). Also mutual assistance societies, savings banks, confessional trade unions (the beginnings of the 'Yellow Unions') were set up and acted as pressure group for new employment legislation.

103

As in much of Europe, education was seen by Spanish liberal reformers as an answer to 'the social question' of how to integrate the working class harmoniously into the existing social order. But it was sandwiched between two violently opposing forces. As well as Catholic conservatism there were the revolutionary workers' movements and particularly Anarchism. University extension was initially and most successfully introduced by Krausists at the University of Oviedo and extended from there to Seville, Salamanca, Barcelona, Santander, Saragossa and Valencia, stimulated by the national crisis of colonial defeat by the USA in Cuba in 1898. But with the exception of Oviedo, despite its intention to promote academic culture and science, serious educational deficiencies at other levels forced a return to elementary and vocational knowledge.

The impetus for promoting university extension dated from Giner's visit to England in 1884 that included Toynbee Hall in his itinerary. Giner believed that English initiatives offered a model for the social mission of the universities urged by the ILE. The first step was made by Rafael Altamira's speech to the *Congresso Pedagogico* in 1892. Solá claimed the universities needed 'more than any others, to leave their homes, to meet the masses, to educate them and to collaborate in the task of national education' (Solá, 1996: 22). This mission was related to the desire for social harmony at the heart of Krausism to achieve a lasting settlement based on the national unity of culture, social justice and the distribution of rights and obligations. But Solá argues that the university intelligentsia also wanted to promote university extension as a challenge to the more radical network of independent popular universities that had swiftly risen on the French model and over which they had no control since they were not formally attached to the university. The liberal reformer, Montoliu maintained quite explicitly that the universities wanted institutions of social culture to promote a single human culture and change through culture rather than through violent revolution. Although this political distinction existed formally, in many instances both university extension and popular universities cooperated in practice.

The first university extension programme was announced in 1896 by the University of Oviedo, a small provincial university with a growing working class population and important group of *Institu-tionalista* professors for whom the potentially uncontrollable, socialist tendency reflected in workers' associations caused great concern (Tiana-Ferrer, 1996). They established the Practical School for Law and Social Studies that gave a series of scientific lectures in a desire to renovate university life and modify the social image of the university. Most of the classes and a summer school were held at the university but some were held in related workers' centres. Oviedo's large programme of activities included outreach courses in mining villages and towns. Following the success of this programme further centres developed in Seville in 1899, Salamanca in 1901, Barcelona in 1902, Santander, Saragossa and Palma de Majorca in 1905 and Valencia and Jerez in 1906, where links between *Institutionalistas* and promoters of university extension were well established.

What could also be considered as informal forms of university extension were often implemented by the local *Ateneo*, as in the Barcelona's *Ateneo Obrero* and the *Ateneo Scientifico, Literario y Artistico* in Madrid. In Valencia University, remarkably, extension coexisted with the independent popular university of Blasco Ibanez and the Republican Party and in Malaga with the Economic Society of Friends of the Country. Thus a variety of institutional forms were involved in providing some form of university extension, although they all centred in the project of social harmonisation as against the class struggle increasingly adopted by workers' movements.

But what counted as true University Extension? A leading reformer at Oviedo, Adolfo Posada, followed the Cambridge founder of university extension, James Stuart, in classifying activities into provision of courses, compendiums or printed summaries of lessons, the written essay and the taught classes, which included class discussion. Posada saw these activities as awakening the student, forming study habits, appreciating sciences and respecting higher things such as culture and, incidentally, the feeling of social solidarity. But there were no university settlements as in England and, it was argued, academic transmission of knowledge tainted with paternalism predominated. The image of Toynbee Hall that so appealed to Giner was beyond reach.

For Posada, university extension was a civilising mission bringing light, culture and spiritual education to the people inspired by liberal intellectuals, whereas by contrast popular universities were based in workers' movements for their cultural and political self-regeneration. Posada argued in 1903 that they should not regarded as opposites otherwise extension would become sealed off from workers' aspirations while popular universities would turn into centres of political propaganda. The worst outcome would be that workers' associations stayed on the sidelines, created their own educational centres and rejected cross-class collaboration.

The first and most successful popular university of the French kind was, as we have noted, established in Valencia and associated with populist republican reformism led by the novelist and political journalist Blasco Ibáñez. Not initiated by the university and frontally opposed by conservatives, it received only wavering support from the anarchists. After an apparently brilliant early few years it faltered and despite being revived several times over the next few years, closed in 1928. Its provision was similar to university extension in that it offered one or two sessional series of lectures and conferences on medical, scientific and artistic topics that attracted workers and the lower middle class. In 1905 a popular university in Madrid was also founded by some young members of the *Ateneo* 'unknowns', who were largely professionals and former Oviedo students but appears to have attracted few workers (Tiana-Ferrer, 1996).

In Barcelona a small group of university professors also established university extension between 1903 and 1909 with a central committee co-ordinating politically and religious neutral education throughout the university's region. It was serviced by a journal called *La Cultura Popular* (1904–1910) which emphasised medical and hygienic issues. Other related institutions included *Institut obrer català* (Catalan Workers' Institute) and the *Ateneo Enciclopédico* which was one of the most important, founded in 1903 with a wide range of activities that included courses, excursions, debates, concerts, sports activities and a library. Although very popular they were regarded largely as compensation for inadequate elementary education and for vocational understanding rather than a liberal civic education. The predominance of illiteracy in Barcelona was and obstacle to liberal education, according to Seitter (1996), due to the lack of systematic primary education and to Catholic forms of socialisation that favoured oral and interactive forms of communication rather than literacy. Despite its academic connection with the university, it more closely resembled late-nineteenth century working class sociable associations, combining education, leisure and welfare and an attempt to maintain political neutrality. Its failure in 1909 was, according to Flecha, due to the radicalisation of Catalan workers. Reasons for the lack of rapport between intellectuals and workers may have centred on the endogamic and bureaucratised university system that spurned Catalan nationalist sentiments but also the limited ambitions of the workers' own voluntary associations (Flecha, 1990; 1992).

It was only later during the 1920s and 1930s that a form of popular education thrived in Barcelona under the *Ateneo*. An impressive number of extension type courses were promoted by the *Ateneo*'s University Studies for Workers section, during 1931–1936 in such subjects as economics, genetics, hygiene, evolution, and astrophysics. For a small fee (excepting the unemployed) and a form of democratic control in which tutors were chosen by students, these attracted substantial interest. The *Ateneo* offered primary and vocational courses, conferences, a library, gymnasium, laboratory, museum, and scientific excursions. Unlike the more narrow sectarian clubs, it also mounted civic campaigns for public health and modern public schools. It promoted 'a patriotic Catalan cross-class, liberal, non-sectarian but progressively engaged, popular culture' and concentrated on literary, aesthetic and folklore subjects (Solá, 1996: 70). Although independent of political parties and freemasonry the *Ateneo* were attended by masons and freethinkers and forswore institutional links to universities.

The dramatic decline of extension around the turn of the century, for Tiana-Ferrer, had a number of reasons: initial enthusiasm drains away; the Tragic Week of 1909 leads to a political crisis for reformers; the 1917 crisis leads to a revisionist period; workers' organisations, especially anarchism, develop in strength and become increasingly disaffected from middle class reformism (Tiana-Ferrer, 1996). The educational reformer Rafael Altamira, in 1905, had already criticised the lack of commitment to the working class by reformers, claiming extension's excessively academic programmes contained little vocational education and did not take account of the length of working day. Eduardo Ibarra in Saragossa noted that although workers initially attended, they quickly dropped out. Even worse, Juan Besteiro, a socialist, claimed in 1907 that the popular university professors had no great ideas and no passion but were 'typical specimens of our middle class, a class without personality and without character' (quoted in ibid.: 32). While the 'Golden Decade' of extension, 1898–1908, ended in failure, a new but unrelated wave of popular universities sprang up around 1919–1920 and in the 1930s initiated by the Republican movement. The relative success of *Ateneos Obrers* during 1920s and 1930s which were neither narrowly political nor a utilitarian 'enlightening' of workers contrasted with the demise of other forms of popular university. This may have been due to the vigour of libertarian and syndicalist activity in the 1930s that emphasised popular education while the Church's inertia until 1936 left the field of popular education open.

Workers' Educational Movements

Independently of formal contacts with the universities but not without political commitment from liberal intellectuals, the increasingly politicised workers' movements were generating other educational forms, creating forms of *educación integral* both anarchist and socialist over several decades. Spanish socialism became reformist around 1895 with education and cultural action an increasingly important part of political strategy. The Socialist Party and the socialist trade unions established and maintained many schools, but unlike the separatist anarchists, campaigned for public schools. Also created were the Socialist Artistic Associations (*Agrupacion Artistica Socialista*), and cultural institutions flourished such as established libraries, conferences, debates and organised moral campaigns against public houses, bullfights and 'decadent' fairs.

The Socialists also organised *Casas del Pueblo* or people's houses primarily for party members often with public authorities' collaboration, some included vocational training and primary schools and around fifty Graduated Lay Schools in the 1920s. Although in Catalonia there was little formal contact with the university formally, university intellectuals connected to the ILE frequently played a part.[2] The *Casas* were aimed as much at workers' sociability as education and included interesting architectural elements, a collectively owned property, autonomous management and multi functional space for mutual aid, cultural and leisure pursuits but also 'resistance' education. These were modelled on the original peoples' house or *Maison du Peuple* established in Brussels for the Belgian Socialist Party by Jean Volders in 1881. This was financially successful and emulated throughout Europe after the practice was adopted by the International Socialist Congress in Brussels in 1891. Although some *casas* had existed informally as co-operatives since 1890s, the first named was opened in Madrid in 1908 and the name was adopted for similar ventures replacing the older 'Workers' Centres' (*Centros Obreros*). In Mora in the province of Toledo a *casa* was opened in 1904 for the 'technical and mixed schools for members and their sons, based on integrated education' for co-operative action for workers (Guerin, 1996: 43). *Casas* were also opened in Valencia in 1903 and Barcelona in 1906 and by 1915 twenty are recorded in the workers' yearbook. They shared the broadly ILE ideals of secularism, rationalism, coeducation and *educación integral* with all republican, socialist and anarchist groups. By 1930 there were sixty Socialist schools in the *casas* but many gave way to reforms in the public school system under the second republic.

2   Solá notes an interesting comparison with Portugal where in Lisbon the Free University for Popular Education played a key role in Popular Education after the proclamation of the republic: 'The ideas of enlightened Freemasonry and positivism were paramount in this popular university which chiefly addressed the members of the lower middle class' (Solá, 1996: 71). Notes the relative success of Popular Universities in Italy many based on the English University Extension model in many of the leading Italian cities but declined with arrival of fascism. Criticised by Gramsci as paternalistic (cf Rosada, MG (1975) *Le Universita popolari in Italia* 1900–1918). The Catalan UP was genuinely cross class and 'light-hearted' (Solá, 1996).

Anarchism and Rationalist Education

Sceptical of Socialist statism and reformism, Spanish anarchists placed a much greater significance on self-education in their revolutionary strategy because of their rejection of the state as a neutral political form. Nevertheless the *Federation Regional Epsilon* (FRE) created international and lay schools with the collaboration of freemasons and freethinkers, such as the Spanish Lay Education Conference and the Independent Confederation of Lay Education, which as commentators have conceded, 'led to a certain ideological amalgam which is not always easy to unravel' (Boyd, 1997: 20). This connection was manifest in Ferrer's *Escuela Moderna*, a meeting place for the radical bourgeois and anarchist workers and a symbol of anarchist cultural resistance to the state apparatus. This had great international influence through the European network established by Ferrer, the *Liga Internacional para la Educacion Racional de la Infancia*. Because of its commitment to scientifically neutral forms of enquiry, anarchist education was known as 'rationalist' education and a number of Rationalist Schools were created at turn of the century, supported by the Spanish trade union organisation the CNT, possibly 160 in all. These were more or less stable according to location and degree of freedom from external political repression and although they were suppressed by Primo de Rivera's dictatorship (1923–1930) flowered again under the Second Republic and during the Civil War.

Caroline Boyd's (1976, 1997) extensive work on the role of education in Spanish anarchist movements has drawn attention to their distinct, possibly unique, role. Drawing strongly on European enlightenment (and especially the French libertarian thought we noted in Chapter 2) anarchists venerated education and especially scientific education. Many were familiar with the doctrines of Darwin, Spencer and Lyell largely through the abundant Spanish libertarian press, which held science and reason to be the key to happiness. But unlike liberals and republican socialists, anarchists were bitterly opposed to the extension of state education which they believed would merely transmit bourgeois values to the workers and make them 'more perfect instruments of labor' – less ignorant, maybe, but just as docile (ibid.,

1976: 128). They resented the intrusion of the state into the lives of individuals who, they believed, when left to their own devices would be cooperative and self-educating. Consequently while sharing much of the Socialist cooperative ideology, they opposed free public instruction through the state.

Anarchist theory embraced a kind of rational economic liberalism that believed men would act in their own self-interests but added to it a belief that cooperation was rational and understood as a way of martialling self-interest for the public good. Anselmo Lorenzo, a leading anarchist militant, went so far as to claim 'Positivism and socialism (*sic*) are twin brothers' (quoted in ibid.: 128) but an endemic anti-intellectualism of Spanish anarchists made them suspicious of too much theorising. But following Proudhon's lead, they took up the formulation of the French utopian socialist, Charles Fourier, of 'integrated education' (the *education intégrale* we noted in Chapter 2) meaning the integration of theory and practice especially through work. Related to this, the international leader of anarchism Mikhail Bakunin advocated the education of the whole man and incorporated integrated education ideals into his International Alliance of Social Democracy. Bakunin was not the first to identify the revolutionary potential of scientific knowledge in theory but he was one of its most articulate promoters and his educational ideas were adopted by the Spanish section of the First Workers' International in 1866. It approved a detailed proposal for integrated education by Trinidad Soriano, a mathematics professor from Seville that advocated a scientific education which would cultivate theoretical mastery of all the natural sciences followed by programmes of technical training for students (Ibid.: 131).

A third influential European anarchist thinker was the Russian Peter Kropotkin, whose theories of mutual aid had gained ground in Spain when Bakuninite terrorism had invited only greater repression from the authorities, rather than the predicted revolutionary upsurge. For Kropotkin 'mutual aid' could be scientifically proven to be an instinctual tendency of all natural creatures but in men it had been warped by centuries of religious superstition and tyranny. Taking elements of these approaches, the anarchist school therefore aimed to eliminate superstition and cultivate a spontaneous natural morality which would permit evolution toward a more cooperative society.

This moved activists away from direct terrorism toward construction of an alternative educational system. Kropotkin's proposal was for:

> The formation of the moral being, the active individual, full of initiative, enterprising, brave, free from timidity of thought that characterises the educated man of our day – and at the same time, sociable, egalitarian, with communistic instincts, and capable of sensing his unity with all men in the entire universe, and thus, divested of the religious strictly individualistic, and authoritarian preoccupations that the schools instil in us (quoted in ibid.: 133).

Anarchists founded Rational Schools from the 1870s, which were largely makeshift classes operating in workers' centres in the towns and villages but regular periods of repression by the authorities and their instinctive aversion to bureaucratic planning meant that a plan of integrated education was rarely implemented. Thus the schools were mostly seen as 'nurseries for revolutionaries' rather than genuinely Kropokinite tools for reconstructing society along lines of mutual aid. Also the workers' preference was for practical instruction in reading writing, arithmetic and training in skills that might lead to social and economic advancement like book-keeping and dressmaking. So, although purely libertarian in principle, the more successful educational initiatives of the anarchists were increasingly pragmatic.

This preference was also adhered to in the schools created by republicans, one of the first of which was founded in Madrid in 1851 and taught probably over 1500 students. In 1861 the workers' cooperatives in Barcelona founded a school and cultural centre the *Ateneo de la Clase Obrera* which thrived past the turn of the century and claimed over a thousand children and adults in classes. It was steadfastly reformist and pragmatic and like Catholic schools received some municipal and provincial funding. Lay schools were also sponsored by the (masonically supported) free-thought movement, of which there were 124 around Barcelona in 1909, which also attracted the progressive middle class. They were stridently anticlerical but politically moderate and pedagogically conservative, emphasising civic consciousness and patriotism. Anarchists learnt from the success of their competitors who adapted the cause of popular education to the need to earn a living.

Schools and *Ateneo* were not the only sources of popular education, though. The anarchist press was important in spreading basic literacy which anarchists saw as having a revolutionary potential. Anarchist newspapers were well written and devoted considerable attention to educational matters and particularly to revelations of scientific truth and lectures, debates and meetings. The itinerant anarchist 'man of ideas' who distributed newspapers and pamphlets was also pre-eminently the local educator. According to Boyd:

> Through the simplified articles on science and art, rudimentary ideas of modern culture filtered down to the Spanish masses. No other group, political or religious, showed as much concern for the intellectual and moral welfare of their country men, who returned the compliment with loyalty and revolutionary ardour (ibid., 1976: 143).

In the 1890s and early 1900s anarchists produced many well regarded literary and sociological journals like *Ciencia Social* and *Natura* and *La Revista Blanca* edited by Federico Morales (to which Giner, Unanumo and Clarín contributed). Anarchists were convinced that science was on the side of revolution:

> There is no work more praiseworthy, more correct, more efficacious, or more revolutionary than to bring to the popular masses, to all individuals, Science, demonstrated truth, love of natural law and enjoyment of nature, since Nature is Science, Science is nature and it is Truth, Beauty, Art and the sublimity of Life (quoted in ibid.: 144).

The journals also devoted much space to pedagogical theories usually labelled 'rational education' which they saw as derived ultimately from Rousseau and developed by Pestalozzi, Froebel and Spencer. By general agreement the most successful proponent was the American, John Dewey while Giner's ILE represented the pre-eminent Spanish model. Anarchists were however; deeply suspicious of French lay education arguing that it merely substituted civic duty and patriotism for Christian virtue and reverence to the bureaucrat for submission to aristocracy and the king. The point of rational education, however, was to subvert the bourgeois ideologies of private property, the nation state and the family and replace obedience to authority with a 'scientific-physiological morality' (Ibid.: 147). Although widespread, anarchist educational activity was at it most efficacious in Catalonia but even here was never a systematic network. Catalonia, nevertheless, was to offer the most influential model of progressive education in the early-twentieth century.

Francisco Ferrer and the Modern School

Born in 1859 near Barcelona, Francisco Ferrer was a singular controversial figure in the history of Spanish educational modernisation. He was a committed freethinker and republican even before he was twenty years old. For the last decade and a half of the nineteenth century during the period when Giner was exercising his greatest influence, Ferrer was exiled in Paris 1886–1901, where he met many French political radicals and crystallised his ideas. On his return to Spain, financed by a bequest from rich supporter, he opened his radical *Escuela Moderna* (Modern School) in Barcelona in 1901 and later offshoots elsewhere in Spain and Latin America. He travelled Europe after 1907 promoting the Spanish revolutionary cause which he linked to his own educational campaign through the *Ligue Internationale pour l'Education Rationelle de l'Enfance*. But because of his association with the events of the 'Tragic Week' of civil rebellion in 1909, he was arrested and executed, a series of events that made him a martyr to the cause of rational education.

Unlike earlier followers of the Krausism, Ferrer was not at all hostile to French intellectual influence and warmly embraced Rousseau's educational idealism. He was also closely associated with the European, largely French inspired, anarchist tradition and the modern schools contained both socialist and anarchist educational ideals common to Elisée Reclus and Peter Kropotkin. Ferrer however appealed to a broad spectrum of enlightened opinion because he offered a genuine educational alternative to the doctrinaire state schools. He also advocated a committed radical education for adults to be undertaken within the factory context (an ideal also congenial to Antonio Gramsci in Italy later). Ferrer was closely involved with Anselmo Lorenzo in editing and contributing to the anarchist syndicalist newspaper *La Helga General* in 1901–1902. He worked constantly for the Catalan labour movement and 'the radical centres of worker's education invariably linked to the *Escuela modernas'* (Fidler, 1985: 107).

The *escuelas modernas* were in many ways a continuation of the pattern of radical education in Spain that had taken place over the previous three decades, specifically the *escuelas acratas* (libertarian schools). Ferrer turned away from direct action politics in 1890s when he became a teacher in the French, masonic-led, *Cercle d'Enseignement laïque*. Here he made links with radical authors including Emile Zola and Anatole France and the English secularist William Heaford. Fidler notes that:

> through the writings of Reclus and the French intellectual orientation of laïcite – a concept evoking not merely laicization and secular education but also a tradition of rationalist and Positivist thought – he became deeply attached to the pursuit of "disinterested" scientific knowledge' (Ibid.: 108).

Despite his attachment to French laïcite, Ferer was not at all impressed by the French *Loi Ferry* of 1882 (the seminal legislation authored by educational reformer and leader of the Radical Party, Jules Ferry). This was because it glorified the *sentiments patriotiques* and the state as *patrie* which for him ran counter to Spanish cherished decentring traditions. He wrote of French lay education:

> If state schooling has gradually come to break away from confessional ideas, it has remained no less dogmatic; it has served an official truth, it has not managed to rise above the prevailing social prejudices. The school today is the image of bourgeois society (quoted in Fidler, 1985: 110).

Ferrer regarded Ferry's kind of schooling as irredeemably bourgeois in that it ignored or overruled working class needs and aspirations. While the *escuelas modernas* attempted to overcome the class divide and offer a genuinely proletarian model, it embraced a potentially incompatible pair of directions. In the first place, in tune with French enlightenment, it advocated the scientific pedagogy of the Rousseauan naturalist and libertarian schools. But it also attempted to marry these principles to the socialist preoccupation with education as an instrument for social and political change.

Although Ferrer wrote relatively little on education, his *The Origins and Ideals of the Modern School* (1913) became widely influential. In common with progressive educationalists, he believed that child centred education should nurture a spontaneous love of learning, not so much book based as experiential. In his article the 'The Renovation of the School' in the *Boletin de la Escuela Moderna* (New Series, May 1908) Ferrer wrote, prophetically:

> Governments have ever been careful to hold a high hand over the education of the people. They know better than anyone else that their power is based almost entirely on the school. Hence they come to monopolize it more and more [...] government wants education; they want a more and more complete organization of the school, not because they hope for the renovation of society through education, but because they need individuals, workmen, perfected instruments of labour, to make their industrial enterprises and the capital employed in them profitable' (quoted in Fidler, 1985: 111).

'Perfected instruments of labour' was the last thing Ferrer had in mind. His modern school was however distinguished from the model of the British 'progressive school' in its commitment to science and neutrality and thus differed from A.S. Neill's Summerhill, to which in many other respects it bore resemblance. It opposed 'possessive individualism' and nourished 'communal individuality' grounded in the principles of solidarity and equality. Ferrer also absorbed the concept of the 'conscious worker' (*obrero consciente*) characteristic of the earlier golden age of Spanish rural anarchism.

By way of illustration, the school Ferrer founded while in exile, the *Ecole Ferrer de Lausanne*, was set up specifically to give workers an example of teaching 'in the interest of the of the child and adapted to the needs of the working class' (Ibid.: 115). It was loosely tied to the Swiss Trade Union movement the *Federation des Unions Ouvrieres de la Suisse Romande* and the Geneva anarchist communist circle associated with the journal *Le Reveil* of which Jean Wintsch (1880–1943) a school doctor and professor at University of Lausanne, was an editor. Wintsch's *Essai d'Institution Ouvriere* (1919), Fidler notes, 'indicates that the school adopted much of the authentic Socialist-materialist preoccupation with human work as a creative social enterprise and central pivot of life, a preoccupation equally present in the social education that Dewey was then developing' (Ibid.: 125).

(Another modern school founded outside Spain was James Dick's school in that 'clerical ridden city', Liverpool, in 1908.)

As important as the school was the publishing house that turned out small, inexpensive, easily understood books on a variety of scientific and cultural subjects. These were distributed widely throughout Spain to peasants, *braceros*, and workers, often by wandering anarchist propagandists. The anarchist historian Murray Bookchin notes that 'It was from these booklets that the poorer classes of Spain acquired their first glimpse into the strange, almost totally unknown world of science and culture that lay beyond the Pyrenees' (Bookchin, 1977). On his return to Spain Ferrer maintained his association with anarchists, taking a number onto his staff and giving employment to his friend, the aged Anselmo Lorenzo, as a translator.

Not surprisingly the conservative Spanish State did not take kindly to Ferrer's activities. Bookchin held the authorities squarely responsible for the mistreatment, questionable trial and eventual execution of Ferrer after the events of the 'Tragic Week' in 1909:

> The growth of the Escuela Moderna and the wide distribution of its booklets infuriated the clergy. But for years there was little they could do beyond denouncing the school and pouring vituperation on Ferrer's personal life. The opportunity to restrict Ferrer's work finally came in 1906 when Mateo Morral, a member of Ferrer's staff, threw a bomb at the royal couple of Spain. The assassination attempt miscarried, and Morral committed suicide. Ferrer and the Modern School were held responsible, although the young assassin had explicitly denounced the Catalan educator (Ferrer) and Anselmo Lorenzo for their opposition to *atentados*. Such was the state of Spanish justice at the time that Ferrer was held in jail for an entire year while police professed to be accumulating evidence of his complicity in the Morral attempt. A review of the case by the civil courts established his innocence, and he was released, but he never reopened the original Modern School in Barcelona (Ibid.).

Boyd, however, believes that Ferrer was complicit in the assassination attempt. Thus in the minds of Spanish conservatives the link between modern education and subversion was wholly confirmed and period of deep reaction set in. For the first three decades of the twentieth century no serious effort was made to provide systematic education for the people and the Church's power over what remained was augmented. Less than one million children attended either the state or

117

private religious schools and few teachers received any sort of training. The result was over fifty per cent illiteracy. Not until the Second Republic in 1931 was any serious effort made to address the educational needs of the country and for a brief period there was an efflorescence of popular educational activity. The Constitution of 1931 separated the state from the church, quadrupled the educational budget and dissolved the Society of Jesus. By the time the radical Azaña government was toppled in 1933 over six thousand new schools had been opened offering places for fifty-five per cent of all eligible children (Bowen, 1981: 468). However, the new coalition of monarchists and Catholicism rapidly withdrew the budget for educational reform and within three years the country was plunged into a civil war the outcome of which was more than thirty years of Falangist repression. Popular education was driven underground and into exile where, despite regular attempts to eradicate it completely, it remained a slow burning fuse.

Popular Education in Italy

As in the movement for modernisation in Spain the Italian movement for national liberation and unity was also widely seen to be led by masons, particularly the intellectual leadership. Moderate and constitutional democratic demands emanated from the northern Italian cities of Milan, Bologna and Rome while in the South Masonic lodges such as that in Naples were alleged to have supported the development of centres of revolutionary activity. The rebellion against Papal governments during 1830s known as the 'Risorgimento' led by Giuseppe Mazzini, Giuseppe Garibaldi, Camillo Cavour and King Victor Emmanuel II was also seen as a masonic-led revolutionary movement.

Garibaldi, who saw masonry as a network for uniting the dispersed forces desiring Italian unity and renewal, was impressed particularly by the possibilities opened up by progress in sciences such as medicine, chemistry and physics. Like many liberal European intellectuals he wanted to create an intellectual network on a European wide basis and ultimately globally that would nourish a brotherly humanity that would transcend national rivalries. Practically, he advocated the formation of international arbitration panels for the prevention of war, universal suffrage, women's emancipation and the diffusion of compulsory free education.

Following the *Risorgimento* masons were prominently involved with the establishment of popular universities in Italy. R.D. Waller noted:

> about the turn of the century Italy seemed on the way to developing adult educational institutions, and made rapid headway with People's universities – *Universita Populari* – which in those days really did attract working men. The idea and name came to Italy from France' (Waller, 1954: 98).

The Oxford based *University Extension Journal* reported in 1902 (Vol.XII, No.61, April 1902, p.102) that 'extension' flourished in the major Italian cities of Milan, Florence, Turin, Venice and Naples and also in a number of smaller towns, Alessandria, Brescia, Crema, Ferrara, Pisa, Rimini and Trieste. The curriculum was marked by an orientation towards 'objective knowledge' included Democracy and Science, Social Morality, Political Economy, Physics, Electricity, Experimental Psychology, Agriculture, Chemistry, Industrial Education, and Commercial Law, with only a few courses on literature and the arts. In 1903 a congress of popular universities was held in Milan followed by the first great national congress in Florence in 1904 which founded the Italian Federation of Popular Universities.

Another contemporary commentator Rusca (1907) argued that their spread during the first years of the twentieth century was important in raising the low standard of popular education in Italy. The largest centre of popular education, in Milan, owed its existence largely to associations belonging to the Chamber of Labour and the organs of the radical and social democratic party which collaborated with the APPC from 1900. Political impartiality was insisted on and the provision was largely scientific and technical but included aesthetic education, by what Rusca calls the application of modern methods, in accordance with middle-class education. It was not intended as paternalistic charity on the part of the propertied classes but an initiative of the lower classes that were prepared to make financial

119

sacrifices. Their annual subscriptions, graded according to ability to pay admitted members to lectures, events, the library, museums and collections. Initially over forty per cent of the membership was workers but between 1902–1904 there was such a noticeable decrease that a special workers' section was planned. The 'truth of science and the purity of art', Rusca believed, would soon overcome empty slogans and political fantasies. But this was perhaps optimism of the will rather than pessimism of the intellect, and he concluded, rather dispiritedly, that the popular university movement had not fulfilled its promise because of insufficient preparation and remained really a sign of working-class aspirations rather than the reality.

The Gramscian Critique of the Popular Universities

By World War One popular universities were regarded by Italy's rapidly growing socialist movement to have lost any claim to progressive intentions. In 1916 Antonio Gramsci several times attacked the popular university movement in the left press as having no understanding of the different needs and background of people who had not been through secondary school; they merely aped the curricula of existing bourgeois universities (Gramsci, 1985: 21n.). In an article in the Socialist newspaper, *Avanti!* considering the need for a workers' cultural association, Gramsci dismissed the popular university in Turin with scorn:

> It is best not to speak of the Popular University. It has never been alive, it has never functioned so as to respond to a real need. Its origin is bourgeois and it is based on a vague and confused criterion of spiritual humanitarianism. It has the same effectiveness as charitable institutions which believe that with a bowl of soup they can satisfy the physical needs of wretches who cannot appease their hunger and who move the tender hearts of their superiors to pity (Ibid.).

Gramsci also delivered a sustained attack on philosophical positivism represented in the work of Daudet and André Maurras of the monarchist (and proto-fascist) Catholic political group *Action Française*

120

(who incidentally claimed Auguste Comte was the last great philosopher to be produced by the true national spirit of France) which he called 'pseudo-science' such as practised by the popular universities and was calculated to appeal to Catholics since it identified God with nature.

Gramsci claimed that although Marx used positivist elements in his work, Marxism was a kind of philosophical idealism. Marxism opposes the idea of natural evolution in society which was dear to positivists claiming that historical change only comes about by 'self conscious and disciplined use of force' (Gramsci, 1994: 78). The experimental positivist method as a dispassionate and disinterested method of scientific research was also the method of historical materialism but, as philosophy, positivism still embraced the obscurantism it originally attacked. 'Obscurantism' claimed Gramsci, 'can also be a lack of education, or an education picked up in a Popular University' (Ibid.: 79).

Then at the extreme moment of his refusal of bourgeois culture, Gramsci demanded that the Turin proletariat should dispense with all bourgeois cultural props and agenda and create its own specifically proletarian institution for its own class ends. It was, he felt, a world historical moment when the proletariat recognises 'that the complexity of its life lacks a necessary organ and creates it, with its strength, with its good will, for its own ends' (Ibid.). Compared with Italy's backwardness, he claimed that both England and Germany had contained powerful organs of proletarian and socialist culture such as the Fabian Society. For Gramsci the value of the Fabian Society was that it offered a forum for thorough and popular discussion of the moral and economic problems affecting the working-class. But just as important was the fact that it had moved a large part of the English intellectual and university world into this work.

Some years later when detained at Mussolini's pleasure in prison he was less dismissive and felt that they were in the end worthy of consideration by those intellectuals who had previously rejected them. He now held that they had in fact enjoyed a certain success in that they demonstrated on the part of the 'simple' a genuine enthusiasm and a strong determination to attain a higher cultural level and a higher conception of the world (Gramsci, 1971: 330). This time he

121

attributed their failure not simply to their lack of proletarian historical objectives but to:

> any organic quality either of philosophical thought or of organisational stability and central cultural direction. One got the impression that it was all rather like the first contacts of English merchants and the negroes of Africa: trashy baubles were handed out for nuggets of gold (Ibid.).

Nevertheless, they persisted and after World War One the British *1919 Report*, concluded that in Italy the chief organisation for adult education was the *universita populari*, which were to be found in most large cities. But as in France they varied widely and there were few working men or women attending: 'the audience is generally more like that of our university extension than like that of the tutorial classes' (Great Britain, 1980: 366). However, it noted that in Milan in 1913 there were forty-five courses in different places and attended almost entirely by working men on such subjects as political economy, heat and light and social hygiene, strongly supported by the 'predominantly socialistic' local authority.[3] In 1925 there were some sixty-one popular universities in Italy which at the larger centres were mainly attended by the middle class and a smattering of workers. But in the smaller towns the audience was often half working men and women and in towns such as Perugia and Salerno the popular university was actually the intellectual centre of the place, without which and the People's Library there was little means of keeping in touch with intellectual life. A series of books was also published jointly by the popular university of Milan and the *Federazione Italiana delle Bibblioteche Popolari* including science, economics, history, current social problems, arts and classical literature.

---

3   As an example of a large centre's programme, the Milan Institute in February, 1924 offered sixteen courses including philosophy, physics, hygiene, history, archaeology, political economy, literature and art. These were accompanied by recitations, concerts and films and classes in reading, writing and stenography (not for illiterates). Subscriptions for workers were 8 lire, ordinary members 16 lire for which all receive the magazine *La Parola e il Libro*. This account would be similar for the other big centres. Florence differed though in that it association was still called *Pro Cultura* but was federated to the national convention of popular universities.

122

Following Mussolini's consolidation of power, however, the popular universities were attacked from another side. The unnamed Italian contributor to the *International Handbook of Adult Education* (1929) was critical of the attempt to set up popular universities which he describes as 'institutions for the diffusion of popular knowledge by means of public lectures of general culture clearly and simply expressed' which were largely frequented by the middle classes (WAAE, 1929: 259). In a similar vein the WAAE's *Bulletin XXII*, on Italy contained a virulent attack on what it saw as the class character of university extension. It claimed that the university towns of Rome, Bologna, Milan, Naples, Florence and Turin:

> will not have remained untouched by the general world trend in adult extension, that of the nineteenth century university extension movement. Therefore Italy too has her "Popular University". But there, more than in other countries even, is modern culture restricted to the bourgeoisie, and the sifting, condensing and popularising of this select culture carries no message with it to the people whose language would be that of myths, legends and song [...] The popular lecture, the diffusion beyond a certain sphere of exactly that which is familiar to all within it, failed from the outset, as it was doomed to fail. The Popular University has served, as in so many other countries, to revive, stimulate and furnish knowledge for those already partially informed (WAAE Bulletin, Vol.XXII: 2–3).

It is clearer now why the popular education movement in Italy appeared so obtuse to later commentators. Although it bore a resemblance to French *universités populaires*, organised working class support was rapidly withdrawn and it appears gradually to have metamorphosed into a mainly middle class cultural association. Initially, at least, an attempt was made by dissenting intellectuals and businessmen in the larger manufacturing towns of the north to combine with active workers in a process of enlightened education. As in Spain and elsewhere in Europe however, the message of class rapprochement through culture failed to appeal to militant workers who turned to the Marxist inspired socialist movement instead. It also lacked the radical liberal generation of educationists from Sanz del Rio to Giner and Ferrer that could translate the need for modernisation into an educational programme. Gramsci might have pursued that line as an element of the cultural struggle he favoured but events caused him to embrace more direct revolutionary means, culminating in the workers' occupation of the factories in Turin in 1919. Mussolini's regime during the 1930s did not encourage further progressive educational reform while the Civil War in Spain and the triumph of Francoism abetted by the Church in 1936 postponed modernisation for five decades.

Chapter 6
French Radical Freemasonry, Comtean Positivism and the Rise of the *Universités Populaires*

Although histories of adult educational movements have generated remarkably full and detailed accounts of the many varied societies, groups and circles which constituted the pre-history of institutional adult education in Britain and have impressively contextualised them in the social history of the last two centuries, less attention has been given to continental influences and cross-cultural connections. Surprisingly, the role of continental freemasonry has hardly been touched on. One of the most contextual accounts in English is Elwitt's analyses of the *universités populaires* (Elwitt, 1982, 1986) which extended and qualified J.E.S. Hayward's earlier work (Hayward, 1963). Accounts of the formation of the Educational Leagues formed by freemasons and backed by the masonic orders in Belgium and France do not appear in mainstream adult educational histories but are located in the history of freemasonry (Headings, 1949), monographs (Auspitz, 1982), or more recently in social histories of radical artisans (Prothero, 1997).

It is clear however, that many of the most effective adult educational movements on continental Europe in the mid-nineteenth century were either directly inspired by freemasons or were indirectly controlled by masonic organisations. They formed a conscious bridge between the republican bourgeoisie and the moderate leadership of the workers' movements. Originating in Belgium and developed by the organising body of French freemasonry, the Grand Orient and often supported by socialists and trade unionists, they were strongly anticlerical in attitude and positivist in epistemology. It is likely that they were popular vehicles for pursuing the 'religion of humanity' inspired by Comtean social science and as such generated a new constituency for social reform. From this stratum came the educated popular support for the radical governments of the 1890s and early twentieth century in France and Belgium. In France they promoted the Durkheimian ideology of 'solidarism' between classes often through the many masonic lodges that rapidly converted themselves into *universités populaires* when that movement ignited during the late 1890s. Freemasons associated with the *Ligue de l'enseignement* were in the majority of the cabinet of Leon Bourgeois's Radical Socialist government of the mid-1890s in France (including Bourgeois himself) and substantially influenced educational and welfare policy. Radical masonic ideas around education and welfare were certainly even more widespread in Europe particularly where the Roman Catholic Church was dominant (as we saw in the previous chapter). Freemasons with positivistic theories led the educational element in Czech anti-Hapsburg nationalist movements and almost certainly contributed to the popularisation of scientific methodology in the Viennese folk high schools.

'Solidarism' and the Harmony of the Classes

During the 1890s a new social doctrine caught hold of the liberal imagination in France. It became so widespread that in 1900, Emile Loubet, the President of the Republic, declared that it was the 'great common inspiration' of the day and amounted to a higher law of morality (Zeldin, 1979: 290). The new doctrine was called 'solidarism' and Zeldin records reactions from further leading contemporaries as follows: for Millerand, the socialist minister of commerce, it was a 'scientific revelation' which contained 'the secret for the material and moral grandeur of societies'; a leading monarchist held that professional advancement required openly embracing its tenets; others compared its philosophical significance with Cartesianism and that its central proposition, 'every man his neighbour's debtor' was as resonant as was Proudhon's 'property is theft' had been forty years earlier.

Solidarism, which is in some ways an antecedent of contemporary communitarianism, represented a critique of the individualism and laissez faire attitudes of liberal capitalist economics, but it seems to have had stronger philosophical underpinnings and included a more trenchant moral critique of bourgeois individualism. It held that the ideals of freedom and liberty, which were so central both to the spirit of the French Revolution and to the entrepreneurialism of the nineteenth century, were inadequate foundations for social justice and solidarity. Freedom, in the shape of the 'Rights of Man' had, according to Leon Bourgeois, the leader of the Radical Party, to be supplemented by a declaration of his duties. Liberty, he held, was frequently only 'force' under another name, which legitimated the oppression of the poor by the rich. The solidarist economist, Charles Gide in his *Principles of Political Economy* (1883) insisted that orthodox liberal economics should be discredited because of their manifest social harshness. Henri Marion's *De la Solidarité Morale. Essai de psychologie appliquée* (1880) argued that morality could no longer be considered simply a matter of individual virtue. He also held that Rousseau's advocacy of the idea of the 'noble savage' ignored the mounting *scientific* evidence that human character was to a large extent socially determined.

As an ideology, solidarism owed a great deal to the growth and development of the methodology of scientific positivism, particularly as it related to the newly devised 'human' or social sciences and shared in the discourse of scientificity being developed by the new generation of 'social scientists' that followed in the wake of Auguste Comte and Saint-Simon. Solidarism also drew on the evolutionary theories of Charles Darwin. But while Darwin had appeared to liberal economists to license the theory of evolutionary struggle as necessarily unequal, individualistic and red in tooth and claw, solidarists argued, to the contrary, that *organic co-operation* was more characteristic of life forms than individualistic competition. Milne-Edwards, an eminent French professor of zoology, for example, argued that the prime characteristic of living organisms was the concerted activity of large numbers of interdependent cells (Zeldin, 1979: 292). The many Owenite inspired co-operators who embraced solidarism were quick to seize on this 'scientific' justification of collectivist economics and social living.

Comte believed that scientific knowledge about human society could be accumulated in the same way as in the natural sciences. In the hands of the enlightened social scientist this material could liberate society from the superstitious authority of religion and abstract metaphysics, both of which in his view had become historically redundant. Solidarism was developed into a set of coherent principles largely through the work of Comte's eminent successor, Emile Durkheim. Durkheim's belief that sociology should study social facts implied that belief systems, customs and institutions of society were just as much *things* as were objects and events in the natural world. Crucially for him, society was not simply a collection of individuals acting independently according to their own unique psychologies but social beings directed by collective beliefs, values and laws which themselves could be scientifically studied.

By the late-nineteenth century, Durkheim was installed in the first chair in Sociology (and Education), in Bordeaux. His major work *De la division du travail social* (1896) argued that the social fabric of the country was crumbling due to an excessive infatuation with individualism and the weakening of the bonds of religion and the family. He argued not only that a new morality was needed but more concretely a new social organisation based on *professional* associations. Jacques Donzelot noted that, 'Durkheim sees the concept of solidarity as encapsulating a general law of social development'. This was further elaborated in his notion of 'organic solidarity' which, 'at once reinforces and overlays the unity which arises from similarities with the interdependence created by the increasing division of labour and the resulting tendency for people to identify themselves as individuals' (Donzelot, 1991: 172).

The conclusions of this pioneer generation of social scientists, however, may not have attained the level of a general ideology without an active political platform. French radical freemasonry it appears was instrumental in laying the organised social base on which this could be raised. Leon Bourgeois, Prime Minister of France, 1896–1898 was himself a leading mason and it was he according to Zeldin, who gave the doctrine of solidarism a political basis (Zeldin, 1979: 293). For Bourgeois, men were not born free but, from their first breaths onward, increasingly indebted to society. Food, education and economic opportunities were all social debts which had to be repaid through a 'quasi-contract' with society. Thus, the rich had debts to the poor which could not be redeemed simply through the old idea of charity. Bourgeois's view, consequently, was that the idea of 'charity' should be replaced by that of 'solidarity' which, in turn, should be legally enforceable with sanctions. Rights were reinforced with obligations, which must be collected in the forms of taxes.

While solidarism accepted that human beings, because of natural and inherited endowments, were not necessarily equal in ability, there was no reason why these should be exacerbated by social factors such as inherited wealth, education and social status. The socially privileged therefore would be expected to pay compensatory taxes. Despite what might be seen as an attack on the newly enriched capitalist class, Bourgeois distanced himself from socialist collectivism because, although he believed in the socialist commonwealth, he still valued the role of the individual within it. It was a doctrine not of *equality* so much as of equality of *opportunity*. Thus once the rich man had paid his debts to society he was free within the law to pursue his own advantage. Taxes would support common services including free education, but not redistribution of wealth, and capitalism would remain the dominant economic form. Society, for Bourgeois, should resemble a mutual insurance society which would in practice operate like a kind of scientifically self-regulating machine. Bourgeois's elaboration of solidarist doctrine was in practice a trade off between the individualist aspects of liberalism and the communalist underpinning of socialism, the political outcome of which was one of the first national programmes of social welfare, sustained by a progressive income tax, introduced by any national government. Because solidarism was scientifically based, Bourgeois argued, it would transform the biologically determined interdependence of individuals upon each other into a voluntary and rational relationship based on equal respect for the rights of all (ibid., 1979: 294). Hence, as for Blair's New Labour government, at the epicentre of his political programme was an almost religious reverence for education, education, education.

The variety of forms and organisations of earlier popular education could be seen in operation across Europe from the mechanics institutes of the UK to the semi-illegal courses in science and culture run by university academics for adults in Russia. Scientific lectures and technical instruction were the most popular forms of adult education during the mid-century. The courses in science subsequently offered by the Ottäkring and Urania folk high schools in Vienna, for example, were of such high standard that they became instrumental in

129

reforming the way the university itself taught science (Stifter, 1996: 180).

When the British system of university extension first became noticed in Northern Europe it was frequently heralded, precisely, as a *scientific* system. In Belgium, for example, it was described even by the founders of the Belgian Socialist Party, Jules Destrée and Emile Vandervelde, as a most interesting example of 'pure science', disengaged from both politics and economics (Destrée and Vandervelde, 1903: 373). University extension teaching, held to be free of both dogma and religion, was promoted in Brussels and other parts of Belgium as the model of disinterested inquiry (as we shall see in greater detail in Chapter 9). Destrée and Vandervelde noted that the Free University of Brussels proclaimed the purpose of its university extension classes as:

> la diffusion de la culture scientifique basée sur la principle du libre examen; elle institue à cet effet des cours populaires d'enseignement superérieur [...] Elle donne à ces cours un caractère exclusivement scientifique' (Destrée and Vandervelde, 1903: 375).

The view that a scientifically-based popular education was the key to a new kind of democratic society in its turn owed a great deal to the work of Auguste Comte.

Auguste Comte and Positivist Social Science

Auguste Comte, conventionally seen as the progenitor of positivist social science, found in the Scottish philosophers the preparatory ground for his own theory. Comte wrote to John Stuart Mill that he regarded the Scottish Enlightenment as the 'most advanced of all (the philosophical schools) of the last century' (quoted in Pickering, 1993: 305). Comte's interest was precisely in how far their ideas contributed to his new 'science of society'. By 1825 he had read Smith, Ferguson and Hume whom he added to his 'Positivist Library'. Comte admired the way they had turned their attention away from the individual as such to the study of society. In his *Essay of the History of Civil Society* (1767) Ferguson had written:

> mankind are to be taken in groups, as they have always subsisted. The history of the individual is a detail of the sentiments and thoughts he has entertained in the view of his species; and every experiment relative to this subject should be made with entire societies, not with single men (quoted in Pickering, 1993: 307)

Comte took from Ferguson the idea that government and society were developed gradually from man's inherently social nature and not as his French forerunner, Rousseau, insisted because of a contract established by strong individuals. He also admired the commitment of the Scots to historical investigation and the idea of continual progress 'from rudeness to civilisation' in Ferguson's phrase. From Smith he took the view that industrial development was dependent on the growth and freedom of the manufacturing and commercial classes and that banks and money played a crucial role. He was also impressed by Smith's concept of the division of labour but like Marx and Comte's student Durkheim he was struck by the debilitating and alienating effects that such specialisation entailed. Like Smith he viewed *education* as an essential remedy to this socially unhealthy condition. From Hume he borrowed his associationist view of causality; that is to say that ideas derive solely from corresponding sensations or impressions. Hume was utterly sceptical of anything that could not be verified by observation and experimentation and in particular he regarded cause and effect as not demonstrable scientifically. Since, he believed, we merely associate a cause with an effect because the two things are connected temporally, there is no necessary connection between the two events. It was pointless therefore to build theological and metaphysical systems on what could not be verified by observation. Although Comte was in the end substantially less rigorous that Hume on the question of causality, he regarded him as his 'principal philosophical predecessor' (quoted in Pickering, 1993: 313).

Comte's attempt to introduce a 'Religion of Humanity' was the ambitious application of these positivist concepts refined from British and subsequently German philosophers and arguably the foundation of the academic study of sociology. As such it became extraordinarily influential on radical and progressive thought in the mid-nineteenth century. We shall return to this shortly. However an important stage in the history of positivist thought especially in its relation to popular movements for education was that of the utopian socialists, Saint-Simon, Fourier and Robert Owen.

Comte's mentor was Claude-Henri, Comte de Saint-Simon (1760–1825) also an Enlightenment freemason who devised a form of what Marx critically called 'Utopian' Socialism (although Marx also acknowledged his debt to it). Saint-Simon applied positivist ideas to the rational organisation of society and conceived of a meritocratic hierarchy, not unlike Plato's Republic, in which education would play a central role. For Saint-Simon education had to be universal in order to initiate individuals into society, create social solidarity and focus all on the one goal of social harmony. This was, firstly, as a mechanism for developing and gaining adherence to a common morality and agreement as to cannons of approved social behaviour. Education, secondly, would have the social function as a sorting mechanism for individual intellectual capacity and positioning individuals in their most appropriate vocations. In addition it was to transmit the special knowledges required by each to fit her or him for the work suggested by their own talents and the needs of society. All should have a 'faculty of feeling' cultivated by moral education and should understand how their talents fitted them for specific social roles (Bowen, 1981: 383).

Both Saint-Simon and Comte wanted society to be re-organised on the basis of scientific understanding of human and social behaviour. Comte in particular took the view that a properly scientific study of history could predict a largely desirable future based on the transformation of the natural world by industrial progress. Thus a new science of society had to be constructed and a complete overhauling of knowledge undertaken as a preliminary to any social reorganisation. The outcome of this point of view was his widely influential work, the massive *Cours de philosophie positive* published in Paris in six volumes from 1830–1842. Of this work Wright claims:

> Comte attempted to show how each of the sciences, first mathematics, then astronomy, physics, chemistry and biology, had become positive, that is, based on empirically verifiable laws. Finally, he claimed, social physics, the historical

study of the collective development of societies, was now sufficiently advanced to join the other sciences (Wright, 1986: 10–11).

From the point of view of popular education, it is significant that Comte explicitly intended his positive philosophy to appeal to ordinary people and he wrote a number of shorter volumes to popularise his ideas. *A Discourse on the Positive Spirit* (1844) was written especially for working men (although not translated into English until 1903). *A General View of Positivism* (1849) dealt with the intellectual and social aspects of Positivism in relation to the working classes, women and art. *The Catechism of Positive Religion* (1852) was addressed specifically to women and was translated into English only six years later. The great interest shown by British feminists such as Harriet Martineau and the novelist George Eliot (Mary Evans) in Comte's work might be directly related to this as was J.S. Mill's influential work on the subjection of women. However, Comte's passionate concern that the educationally excluded working class should take note of his work was demonstrated by his argument in the *Discourse* that:

> the proletariat was the most disposed of all classes to accept Positivism on account of their common sense, their freedom from the taint of the metaphysical and literary speculation, their appreciation of science and their lack of self-interest (quoted in Wright, 1986: 13)

In short, the proposition put forward by Comte in the *Cours* is an evolutionary view of the development of man's intellect and society. He argued that there were three states through which thought and development had historically passed namely: the theological, the metaphysical and finally the positive. In the theological state men had tried to explain phenomena by reference to supernatural agency. From this, explanation had then passed to the abstract entities of metaphysics and finally had 'emerged into the clear light of a scientific positivist approach' (Webb, 1960: 306). In this last stage phenomena were observed not to find ultimate explanations, which were characteristic of earlier phases, but to discover the laws controlling them. Comte constructed a hierarchy of sciences according to their degree of positivity, beginning with mathematics and progressing through astronomy, physics chemistry and biology to be crowned finally by the science of society to which Comte gave the term 'sociology'. To this he added a substantial philosophy of history and an account of the organic society that might be achieved if the positive principles of sociology were discovered and applied. How, then, did Comte's Religion of Humanity achieve its popular impact? One very important vehicle was the French masonic organisation the Grand-Orient and Comte's pupil Emile Littré.

'A vast school of propaganda for materialistic philosophy'

French freemasonry, as we have seen, dated from the reformed Scottish lodges of the eighteenth century, and took the 'Scottish Rites'. But, organised by the Grand-Orient, it had flourished from before the French Revolution and perhaps more than any other national branch of freemasonry (following freemasonry's proscription in Austria) had embraced Enlightenment principles. Although it originally supported a form of deistic philosophy, or belief in the 'Great Architect', by the 1860s the more radical elements had become impatient with all theistic forms and were attempting to replace them by Comte's doctrine of scientific positivism. Mildred Headings noted:

> In the eighteenth century they, like their English brothers, had adopted and propagated the philosophy of the Enlightenment, a philosophy based upon faith in reason, belief in the perfectibility of man, and the assumption that a Supreme Being or Power gave purpose to the universe; but in the late nineteenth century the French Masons (who then represented the anticlerical bourgeoisie), influenced by the development of science, discarded the conception of a Supreme Being and openly accepted positivism, a philosophy which tended toward a materialistic and mechanistic conception of the universe. It is also evident that masonic leaders used the lodges as schools to convert Masons in general to positivism: and that through their relation with teachers and with the department of public instruction in France, they aided in popularising positivism to the outside world (Headings, 1949: 282)

Freemasonry was therefore one of the most important vehicles for the development of positivist ideas especially as they related to social and

134

political concerns. It was in fact Comte's pupil, Emile Littré, who led the radical educational movement and also the campaign to replace deism. Littré encouraged a materialistic and mechanistic interpretation of the universe based upon an evolutionary concept emphasising reason and science. What he, and a growing section of French free-masonry, saw as a 'positive' knowledge based on 'fact', they insisted, should prevail over all forms of theological and metaphysical conceptions. Neither should they be concerned with 'first causes', which could not be rationally proved or disproved. As for morality, Littré believed that a powerful science would inspire a new form of humanistic morality and that humanity itself would become a religion. He also advocated republicanism and social revolution as a swift and progressive cure for social ills.

None of this could be achieved without education. Another leading protagonist was André Massol, who as a member of the governing body of the Grand Orient, urged that lodges should co-ordinate educational programmes which should be open to the public. A Saint-Simonian and sometime collaborator with the anarchist theorist Proudhon, he too advocated a morality free of religion. In his book *Le Morale Indépendante* (1865) he argued that social harmony should be based upon self-respect and respect for the rights of others. Under pressure from Littré, Massol and a growing positivist faction the issue of positivistic education began to split French masonry deeply. In the heat of these disputes one lodge, *L'Avenir*, jumped the gun and, in 1866, replaced the phrase 'to the Great Architect of the Universe' with 'in the name of right and justice' in its rituals, only to find itself swiftly closed down by the Grand Orient. Despite this rebuff, the initially small left-wing movement grew and continued openly to dispute the existence of God and first causes. Fearful of Massol's fight for a practical religion-free moral philosophy, the traditional deists warned that these new positivists were dedicated to turning masonry into little more than 'a vast school of propaganda for materialistic philosophy' (Ibid.: 43).

By the mid-1870s, at about the same time that university extension in England led by the Scot James Stuart, was taking its first tentative steps the tide in French masonry had decisively turned in the positivist favour. Another prominent mason, Jules Ferry, who was then leader of the Radical Party, referred to the initiation of Littré into the Grand Orient in 1875 as marking the official entrance of positivism. Showing perhaps that the old habits of esoteric thought die hard, he also revealed there was 'a secret and intimate affinity between masonry and positivism' (Headings, 1949: 44). The founder of the Third Republic, Léon Gambetta, whom Ferry succeeded as Prime Minister, endorsed this sentiment. By 1877 at least one half of the 307 French lodges had voted to reject God and immortality and the General Assembly of the Grand Orient voted that 'Freemasonry had as its principles absolute liberty of conscience and human solidarity' (Ibid.).

Acutely alarmed by 'the cult of science' across the channel, freemasonry's more conservative Anglo-Saxon brothers swiftly severed relations with the French and Belgian lodges. With the adoption of positivism as a doctrine the gulf between French masonry and Roman Catholicism, which had widened since the Revolution, consequently became a canyon. Pope Leo XIII issued a Papal Bull in 1884, *Humanus Genis*, which warned of the overthrow of civilisation by socialists and communists and, unofficially, he encouraged the formation of militantly anti-masonic groups.

Citizenship Education: the *Ligue de l'Enseignement*

Along with the adoption of positivist modes of thought, leading masonic figures such as Babaud-Laribière now began promoting radically liberal social doctrines and in 1871, in a surge of democratic spirit, the office of Grand Master was abolished. But it was not until the Dreyfus affair in 1896 that racial and religious discrimination was outlawed in French lodges. However it was agreed that through its educational programme of positivist and rational thought masonry should take the lead in the formation of the *citizens* of the future.

By the time of the Third Republic in 1875, French masonry had agreed on a total political programme of reform, at the heart of which was the goal of a completely läic state. In many ways this was the culmination of French masonic anti-clericalism, which was now close to becoming a thorough going anti-Catholicism. But in line with Comte's historical theory it also frowned on all forms of metaphysical thought, including German philosophical idealism. The large numbers of masons represented in Léon Bourgeois's Radical Party government of 1895 had for some time pursued an educational campaign throughout the country and masonry already supported a number of educational agencies. The most important of these was the *Ligue de l'Enseignement*, a popular education organisation that held regular courses and conferences for adults.

The League, which was formed in 1866, was the project of Jean Macé, who in his youth was a follower of the utopian socialist, François Marie Charles Fourier (1772–1837). Along with the Saint-Simonians he adopted the aim of moving freemasonry on from its previous ideology of revolutionary individualism towards a reformist socialism. Described as 'a prolific vulgariser of läic and anti-clerical doctrine' (Hayward, 1963: 3) Macé was inspired by the Belgian *Ligue de L'Avenir* which had been founded two years earlier. Its aims, reflecting Fourier's feminism (a word he coined in 1837), were 'to offer young women a more serious curriculum, improve the social position of teachers, and encourage adult education' (Auspitz, 1982: 76). His concern for promoting popular education was that 'the people themselves prepare their entry into political life, by organising societies of instruction, as in England and America, where the bourgeoisie figure only as supporters of the popular effort' (quoted in ibid.) in effect calling for middle class patronage. Unwisely, the Second Empire under Louis Napoleon was profoundly suspicious of his republican allegiances and refused support.

But masons were more consistently anti-clerical than anti-Bonapartist and under the liberal empire the *ateliers* or educational groups associated with the League, increased by over fifty per cent in ten years (from 244 in 1858 to 392 in 1870). Masonic newspapers backed Macé's insistence on the local self-determining nature of these local circles and lack of imposed direction. *L'Action Maçonique*, the more radical and atheistic of the masonic journals quoted Comte's words 'Toute idée doit passer dans les moeurs avant de s'affermer dans les institutions' to announce 'their intention to accomplish through freemasonry the incorporation of righteous ideas into French life' (Ibid.: 80).

Macé's educational project, according to Hayward, significantly changed the emphasis in French freemasonry:

> from a quietist, mystical theosophy towards a positivistic scientism and a practical preoccupation with popular education, friendly societies, co-operatives and legislative measures to reduce social conflict and social injustice within the nation, combined with efforts to reinvigorate the ideals of international brotherhood' (Haywood, 1963: 4).

This momentum, which allied elements of radical freemasonry with the broader republican left, was attractive both to the skilled worker and to the newly emergent profession of schoolteachers that joined the League in great numbers. (School teachers, it should be noted, also formed the backbone of the university extension movement in Britain, which by the 1890s functioned in some ways like a professional development body, holding courses especially designed for curricular and pedagogic development.) In France the *avant-garde* of the school teaching profession were the most enthusiastic in disseminating the idea of solidarity in the new popular education movements. Macé encouraged the growth of the League until, in 1881, it became a fully national institution and modified its name to the *Ligue Française de l'Enseignement.* By then, the League incorporated 1298 *Sociétés républicaines d'instruction* and founded a number of *bibliothèques populaires.*

As part of a network of masonic-led institutions with an educational function the League jooined the *Libre Pensée, Denier des Ecoles Laïques* and *Sou des Ecoles* supported by a journal called *L'Ecole Nouvelle.* The Grand Orient itself offered free courses to the public in German in 1871 and by 1885 these included English, Spanish, stenography, commercial law and French language and literature. All lodges were encouraged to undertake educational work and by 1879 there were an estimated 1400 students. Although the proposal for a masonic university was turned down, despite strong support, on the ground of expense and a fear of becoming a teaching corporation, several lodges established a Syndicate of Members of Instruction which taught advanced courses in philosophy, sociology and pedagogy. So successful was the programme of positivist pedagogy that the masonic paper *Chaine d'Union* asserted that masons were now in the vanguard of läic and republican instruction (Headings, 1949: 126).

Thus, by the turn of the century the drive for lay education had laid a foundation for the educational reforms of the Radical Party governments of Jules Ferry and Léon Gambetta. Auguste Comte was adopted as the leading philosopher of the republican regime and his writings were compulsorily studied in school. Littré, whose role in freemasonry Ferry had earlier praised, was now appointed philosophical adviser to the government (Zeldin, 1979: 260). Ferry's view of the 'religion of humanity' was lyrical. Humanity was no longer a fallen race, doomed by original sin, 'but a ceaseless cavalcade marching forward towards the light', a great imperishable Being of which he felt himself part (Zeldin, 1979: 261). *Sociabilité*, which for him replaced the revolutionary idea of *fraternité*, would be the means by which a common human consciousness beyond class divisions would be generated and become the precondition of solidarity.

But, for Ferry, a truly egalitarian society was not possible without a universal education system directed towards forming a common morality. This demanded, moreover, a professional body of lay teachers safely withdrawn from the hands of the Church. As Education Minister, he made primary education free and compulsory, abolished the teaching of the catechism in schools and replaced it by 'civic and moral education', turned teachers into civil servants and gave state help for new schools. Touched by J.S. Mill's plea for the emancipation of women, Ferry placed great emphasis on their education by establishing secondary state schools and established regional teachers training colleges for women. The curriculum was reformed for all pupils, gymnastics made compulsory and military training introduced. The Catholic universities were suppressed.

A prominent role in this reform was taken by another prominent mason, Frederic Buisson, who believed that man could find enough miracles in nature without having to resort to religion. Buisson served under Ferry as Director of Primary Education and subsequently became Professor of Pedagogy at the Sorbonne in 1896. He became President of the League of the Rights of Man and won the Nobel Peace Prize in 1926. Buisson was also a former president of the *Ligue de l'Enseignement*, which the masons now claimed as 'their eldest daughter and as an example of Masonry in action' (Headings, 1949:

97). His educational reforms promoted equality of opportunity, scholarships for the disadvantaged, technical and vocational training, locally-developed syllabuses and the achievement of social advantage only through merit.

Like Ferry, Buisson was not opposed root and branch to capitalism as such but only to its socially dysfunctional aspects which, he was convinced, could be repaired through an egalitarian educational system which stressed equality of opportunity. He was convinced that a sea change had come over the French middle classes who were now disposed, *in their own interests*, to throw in their lot with the working classes, claiming: 'the petty bourgeois, small employers, small tradesmen, small landowners, small employees, small civil servants have discovered that they are nearer the working class than the great bankers, the great capitalists and the great ones privileged by wealth' (quoted in Zeldin, 1979: 353). He claimed the Radical Party was 'a bourgeois party which has the soul of a people's party' but, although they had adopted the doctrine of solidarity, they had yet to feel it! (Ibid.) According to Hayward, it was Buisson too, who was most influential in winning the acceptance for the doctrine of 'solidarism', achieved in the Radical-Socialist governments following that of Leon Bourgeois of 1895–1896, as an official state ideology. In effect these governments laid-down the basis of the French welfare state.

The Rise of the *Universités Populaires*

The relationship of French freemasonry and positivist ideology to the efflorescence of the *universités populaires* is intriguing. As we have argued, education as such was central to the progress of social reform as proposed by the radical positivist tendency within masonry and, while the reform of the, Church dominated, school system was also seen as a priority, workers also had to be transformed into citizens. Many masons were impressed by the 'social education' provided by philanthropic groups in Britain and agreed that Toynbee Hall and the

140

Working Men's College in London, as well as university extension, were models to be emulated.

One problem confronting any notion of university *extension* in France, however, was that the French university system was all but dysfunctional and could not therefore be easily 'extended' (Zeldin, 1967). The old medieval system of universities had been abolished by the Revolution and, after the restoration of the Bourbons, many professors contented themselves with issuing degrees without undergoing the exertion of having to teach their students - a practice against which only a minority of students rebelled. The Master of Arts degree was largely of secondary school standard, children entering faculty at the age of ten and leaving at seventeen or eighteen. Latin was the main subject taught and the universities were almost entirely untainted by contact with current scientific thought. Fragments of the older universities were regrouped into institutions misleadingly known as faculties since they were in fact entirely independent of each other. These 'faculties' were situated in sixteen provincial towns and also specialised in professional training. Standards were low, scholarship was not encouraged and research was almost unknown. Scientific education was marginal and frequently scorned. Even in the 1870s, science at the Sorbonne was taught merely in a few small rooms and an enquiry in 1885 found that the scientific equipment used in faculties was virtually identical to that used in 1847 (Ibid.). Reformers, such as Victor Duruy, consequently found that it was more practical to establish entirely new institutes of higher education than attempt to reform the ancient system of independent faculties. Thus, new research institutes, such as the *Ecole Pratique des Hautes Etudes*, were established as completely independent foundations.

The university reform movement was ironically boosted by the intervention of war. Ernest Renan, the philosopher, declared in 1870 that the Franco-Prussian war had been won by the German universities. A group of French reformers denied that there was any higher education in France at all and that the isolation of the faculties made the holistic treatment of knowledge impossible. The new legislation to reform the faculties was eventually introduced in 1877 under the Third Republic, when Jules Ferry quadrupled the budget spent on higher education compared with 1847. Only in 1896 did the Radical government of Léon Bourgeois create a united university system in which the ancient faculties were integrated and the provincial universities were established.

Thus, almost until the twentieth century the idea of university extension was somewhat oxymoronic. Even so it did not prevent considerable disdain for the English project. Some French academics, who examined the English extension system, were dismissive of its potential claiming that it merely made amends for a defective secondary system. Alfred Espinas, a social psychologist in the Spencerian mould, who visited England in 1891 to study extension, declared that:

> the English urgently needed a properly co-ordinated national system of secondary and technical education, but meanwhile Extension was dabbling inappropriately and inefficiently in what was really a public, governmental responsibility' (quoted in Marriott, 1987: 7).

Espinas concluded that extension 'was to a considerable extent a diversionary misapplication of resources' (quoted in ibid.: 8).

So except for a few enthusiasts, the idea of popular adult education attracted little interest in French universities until the period of radical reform in the 1890s. As a consequence the commitment of French freemasonry to scientific positivism, which directly opposed the values held by the antique faculties, enabled it to appear as the very acme of modernity. While the masonic lodges, generally, were encouraged to establish their programmes of membership education under the guidance of dedicated reformers, some particular lodges established a model of popular education.

The *universités populaires*, Hayward argues, originated in the town of Nimes (Hayward, 1963). Here the economist, Charles Gide, established a reform group, the Protestant Association for the Practical Study of Social Problems, in 1887. A friend of Charles Fourier, a champion of Social Protestantism and an ardent advocate of solidarism, Gide was both a freemason and Christian socialist, who was genuinely interested in ameliorating the condition of the working class. As a Professor of Economics at the University of Montpellier in 1886, he was inspired by his contact with the co-operative movement at Nimes, the *Société d'Economie Populaire*, and was very impressed by the English originators of the movement, the Rochdale Pioneers.

The co-operative movement at Nimes had been founded by another Fourierist, August Fabre, who had organised a workers' discussion group in 1878 called *Chambrée la Solidarité* which, in turn, had spawned a small Rochdale type co-operative, called *la Solidarité*. The relative success of this initiative gave rise to a study group known as the *Societé d'Economie Populaire*, in reality a businessmen's group to which workers were invited to discuss social and economic issues on condition that politics were excluded (Elwitt, 1982: 57). The first congress of the French Co-operative Union was held in 1885 in Paris which both Vansittart Neale and the historian of co-operation G.J. Holyoake attended.

This was, in effect, an early form of Third Way politics, a form of co-operation opposed both the laissez-faire rule of market forces and the Marxist doctrine of class struggle. The leaders considered themselves as *evolutionary* socialists opposed to the fashionable idea of the competitive struggle for life and active proponents of the solidarist morality of 'union for life'. For these pioneers:

> the peaceful solidarity of all classes could be achieved through their co-operative emancipation from the evils of the wage system, the root of the conflict between those two evils, capitalism and collectivism. In this task, the co-operative movement did not discriminate between bourgeois and proletarian; on the contrary, 'its doors are wide open to all those who accept the principles of solidarity' (Hayward, 1961: 7).

The initiative then seems to have passed from the Nimes to Paris, where Georges Deherme founded the first *université populaire* in 1898. Deherme regarded Charles Gide as his mentor and also recognised the *Societé d'Economie Populaire* in Nimes as the progenitor of the *universités populaires* movement in all but name and, in the following year, proudly presided over the transformation of that society into a *université populaire*. Deherme was by trade a printer and sculptor and had spent a spell in prison for his activism as an anarchist. That time for reflection, however, had convinced him that violent class struggle was not the way forward and had given him a thirst for knowledge. He believed that the positivism of Comte gave an impartial and objective account of human society distinctly different from the partialities of both Marxism and Catholicism.

As a result of this turning away from political activism, Deherme assumed instead what Lucien Mercier calls a 'cultural militancy' and took up the cause of education (Mercier, 1987: 171). His first enterprise, with Paul Desjardins, was an educational body called *l'Union pour l'action morale*, which echoed the solidarist belief that social problems were at root *moral* problems. Throughout 1896 he contributed a page to the co-operative journal *Coopération* and then in February 1896 founded a journal called *Coopération des Idées*, which, as a monthly review of positivist sociology, was to become the vehicle of his ideological campaign. It signalled clearly his relationship to the masonic movement's reformers and like them, Deherme wanted to regenerate the individualist spirit and improve the social state. But his overarching political ambition was to rescue the working class not only from laissez-faire capitalism but from a socialism of 'sentiment and appetite', which was blinding and corrupting it.

His next step was to propose a programme of popular education for trade unionists and working-class activists to form what he called 'une puissante elite proletarienne' (Mercier, 1987: 172) which would form a living kernel of a future society. His first *université populaire*, also called *Coopération des Idées*, was founded in a suburb in Paris in 1898–1899 where workers and intellectuals regularly met. A number of leading academics and artists were attracted onto this programme including the Sorbonne philosopher Gabriel Seailles, and novelists Anatole France and Emile Zola. Seailles became the *université populaire*'s president and the committee included Charles Gide, Paul Desjardine, Anatole France and Charles Wagner. It was the first moment of a movement that, augmented by the heightened political tension generated by the Dreyfus affair, swept through metropolitan and provincial France.

The presence of well-respected intellectuals like Seailles suddenly gave the movement a legitimacy among otherwise jaundiced university men. At the same time as Deherme was establishing his group in Faubourg St Antoine, they made the first attempt to associate the university with the cause of workers' education a few miles away, in Belleville. Jacques Bardoux and other colleagues from the Sorbonne were preparing a university settlement on the Toynbee model, called the *Fondation Universitaire de Belleville*. Described by Elwitt as 'an incarnation of social education's spirit of class reconciliation'

(Elwitt, 1982: 66), it was also supported by public figures including the philosopher Henri Bergson[1] and subsequently it too became a *université populaire*.

Caldwell makes it clear that *université populaire* was not a term invented by Deherme since the very idea of 'university' smacked of unwelcome officialdom and, even while encouraging sympathetic intellectuals, he jealously protected workers' autonomy. But like many self-styled anarchists, he was also an autocrat whose authoritarian tendencies resulted in his being ejected from the leadership of his own group some years later. His relationship with masonry also appears to have been at times distanced, since when he tried to introduce a Catholic priest into the *Coopération des Idées*, he was abruptly challenged by two other *universités populaires*, the 'Diderot' and the 'Voltaire', which were formerly freemasons' lodges (Caldwell, 1962: 245).

In the provinces, the rapid growth of *universités populaires* in the years following the Dreyfus affair was something of a social phenomenon. Between 1899 and 1914 over 230 were formed, mostly in the two or three years immediately following the affair. Mercier estimates that, by 1901, there were 50,000–60,000 adherents (Mercier, 1987: 176). However these figures need to be treated cautiously because, in the provinces, it is likely, as Caldwell, Elwitt and Mercier argue, that many of the new *universités populaires* were in fact based on pre-existing discussion circles, social education groups and radical masonic lodges. Inspired by Deherme's example, they may well have adopted the new name, much in the same way the name 'university extension' was adopted in other parts of Europe (as we shall see in the following chapters). One third of all provincial *universités populaires* were in rural villages and of these many were in practice little more than extensions of the *cours d'adultes* initiated by local authorities. In the industrial north, where the biggest growth took place, many grew

1   Anyone further from the spirit of Comtean positivism it is hard to imagine. Bergson's intuitionist philosophy of the *élan vitale* was almost directly opposed. However he may have been known to the esoteric wing of freemasonry and certainly it was true that at this time he was being courted by his brother-in-law Magregor Mather to join the Hermetic Order of the Golden Dawn, a small but influential magical society which included W.B. Yeats and Aleister Crowley.

out of the *societés d'instruction populaire* for the social instruction of workers. Elwitt claims that by the end of the century there were over 700 of these of which seventy-five became *universités populaires*.

The rise of the *universités populaires* is also sometimes characterised as a spontaneous workers' movement, particularly evident in those industrial cities where there was also a well established trade-union movement or *Bourse de Travail*. By the 1890s, the *bourses* in many towns had already developed elements of workers' educational programmes, which were often well-financed by both by workers' levies and publicly recognised, attracting state subsidies (Caldwell, 1962: 247). Caldwell argues that these already acted as a focus for workers' educational activity and in many cases offered a more technical and vocational programme of instruction so that, even before the rise of the *universités populaires*, there were many examples of co-operation between the *bourses* and the university faculties in educational activities. Subsequently, it was usually the *bourse* or a local trade union which decided to inscribe these activities under the banner of *université populaire*.

But there was also substantial evidence of cross-class collaboration especially where masons' lodges were involved. In Tours, for example, the local lodge proposed forming a *université populaire* and it was supported by both the *bourse* and the trade unions. In Toulouse the lead came from the local branch of the masonic *Ligue de l'Enseignement* where a local teacher inspired by English University Extension, Paul Crouzet urged his fellow teachers to 'immerse themselves in adult education'. His slogan, 'my duty to my pupils, my labour to my subject, my leisure to the people' became a catchcry for the *avant-garde* of the new profession (Ibid.: 263–4). In this instance of collaboration, it was the *Ligue* that ran courses for the *bourse* during 1898–1899. However the *bourse* subsequently played no part in the *université populaire*, the *'Foyer du Peuple'*, which it regarded as rather shallow. In Lyons, the *université populaire* was composed mostly of businessmen and teachers associated with the local Radical-Socialist leadership. In Lille, after some collaboration, the trade unions split with the masonic radicals in the *université populaire* over their commitment to the principle of private property. In Marseilles, a different kind of collaboration came about with the local municipal authority, probably inspired by local freemasons, from which a *université populaire* emerged. Here, however, the programme was more intensively technical and vocational. In other towns, like Toulon, *universités populaires* were the result not just of collaboration between trade unions and masonic lodges but also with the political opposition. Some *universités populaires* would offer educational programmes for trade union members that attracted trade union support but, on the whole, the working-class political groups were ambivalent and remained suspicious of the intentions of their middle-class sponsors. This foreshadowed the attitude subsequently to be taken by left wing groups to the Workers' Educational Association in Britain, who eventually formed the Plebs League and National Council of Labour Colleges. Significantly, the masons in Tours blamed the workers' suspicion of their intentions on reactionary clerical organisations, which had their own reasons for breaking up the alliance.

Educational Laboratories

In a downbeat comment, Elwitt saw the *universités populaires* as 'a good example of how solidarist ideology helped to shape popular education and make it a kind of laboratory for experiments in class collaboration' (Elwitt, 1982: 57). This may well have been the intention on the part of many of the leading masonic businessmen and also the political programme of the Radical governments of the late 1890s and early 1900s. But, as we have seen, this was not necessarily Deherme's programme, which sought to establish autonomous working-class elite. What is characteristic of at least the earlier *universités populaires* was that they cannot be separated from the masonic drive for popular education, the doctrine of solidarism and the adoption of sociological positivism, much of which was attractive to working class leaders who wished to avoid revolutionary socialism.

Despite their high moral tone, the *universités populaires* appear to have fallen between the two stools of serious study and good fellowship and consequently never emulated the programmes of study found in the best of university extension and in the university settlements. Bardoux, the founder of the Belleville settlement, noted a profound difference in attitude between the preference for disciplined study he found in the students at Ruskin College, Oxford, and those at the *Fondation Universitaire*, who, he said, were 'just anarchists'. Deherme had in truth wanted more serious study, courses of lectures and appraisal of written work, as was the case in university extension. But in effect the lack of serious funding and institutional commitment meant that the single lecture and self-help discussion group became the staple fare. As a medium for the higher education of working men, Caldwell suggests, the *universités populaires* were not successful. Increasingly, the aspect of *sociabilité* became dominant over serious study and by World War One most universités populaires were little more than social clubs.

Their symbolic importance was nevertheless much greater. By their more directly political aspect and relatively democratic control, they represented a new stage in the development of popular education. They were not merely the products of middle-class paternalism but a genuine meeting of the aspirations of workers for 'really useful knowledge' and the liberal professions' desire for class harmony and social justice. Positivism, which claimed to offer a model of unbiased social education, made a critique of both capitalist economics and Marxism and other socialist ideology from an apparently neutral scientific standpoint. The effect of the movement upon higher education was probably significant, and shadowed the formation of the specialist social science school in France, the *College Libre des Sciences Sociales*, which later became the prestigious *Ecole de Hautes Etudes Sociales*. It established the utility of social science as a 'politically neutral' alternative to metaphysics and religion, on the one hand, and social revolution on the other. Nevertheless, Mercier's comment that they offered the workers cake when they really wanted bread opened the way for the revolutionary syndicalist movements of a few years later.

Chapter 7
German and Austrian Popular Education: Science, Marxism and the *Neue Richtung*

The rise of popular education in Germany in the mid-nineteenth century corresponded with one of the most dramatic and crisis ridden periods in the history of that or any country. Not even at the start of our period a political unity, what became Germany only in 1871 was in effect the burgeoning state of Prussia embellished by a collection of princely states and duchies (Roberts, 2001: 9). By the end it had become the most powerful European nation and one that had already undergone a devastating war, an unsuccessful and bloodily suppressed Socialist Revolution, the installation of a Nazi dictatorship dedicated to systematic annihilation of the Jewish people and stood on the brink of yet another global apocalypse. Yet, curiously, popular education had flourished to high degree both in its attraction to ordinary people and in the quality of it provision. Arguably, the liberal intellectuals were fully engaged in the educational project they hoped would bring enlightenment, stability and national unity to the people. Those that turned towards socialism and Marxism were equally serious in their objectives and no mere propagandists. Nevertheless, a number of issues lay as snares in the path towards the ideal society – national, liberal or socialist – that each party desired. Undoubtedly the most important was the drive to national unity under the pressure of a poisonous ideology of 'blood and soil' that systematically marginalised and demonised 'inferior' races. The suppression of socialist parties fuelled workers' resentment internally while the imperialist race for colonies brought Germany into cataclysmic conflict with the other European powers and drew in the New World as well.

Was there was also something about the nature of high German culture in the later-nineteenth century that may have intensified the heroic and tragic concept of destiny that swept it along so recklessly? Richard Wagner celebrated, in the most passionate music of his time, a mythical history of the conflicts of gods and giants over Rhenish gold that brought down the paradise they were building on their heads, while Friedrich Nietzsche generated an egoistic philosophy of nihilism that cast out gods, morals and 'all too human' men from the future he desired. The cult of the heroic superman when allied to racial domination may not have been exactly what Nietzsche or Wagner had in mind but it appears dangerously to have fuelled the fantasies of a race of young Hitlers as they sat transfixed by Wagner's *Ring* at Bayreuth or immersed in *Thus Spake Zarathustra*.

Germany's unique intellectual tradition stood at the heart of Europe's Enlightenment and also bred its counter-tradition in the shape of the Romantic movement. Its reformed universities dedicated to research and the almost mystical concept of *Bildung* were at the beginning of the nineteenth century undoubtedly the best in the world. They were profoundly elitist institutions however not simply because they served only a small privileged fraction of the population– that was common to the rest of Europe – but because of their active disdain for the connection of knowledge to the sordid needs of everyday life. They appeared to dwell in the clouds of speculation and research rather than sordid application. But by the latter half of the nineteenth century this elitist isolation was becoming a severe handicap to the ideals of equality and social justice nurtured by the liberal elements of civil society. In this respect they contrasted interestingly with the situation in France where a wholly different intellectual climate (as we have seen in the previous chapter) predominated.

The German Universities and *Bildung*

Before we turn to the growth of popular education in Germany proper it is important to look at the state of the universities in the later nineteenth century in Germany. Ringer (1987) has made an informative comparison of the views of conservative orthodox majority of German professors and French humanist and social scientists of the Sorbonne and *Ecole Normale Superieure*. The decades around 1900

150

saw major structural transformations in both systems around three headings: democracy, modernisation and specialisation. The problem of specialisation in the universities was anxiously discussed in Germany, some arguing that subdividing older specialisms would further widen the gap between experts and the public. Others believed specialisation would open an even deeper chasm between the specialised and largely instrumental knowledges on one hand and the personal evaluative knowledge or wisdom (that was seen as fundamental to *Bildung*) on the other (Ringer, 1987: 182).

The German concept of *Bildung* meant education in the broad sense of cultivation or 'self-development' based on the individuality of 'the soul', described by Simmel as 'every kind of learning, virtuosity, refinement in man' (quoted in ibid.: 182). This highly personal cultivation comes about only if new learning unfolds in the soul as an instinctual tendency leading to subjective perfection, a kind of transfer of grace from text to learner. German universities were rooted interpretative disciplines and the German idealistic tradition of *Geisteswissenschaften* (or humanistic disciplines conceived as non-intervention or instrumental) has encouraged a suspicion of instrumental knowledge down to Gadamer and Habermas in the later twentieth century. The ideal of a pure *Wissenschaft*, designed to protect German universities from such demands for immediately applicable, utilitarian, knowledge becomes urgent around 1900. A second implication of *Bildung* is personal or integral knowledge leading to a 'value saturated personality' not wholly dissimilar from what English public schools would label as 'character building'.

Thirdly, *Bildung* conceives the individual person as a wholly unique totality and resists idea of education as socialisation. The unique individual of *Bildung* has little in common with the hypothetically rational individual of English classical economists, utilitarians and liberal contract theorists. It owes a good deal more to Romantic conceptions of the individual, wholeness and of change as unfolding potential. It also resists democratisation which, it was argued, falsely assumed that the unique individual potential for *Bildung* could be measured in a uniform and mechanical way, an idea fiercely opposed by German academics. They also feared that specialisation would increase intellectual fragmentation, and cognitive incoherence leading to a collapse of personal integrative knowledge

151

and losing the connection between *Wissenschaft* and *Weltanschauung* (the English translation as 'world view' does not quite get the semi-mystical profundity of the idea). Yet, despite the high cultural rhetoric surrounding the argument against specialisation and in favour of *Bildung*, a more sordid political reality underpinned it. In practice it linked German universities to the Prussian bureaucracy via a politics of direct influence and social paternalism rather than to the electorate through liberal policy or influence on public opinion.

By contrast in France leading academics and especially the sociologist and educationist Emile Durkheim took diametrically opposed positions. As we have seen (in the previous chapter) these nurtured the left liberal republican tradition of the French university closely linked to Dreyfusard and laic positions. This Positivist inspired tradition took a deeply sceptical view of *culture générale*. As frank proponents of specialisation French academics posed an alternative model of education, Ritter claims, 'based on frankly positive image of the division of intellectual labour, in the context of a left-liberal conception of civic solidarity' (Ibid.: 185). There were of course significant differences between *culture générale* and *Bildung* since the French never fully developed the German hermeneutic tradition that emphasised the interaction of learner and text and a person's unique individual potential.

The German bourgeois monopoly of secondary and higher education and perpetuation of privilege clearly posed problems for egalitarian progress. French academics on the other hand joined the argument for democratisation to a broader concept of modernisation. This was not primarily to accommodate economic and technological change but because of the complexity and diversity of modern societies: 'A simple binary pattern of classical *culture générale* for a tiny elite and rudimentary literacy for the rest of the population, they believed, was no longer adequate to this diversity' (Ibid.: 186). Growth of knowledge, for the new breed of French sociologist, had to be based on specialist research and empirical findings or *connaissances positives*. Durkheim's view could not be at a further extreme from that of the conservative German academic; in his *The Division of Labour In Society* he insisted that: 'We must contract our horizon, choose a definite task and immerse ourselves in it completely, instead of trying to make ourselves a sort of creative masterpiece, quite complete, which contains its worth in itself and not in the services that it renders' (quoted in ibid.: 187). Scholars as a *community* could achieve far more than was possible to the individual alone and should be actively engaged in educational reform as a form of socialisation to compete effectively with the sectarian moral education of the Catholic secondary schools.

Durkheim believed his form of scientific analysis 'could rationally ground a new secular morality of social solidarity, a reasoned *Weltanschauung* to replace irrational faith and tradition' (quoted in ibid.: 188). German conservatives might well however have sympathised with Durkheim's study of suicide in which he held up the value of knowledge but it is unlikely they would concur with his separation of knowledge from some profound religious underpinning.

> man seeks to learn and man kills himself because of the loss of cohesion in his religious society; he does not kill himself because of his learning [...] Knowledge is not sought as a means to destroy accepted opinions but because their destruction has commenced [...] Far from knowledge being the source of evil, it is its remedy, the only remedy we have [...] Once the social instinct is blunted, intelligence is the only guide left us and we have to reconstruct a conscience by its means [...] Let those who view sadly and anxiously the ruins of ancient beliefs, who feel all the difficulties of these critical times, not ascribe to science an evil it has not caused but rather which it tries to cure! (quoted in ibid.).

Wagner and Nietzsche in their different cultural expressions would also have agreed with Durkheim's perception of the decline of a cohesive faith but would have had little taste for his unheroic and pragmatic solutions. Many German liberals on the other hand were attracted to his emphasis on 'scientific' solutions which had a resonance for popular education.

Popular Education and the Enlightenment

A leading historian of German popular education Reischmann (2000) asserts that historians of adult education have claimed different times and traditions as the beginning of adult education in Germany according to their own perspective. Most agree that the reading societies (*Lesegesellschaften*) in the second half of the eighteenth century were an important root of the adult education idea. Here, in a prime example of Habermas's expansion of the Public Sphere (as we saw in Chapter 1) intellectual citizens met and exchanged views on art, science, and politics. Libraries were established and journals were discussed. 'These intellectual circles which often included contributions of the leading philosophers of that time are seen as the root of enlightenment in Germany' and is still a basic idea of adult education in Germany today (Reischmann, 2000). The profile of speculative freemasons in these associations was also high and subsequently a liberal masonic left dedicated to popular education and better organised than any political parties pursued a republican belief in a European association of states, class harmony as opposed to class struggle, anti-clericalism and opposition to a militarist monarchy (Fejto, 1998).

Roehrig (1975) finds another source of popular education in the workers' educational societies (*Arbeiterbildungsvereine*) in the first half of the nineteenth century that also sought emancipation through access to the scientific knowledge from which they felt excluded. This contributed to forming the plebeian sphere in contrast to that of the bourgeois (as we saw in Chapter 2) which turned to emancipation through political action. While workers themselves generated this movement, liberal intellectuals and philanthropists frequently played an active part within it.

The Catholic social movement founded in the first half of the nineteenth century by Adolph Kolping, a Minorite priest from a rural family in Cologne, and its journeymen's association (*Gesellenvereine*) was yet another source (Pögeller, 1992). Seen by many as a forerunner of the folk high school movement, this association offered houses for young workers not only for living, but also for further education in religion, vocation and politics. Based on common religious values, learning and education took place in a social context, including work and leisure time activities, organized by the 'Kolping-Family'. In the later nineteenth century Kolping Communities gradually developed into Catholic-orientated trade unions, coops and political parties.

A largely neglected source in many accounts of adult educational foundations is 'vocational' (or more correctly 'technical') adult education. The Navigation School (1749), the Trade Academy (1767), and the Agricultural Learning Institution (1797) aimed to develop adults' employability in a pragmatic way and laid the basis ultimately for the creation of the technical institutes of the late nineteenth century. This had resonance for the countryside as well. During the nineteenth century rural adult education in Germany, such as it was, was in the hands of the clergy but, mirroring Grundtvig's lead in Denmark, residential folk high schools were formed in Schleswig Holstein, growing to around forty-five nationally by 1929. Nevertheless, the peasantry generally took little interest in education until times grew hard, distrusting what they saw as the superficial distribution of knowledge and works of 'enlightenment' and were directly opposed to any education that was likely to distract youth from the laborious business of agriculture or calculated to cause distrust with existing conditions. Thus technical education had to form the basis of adult education in the country side but, as in Denmark, the folk high schools were advised to make contact with the traditional 'spiritual' life of the country side and adapt to peasant ways of speech and thought. For Adickes, reporting the WAAE in 1929, the folk high schools 'must learn how to ennoble the rude customs of the country side, to deliver country life from the dangers of spiritual desolation and reveal it all seekers as a source of serene, unclouded happiness' (WAAE, 1929: 191). Reischmann offers the important observation that:

> These differences in defining the historical beginning of adult education suggest different perceptions of this field: Some authors insist that political emancipation through action in solidarity is the core of adult education. Others see intellectual enlightenment together with liberal-holistic development of all potentialities of the individual as 'real' adult education. Some emphasize social, value- and religion-based themes. Yet others argue in favor of pragmatic and utilitarian justifications. Authors who advocate for one of these four roots

155

generally disregard the others. Perhaps the conclusion is that the idea of adult education originates from different roots. Perhaps these different roots account for the sometimes confusing diversity observable today in German adult education and andragogy (Reischmann, 2000).

This diversity of origins of course reflects conditions elsewhere in Europe, though possibly in sharper focus.

From the late nineteenth century to the early twentieth century, adult education provision in Germany could be described as 'extensive' in operation, with 'knowledge' disseminated widely through the medium of the lecture to an audience. During the early twentieth century this 'old direction' came under criticism from reformers who favoured more intensive methods. In what became called the *Neue Richtung* (new direction) small groups worked together (*Arbeitsgemeinschaft*), discussed, and developed ideas and problems together, reflecting the tutorial class movement in the British WEA. Catholic groups were also formed in the 1890s inspired by educational theories of Anton Heinen, who saw 'people's education as people's reconstruction' (*Volksbildung* as *Volk Bildung*). Thereafter, according to Pögeller, German popular education bifurcated in two main directions: the extension of scientific education by means of People's Academies and 'Urania' in the older Enlightenment tradition, on the one hand. On the other, the new intensive people's education *Neue Richtung* and *Arbeitsgemeinschaft* to form a 'new People' led by Robert von Erdberg, Theodor Bäurle and Wilhelm Flitner, as we shall see.

One very important strand of popular education that is frequently left out of mainstream accounts is that of socialist political education, sometimes called Independent Working Class Education (IWCE). This became more highly developed in Germany than in any other country possibly because of the German prohibition on intellectuals who joined the Social Democratic Party (SPD).[1] Samuel and Hinton-Thomas (1971) argue forcefully that the suppression of revolutionary tendencies and integration of the working masses into national values had by the later nineteenth century became *the* most pressing problem for the German state and it was more evident in adult education than

1   Which contrasted markedly with the freedom allowed by Austria that stimulated Austro-Marxism of Renner, Otto Bauer, Max Adler, Gustave Eckstein and Rudolf Hilferding.

156

anywhere else. Alarmed by the growth of independent workers' associations, liberals desperately sought other solutions and in 1871 formed the Society for Adult Education (*Gesellschaft für Volksbildung*) to counter socialist progress.

The key political event, however, was the foundation of Lassalle's socialist organisation in 1863, which marked the beginning of the modern movement in German adult education. From this time the Worker's Cultural Societies (*Arbeiterbildungsvereine*) play an increasingly important role in popular education. The German Socialist Party founded in 1875 developed a militantly anti-bourgeois culture and stimulated popular education. Although almost fatally inhibited by the Anti Socialist Laws of 1878–1890, their repeal led to re-intensification of efforts by socialists for a cultural alternative. Even more significant is the fact that Jews played a disproportionate role in German and other European Socialist educational movements because of exclusion from many universities and professions and were likely to be socialised into critical and oppositional cultures (Levy, 1987). We shall take a closer look at SPD education later in this chapter.

The British Connection and University Extension

The British model of university extension, for reasons that have been widely debated, never took root in Germany. During the early nineteenth century there was extensive mutual contact between German and British intellectuals and while, until halted by unification in 1871, English liberalism attracted the interest of German intellectuals, German transcendental philosophy greatly influenced British poets and writers like Coleridge and Carlyle. There was great interest in the Mechanics Institutes as models for popular education during the 1840s and 1850s while subsequently German free thought dissidents fled to England and established Secular Societies in many British industrial cities.

The pressure for mass *Volksbildung* spread during the mid-nineteenth century resulting in many educational associations. During the 1860s education became a substitute for open politics for liberal intellectuals, who admired English scientific culture, and they formed the Society for the Promotion of Popular Education 1871. This was grounded in bourgeois associational ideas which were in effect really a compensation for political weakness. While they then took a great interest in the development of English Working Men's Colleges and university extension comparatively little notice was taken by the British in *Volksbildung*, which seemed to have no resonance in Britain. German liberals like Brentano also saw the potential in British Christian Socialism as an attractive third way between the laissez-faire economics of 'Manchesterism' and Marxism which offered the possibility of peaceful social evolution rather than class struggle (Marriot, 1995: 13). The elements of character building, self organisation, fellowship and transformation of attitudes rather than a simple mechanical popularisation of knowledge, chimed in well with the ideal of *Volksbildung*. Many like Ernst Schulze preferred university extension to the Danish model of folk high schools because they held out the hope of a more 'gentlemanly' culture. Toynbee Hall settlement work also appeared later to Schultze – Gaevernitz and others to offer a way of incorporating the lower classes into the 'national culture'.

University extension first took hold in Austria, however, under the leadership of Ludo Hartmann and then in Germany by Wilhelm Rein who was Professor of Pedagogy in Berlin. In Austria university extension was largely concentrated in Vienna where the *Volksheim*, permanent and properly equipped was the one of the most impressive and intellectually significant centres for popular education anywhere. It adopted a liberal constitution and may have reflected anxieties about franchise and popular democracy. Austrian university extension was the most durable of all the continental and Nordic adaptations in part perhaps due to direct recognition from the state and official regulation. In Vienna, regular university lecturers were used (even more correctly than in Britain) to staff university extension and Ludo Hartmann, the guiding spirit of the Vienna movement, insisted on respect for knowledge and an active pursuit of research. Undoubtedly a key figure was Ernst Mach who held the chair in Theory of the Inductive Sciences at Vienna University and who from 1895 was a practising populariser and proponent of the theory of 'empirio-criticism' (which was greatly influential and of great concern to Lenin who wrote a tract denouncing

158

it). Hartmann and Emil Reich were also ardent rationalists who believed in the 'total neutrality' which was written large in the statutes of the University of Vienna's committee of management for university extension in 1895.

In Germany, academics in the University of Berlin closely studied Mackinder and Sadler's published report on British university extension, which they both generously championed and hotly attacked (Mackinder and Sadler, 1891). Prime movers were established figures like Lujo Brentano, Wilhelm Rein and Paul Natorp, concerned by the rift between the academy and popular cultural practice. Rein argued for 'objectivity, social commitment, class-reconciliation and opposition to Social Democracy' and in 1894 recommending the adoption of the English model, he wrote of the 'false refinement' of the conservative university opposition to university extension and demanded an end to elitist isolation (Marriott, 1994: 96–7). Berlin was followed by Natorp's plea for university extension in Munich in 1896 but in both cities no public aid was forthcoming and the ventures relied entirely on the voluntary work of a small minority of university teachers supported by some of the popular scientific associations, largely organised under the *Gesellschaft für Verbreitung von Volksbildung* founded in 1871. *Universitätsausdehnung* (university extension) erupted briefly in the late 1890s but did not bring the universities significantly into play and was shortly roundly criticised by Robert von Erdberg (of the New Direction) as piling up 'unproductive intellectual capital'. Curiously this brief movement helped to establish the term *Volkshochschule* – literally but misleadingly translated as folk high schools.

In Vienna, as we have seen, the atmosphere was subtly different and the appeal to stringent neutrality was an irruption of explicit theory into popular education. Its special philosophical climate of opposition to idealism and romanticism (as well as its masonic anticlericalism) drew intellectual strength from Mach's empirio-criticism. Reich and Hartmann saw themselves as involved in a deeply rationalist enterprise deriving from Enlightenment ideals concerned with banishing superstition and enabling men to form independent judgements. Hartmann, despite his attachment to Mach's anti-Marxist monism became increasingly attracted to the SPD and saw socialism

159

as a 'cumulative progressive work of education rather than climactic class warfare' (Marriott, 1994: 97).

The clarity of Hartmann's approach to university extension is illuminating: he attempted to ban worldviews and philosophical presuppositions from the intellectual work place and laid stress on radically independent thinking. He believed this was the essence of the 'university approach' and that the value of popular education had to be guaranteed by its connection with university. This overlap of the liberal middle class and social democratic domains enabled popular education to offer a viable intellectual space for progressive intellectuals. The older style *Volksbildung* they rejected was either incurious or sceptical of the positivist optimism that university extension could deliver the goods, since it started from a simplistic regard for the cosmos of science and authority of learning rather than needs of learners. Hartmann and his colleagues, however, appeared well aware of the distinction between dogmatic and developmental approaches and the need for intellectual method and process. Marriott holds that their optimism only seems naïve if the competing stance of crisis and cultural pessimism was seen as offering a more profound way of thinking. But although their impulse was undoubtedly one of good organisation and pedagogical practice, what they might have lacked was inspiration, fellowship and sociability and as evidenced in the English missionary settlement.

Connections between British and German liberal educators were nevertheless ongoing and there was much mutual interest. It was *de rigueur* for progressive Germans to be interested in English workers' education. Werner Picht's (1914) dissertation on Toynbee Hall was widely read (and its comments on the failure of university extension duly noted). The German Free student Movement during the 1910s attempted to emulate elements of the settlement and university extension idea though in a context of strong Protestant religiosity and, more alarmingly, political anti-Semitism. Their concern over the 'social question' lent their version of university extension a strongly social work character. Alice Salomon a pioneer of German social work was closely connected (though not with the same political tastes) to adult education. As a leading exponent of *Wohlfahrtspflege* 'welfare work' Salomon, a Jewish convert to Christianity in 1914, advocated 'public health, education, morality and culture in the broadest sense'. She founded several schools including *Deutsche Akademie für soziale und pädagogische Frauenarbeit* (1925) and was the founder and president of International Committee of Social Schools in 1929. She was very influenced by English Christian Socialist tradition of Carlyle, Dickens, Kingsley and had a personal relationship with Lady Aberdeen from 1896. She wrote engagingly about settlements, People's Palaces, Women's Co-operative Unions and the education of female social workers and also Walter Besant and the *Volksheim* movement (Zellhuber-Vogel, 1992). The English WEA in a complementary spirit sent a delegation to visit the *Rhein-Mainische Verband* in Frankfurt which they saw as an equivalent kind of association to the WEA, though in fact it was fourteen years its senior and larger in scale.

By the 1910s Marriott describes *Volksbildung* as a something of a vast but superficial and loosely articulated provision of welfare, libraries, cultural enlightenment and direct instruction, that, although well-meaning, frustrated the ideals of the liberals for progressive social change. It was moreover clear that the WEA in England had overtaken and exposed the limits of university extension in what was seen as a more intensive popular education. Indeed its attempted neutrality was not always welcome in Germany, where Professor Titius of Kiel asserted that committed positions were the only defence against superficiality. Titius also argued that popular education entailed the acquisition of *Persönlichkeit* through exposure to different but sincerely held views, not merely intellectual but emotional and he opposed Hartmann's objectivist stance that excluded religious and political discourse. Hartmann responded by identifying in Titius's remarks 'a new kind of metaphysics of popular education' which he encouraged colleagues to oppose as '*ganz flache Empiker, ganz flache Rationalisten*' (quite plain empiricists and rationalists) (Marriott, 1994: 107). However, the new metaphysics gathered pace and following World War One swung the popular education movement away from universities and to a non- even anti-intellectual position. Unfortunately, the universities responded in kind by removing intellectuals from popular education. A quite decisive shift, as we shall see, was taking place.

Modern German Adult Education – the New Direction

The New Direction in German popular education was pioneered by the energy of one man in particular, Robert von Erdberg, who led a dramatic resurgence of militant nationalism. His self-defined task was the integration of the workers into the community of the nation (*Volksgemeinschaft*). Von Erdberg 'revealed in his stress on the emotive and subjective elements in human nature and on inner "experience"' against the 'accumulation of unproductive intellectual capital' and the mechanical transmission of knowledge an 'irrational and quasi-mystic belief in the folk-community of Germans' (Samuel and Hinton-Thomas, 1971: 138). In 1909 he founded the journal *Volksbildungsarchiv* for a deeper conception of adult education, which became the influential instrument of the new direction. His writing projected a difference between education that merely disseminated knowledge and that which moulds personal life through the experience of values (*gestaltende Volksbildung*). While one of his close associates, Walter Hofmann, established the Central Agency for Popular Literature in 1914 to promote guided reading in the New Direction another, Theodore Baurle, founded the Society for the Encouragement of Adult Education in 1918, to further the new trend another. The Popular Library Movement promoted by Hoffman was consciously part of the adult education movement taking notice of developments in Britain and between 1910 and 1920 he campaigned successfully to reorganise libraries as places of education, signalled by what was called 'educationally correct distribution' (Hofmann, 1929).

However, in opposition to the scientifically orientated rationalism of university extension, the new *gestalt* embodied in the *Volkshochschule* was borrowed from Grundtvig's model to regenerate the peasantry in Denmark. The first, as we have noted, was in Schleswig-Holstein where German border nationalism was strong, and clearly inspired by the Danish folk high schools' spiritual nationalism in which the peasantry was seen as a real source of national strength. By 1906 there were seventy-one institutes in Germany with around seven thousand students and although in some respects resembling university extension the emphasis was on the formation of student's character and will rather than gaining knowledge. It was a curious mixture of the nationalist and reactionary doctrines of the Empire with progressive ideas of education, concentrating less on the inculcation of facts and more on 'inward assimilation' of material.

These new style German folk high schools however reached their full development under the Republic and changed their character somewhat, when liberal elements came to the fore to promote progressive adult education against the legacy of authoritarian forms. The new trend and the Republic were mutual elements in attempting to foster a new type of citizen that could not have been produced by the *Kaiserreich* and could not wait for next generation or the universities to take part. Von Erdberg was appointed head of special department of adult education in the Prussian ministry of Education in 1919 and immediately wrote its 'Ten Commandments' on the character and formation of the folk high schools. Particularly questionable, for liberals, was the fifth commandment, which dedicated the people to revere the spirit and to value spiritual work which would redeem it from the 'one-sidedness of a barren intellectual culture'. The tenth commandment, moreover, committed the folk high school to be 'bound together by the consciousness of the common spiritual struggle for a cultural unification of the nation, and this raises it from an educational organisation to a cultural movement' (Samuel and Hinton-Thomas, 1971: 141). Thus von Erdberg elevated the ideal of the spirit over intellectual progress and the idea of the nation founded on quasi-mystical, common experience, rather than reason and scientific investigation.

Of the two types of folk high schools that were founded during this period, the residential type of which there were eighty was the purest expression while the 215 non-residential schools were seen as essentially urban evening class education. Other reformers who did not necessarily share von Erdberg's ideology, like Gertrud Hermes in 1929, attempted to combine the advantages of the two types by creating a residential group of workers who worked during the day but studied in the evening using the discussion group (*Arbeitsgemeinschaft*) as a basic method. These were influenced by the new WEA university tutorial classes but also promoted independence of thought and self-expression through music and drama. Gertrud Hermes was dismissive of old-fashioned practices based on the lecture and discussion because they failed to encourage development of personality through an appeal to the learner's central life-interests. She advocated the 'structured conversation method' where a new realisation was to emerge between tutor and students based on joint educational work. The experimental *Volksheims* founded by Hermes in Leipzig initially were linked with the working class and youth movements to provide an 'intensive' education not provided by the normal evening classes which, she claimed, lacked a concrete aim of study strong enough to provided student with a lifelong purpose. Instead, she proposed to accommodate small groups who wanted to live and work together communally to develop a group spirit and corporate will. In them the students followed their normal work during the day and then 'Home Life', with three evenings a week given over to instruction. They were financed mainly by contributions from inmates who paid two thirds of their income, supplemented by grants from local and national state (WAAE, 1929: 183).

Academic freedom from state control was agreed in 1919 by the Prussian Ministry of Education which maintained that the promotion of folk high schools was an essential duty of the state (the *1919 Report* in Britain had similar aims). A Reich League of Adult Education to coordinate activities was also attempted in 1925 but it foundered and led to a 'Heritage of particularism' in which conflicting interests squabbled over the heart of adult education. For alter commentators the consequence was that: 'German adult education under the Republic did not succeed in discovering the necessary combination of democratic freedom and organised direction' (Samuel and Hinton Thomas, 1971: 144). The folk high schools were split ideologically so that while many residential peasant colleges leant towards 'blood and soil' racialism, other residential colleges were either socialist, catholic, evangelical or even, in principle, neutral. But not only was there no agreed purpose the hostility between the camps made it impossible to achieve the 'objective teaching', which all agreed should be the essence of the movement.

The folk orientation had not gone unchallenged, though, since Alfred Menzel in 1919, had rejected the Danish model and argued the German 'folk' high schools should evolve out of university extension as had the WEA in England (Marriott, 1994: 113). Claims that the English adult tutorial class was the direct progenitor of *Arbeits-*

gemeinschaft were however disputed because the 'intensive' study group methods were used some years before the WEA was talked about in Germany, as in the Frankfurt *Rheine-Mainische Verband.* There is some similarity with Mansbridge's view that the working class could not generate a new social order, which was not based on existing culture.

Von Erdberg's own theoretical understanding and justification for his project was eloquently stated in his address to the World Association for Adult Education in London (WAAE, 1929: 163–70). The Society for the Extension of Popular Education (SEPE) (*Gesellschaft für Verbreitung von Volksbildung*) founded in 1871, he claimed was probably the largest in the world of it kind and succeeded a range of groups involved in denominational and vocational education. Its aim was to create a united people sharing the same ideals and thus support a United Germany. It was necessary in his view to attack the rise of Social Democracy and to disregard all denominational and political conflicts by not allowing discussion of political or religious substance and was therefore in itself a political act (although this was openly disavowed). This inner contradiction resulted in the decline of the movement owing to its failure to participate in the spiritual conflicts of the time such as the anti-Socialist laws. Thus it could never become a vital movement of the people because it ignored just those issues that most deeply concerned them. After the anti-Socialist law was repealed, the working-man founded his own educational institutions, mainly for educating a party leadership. The SEPE continued to hold to its principles of neutrality but in a dramatically limited role. The Humboldt Academy in Berlin, founded in 1878, for popular enlightenment and education and cultural activities like music and art was similarly restricted in its appeal. Although these were inadequate to the ideals of United Germany the society was unable to adapt, particularly to the demands by workers for cultural advantages as a right and the right to contribute to the formation of a new culture. Von Erdberg then turned to the New Direction: 'At this juncture adult education took a new turn. The old methods, by which the older educational organisations had hoped, through a wholesale diffusion of knowledge, to produce good citizens, were dropped' as well as the ideal of pouring out the blessings of culture (von Erdberg, 1929: 166). 'Behind this lurked the belief, it must be admitted, that by this new

165

method a spiritually united people would be gathered as one flock, and *all danger of revolution be avoided*' (Ibid., my emphasis.).

He saw the central problem as the decentralisation of the work through a variety of independent institutions like libraries, community centres, university extension courses and so on that allowed a plurality of aims and methods. In opposition to the idea that knowledge and education were the same thing and the failure of this movement to produce a unified ideal, a new movement had developed. This affirmed that education did not mean simply the accumulation of knowledge:

> but the freeing of that vital principle more or less latent in every individual, and helping it to find expression in adequate and happier forms of life [...] Knowledge according to Ruskin, must not only bring a man something, but make of him something that he was not before (Ibid.: 166–7).

SEPKA changed it name to Society for Adult Education (SAE) but was not capable of sifting the cultural products of a nation from a scientific, political or aesthetic point of view.

For von Erdberg the New Direction was formative and constructive in striving for a definite ideal and, in a phrase reminiscent of Nietzsche's revaluation of all values, 'submitting all existing culture to the test'. The aim was both personal and collective, to enable the individual to develop all his latent possibilities to the highest standard but also to 'evolve him in contacts with the members of his own groups, and to weld these groups to a nation' in which both religion and politics might have a role to play. Thus von Erdberg's ideal was not to ignore religion and politics but to confront the deeper concerns of religious and political commitment and attempt to create a unified (national) consciousness. But the 'tragedy' of adult education was that it did not 'yet possess a criterion based on the recognition of a universally accepted idea' (Ibid.: 169). The government properly understood that it could not impose such an idea from above and should not interfere or regulate adult education. He believed there was a deep conflict between those formative educational associations that wanted to instil certain (religious and political) viewpoints and those that held that 'a man should be led through development of his critical faculties and disinterested valuation, to form his own independent views' (Ibid.: 170).

There was no doubt however that despite (or perhaps because of) the enormous ideological burden imposed by von Erdberg and his close associates, popular education flourished. His colleague Flitner reported to the WAAE that in the Evening High Schools there was an enormous increase in attendance at popular lectures and course during the years of 'War and Revolution' in Germany in industrial towns (WAAE, 1929: 170–4). Enthusiasm for the democratic state and full share of the 'treasure of spiritual culture' was passionately expressed in the movement for folk high schools during 1919–1922 which became better organised and financed. The folk high schools continued to shadow Grundtvig's Danish creation but with a new emphasis of providing 'a basis for mutual understanding and co-operation between the different classes' (Ibid.). Students' councils and administration should not be simply democratic arrangements 'but a living working body' expressing the sense of the student body (Ibid.).

Flitner also articulated how the German folk high schools differed from British university extension. The object was not the study of any particular branch of knowledge or scientific instruction as in English tutorial classes but the training of the lay person. Education should centre on controversial matters that arouse groups and individuals not simply scientific 'facts':

> The aim of popular education is attained if the clarification of such problems has revealed the deeper human motives and discloses the moral and political antagonisms on which the workaday differences rest, provided that in the discussions a polished and sincere relationship between the disputants has been established (Ibid.: 172–3).

The sciences Flitner preferred were sociology, economic and political science (which in fact had become the staple contents of WEA tutorial classes). These should be complemented by practical vocational classes; courses for representatives on workers councils and Trade Unionists and courses in social work and political work. Courses for the 'purposes of popular reflection' like music, art and literature were also important (and ironically altogether with the exception of vocational course were remarkably similar to what the WEA provided in many districts). For Flitner the overriding rational was that: 'The

167

supporters of out and out nationalism and of the idea of class warfare will thus be brought into opposition, but nowhere will it be suggested to them to sacrifice their idea of warfare; they will however, be asked to infuse it with moral ideas' (Ibid.: 173). Above all the folk high schools will encourage self-help and mutual practical responsibility, with ultimate aim to:

> try to give the ordinary man a spiritual confidence that harmonises with a respect for the established spiritual order, while it produces in each individual self-reliance, independent thought and feeling, and fosters a genuine intercourse between the classes with varied culture (Ibid.: 174).

While the theory was energetically debated in these terms, the practice was more diverse. Within the broad highway of folk high schools a form of Catholic popular education was also pursued by the National Society for Catholic Education funded by Windthorst in 1890. They founded a folk high school in which Catholics were trained to be good citizens and socially minded active Christians (WAAE, 1929: 185). Through courses on social welfare, juvenile aftercare, municipal politics, civic education, political economy a new generation of catholic popular leaders grew up. Natural Catholic suspicions of pure rationalism and its devotion to pastoralism was in tune with new spirit but Catholics took little interest in the intense debates about adult education after the War and did not to contribute anything new to the methodology (Ibid.: 186). As always, the central problem for Catholic Education was the realisation of the relation of the natural to the supernatural. They did not attempt to create a Catholic culture in Germany but addressed the question of how to contribute to the national culture, German heritage first.

Mass unemployment in 1930s brought into focus a new kind of people, 'the masses' no longer the wise *Volk* of rural myth and made von Erdberg's desire for spiritual elite impossible (even if it was ever desirable). Neither was it possible to find a scheme to make the folk high schools both independent of sectarian support and also free of state control. Unlike Britain, universities were unable or unwilling to act as intermediaries between central administration and the educational sphere to allow regional differentiation. This is because German universities still clung obstinately to their inherited methods and *Lernfreiheit* which were not seen as suitable for adult education. Universities moreover were dominated by conservative and nationalist professors, uncomfortable with democratic ideals, who held that the purity of universities would be poisoned by prolonged contact with the masses. Their reluctance to engage in popular education throws into perspective the achievements of the folk high schools, even the more conservative ones, in reaching out democratically:

> the folk high schools, in their best manifestations, showed a remarkable enterprise in thinking out new methods of teaching, free from the dangers of ex cathedra pronouncements and exploiting the advantages of the discussion group, and in devising new forms of community life, stressing self-government by the students and the liberal relationship of student to teachers (Samuel and Hinton, 1971: 147).

Their success was confirmed by the fact that the Nazis soon decided to abolish them and replace the by a new system on the lines of the Italian '*Dopolavoro*' which were called *Volksbildstätten*. The name implied a dropping of the high school educational priority in favour of something that had unhealthy associations with neo-pagan ritual. These were virtually controlled by the party though nominally under the wing of the Ministry of Education through the Strength through Joy department (*Kraft durch Freude*) which was part of the German Labour Front. They specialised in racial history but the most popular courses were in practical subjects like languages and domestic science. The Nazis claimed that in 1940–1941 over ten million students attended 75,000 adult education meetings. While clearly some elements of von Erdberg's ideology might be seen as predisposing the folk high schools to Nazi racism, their liberal educational methods were quite at odds.

Independent Workers Education and the SPD

The object of von Erdberg's earlier concern was the German Social Democratic Party (SPD) which was the largest and most well organised of any of the new European workers' parties. Its educational activities, particularly between 1890 and 1914 were at the core of its attempt to create ideological clarity among organised workers and it was this project that caused such consternation among liberal intellectuals and conservatives alike.

In fact the SPD's programmes drew heavily on the common liberal inheritance of Humboldtian *Bildung* which they understood as learning and cultivation as means for the development of the complete individual (Lidtke, 1985: 159). But they also intended to disseminate the principles of the SPD and the free trade unions through serious study which they called *Arbeiterbildung*. The historian of the movement, Lidtke, notes that: 'The German socialist labor movement began within the framework of workers' educational societies that had been founded by liberals as early as the 1840s and then detached themselves to form independent workers' education' (Ibid.: 160). Originally these societies had provided a kind of 'deficit' education intended by liberals to compensate for poor primary education and to contribute to general progress of humanity. As we have seen they consisted of two kinds of provision: systematic courses and public lectures, which had a considerable popularity such that in 1864 there were over 1000 lectures sponsored by thirty-three workers educational societies in Prussia. Of these roughly half in the sciences and half arts and social sciences.

The major break from liberalism by the organised workers' movement began in 1870–1871 when under the pressure of increased politicisation through the anti-imperialism campaigns of the young socialist movement and the public prominence of the two socialist parties, the liberal educational societies were overshadowed. Losing their contact with the working class, they became increasingly lower middle class in character. This erosion was temporarily halted by the Anti-Socialist laws of 1878 in which all Social Democratic organisations were abolished, while the liberal educational organisations

170

were left in place. But when the SPD's educational programmes were re-established when the laws were repealed in 1890 they rapidly expanded in the decade before World War One.

The most important figure in defining the SPD attitude to education was Wilhelm Liebknecht, who devised a mixed programme of liberal, Humboldtian neo-humanism and quasi-Marxist education. In 1872 he published a popular pamphlet *Wissen ist Macht – Macht ist Wissen*, the oft quoted 'Knowledge is Power – Power is Knowledge' parallelogram, derived from Francis Bacon, whose principles he continued into the 1890s. Liebknecht's defiant argument was that the state simply exploited *Bildung* to support the ruling class and that as a consequence the school system only generated idiocy, maintaining that: 'As long as the present state and society continue to exist, there is no *Kultur*, no *Bildung*, no popular education' (quoted in ibid.: 162). Only the SPD could deliver *Bildung* and that was through political emancipation.

The leading arm of SPD education was the Berlin Workers' Educational School (BWES) founded in 1891 and its aim, 'to prepare the workers to carry on the struggle for emancipation, not to make them learned specialists filled with superfluous information' contained not a little of the holistic anti-particularistic rhetoric of the liberals (Ibid.). Liebknecht drew on his experience of the Workers Educational Society at Leipzig where he had been an active member for a 'kind of agitational school'. This 'Temple of Knowledge' was quite specifically *not* to ameliorate class differences but on the contrary to intensify class consciousness. While it offered an alternative programme of instruction for members of the German Labour Movement, it was not intended as a systematic programme of Marxist study. The curriculum emphasised social sciences, history, public speaking and natural science but not literature despite being taught largely by journalists, writers and intellectuals in Berlin. The most influential teacher, in fact, was probably the anthroposophist, Rudolph Steiner, who lectured the most and introduced a large element of religious study into his classes. The students, mostly in their twenties, were drawn largely from organised labour and ninety per cent held membership of the SPD or a trade union. Women were a significant proportion of students up to 1900–1902 but their numbers dropped markedly afterwards, possibly due to the growth of socialist women's organisations or more likely because little in the programme may have directly appealed to them.

For a few years after turn of century, probably in tune with the *Neue Richtung*, there is an increased commitment to 'intensive' programmes for education and cultivation led by Clara Zetkin, Heinrich Schulz and Otto Rühle. These took two main orientations; firstly a Liebknecht-type ideological and political cadre education with a Marxist orientation and secondly a more general and pluralist education that encouraged workers to think for themselves (Ibid.: 165). According to one leading figure there was a 'significant debate hinged on whether our party should be directed toward instruction in the ideology of the party or toward general enlightenment' (quoted in ibid.: 166). Many like Vollmar, argued that socialists should not condemn all bourgeois educational endeavours. Zetkin wanted the curriculum to be broadened to include the Arts because they were a functional substitute for religion and might prevent the workers from being driven into the arms of religious mysticism (an implicit attack on Steiner?). The Central Educational Commission wrapped up the debate by concluding that a 'politically inspired, propagandistic educational programme within the labor movement' should be carried out by a system of extension courses (*Wanderkurse*) and practical publications.

Nevertheless, a questionnaire designed to discover what educational programmes were already being carried out by the SPD in 1907 returned discouraging results and it was decided to build education on trade union organisational base instead. A Party School opened in 1906 was also shaped by the Marxist tendency. Rosa Luxemburg, one of the most influential teachers at the School, feared the possible dominance of reformist cultural advocates and the function of 'bourgeois knowledge' (*bürgerliche Wissenschaft*) understood rather narrowly as anything not officially prescribed. Franz Mehring and Heinrich Knauf saw the school as essentially providing armaments for agitation while the revisionist Eduard Bernstein and others criticised such a one sided approach to the study of society. This debate was fought out trenchantly at party congress of 1908 with victory going to the radicals over the revisionists.

Not surprisingly, the trade unions themselves were concerned about the dominance of the theoreticist and historical bent of the

172

School's programme over the practical needs of unionists but were slow to develop their own programmes. Tischendörfer in the 1902 Congress of Free Trade Unions in Stuttgart argued for intellectual pluralism and chided members for anti-intellectualism. He found ready support among members who were not worried about 'bourgeois knowledge' and were keen on practical educational programmes. But it was clear that the trade unions lacked the ideological passion of the party and a comparison of the Party School and trade union school shows a more highly organised and intensive PS curriculum. The Party School used as teachers a galaxy of internationally renowned theorists such as Luxemburg, Mehring, Heinrich Cunow, Heinrich Schulz, Artur Stadthagen, Emmanuel Wurm, Hugo Heineman, Kurt Rosenfeld and for short periods Hilferding, Pannekoek and Duncker, while the trade union school depended largely on the contribution of Bernstein.

The number of graduating Party School members was relatively small and only 141 in 1906–1907 and 1910–1911, successfully graduated to positions in the labour movement. Moreover there was no reason to suppose they shared the ideological line of the teachers and substantial revisionist views were expressed. Lidtke notes: 'Even under the best conditions, that is, within an institution controlled by the left wing of Social Democracy, orthodox Marxist were unable to exercise the sweeping kind of ideological influence that they believed should permeate the whole social-cultural milieu of the labour movement' (Ibid.: 174). Larger numbers, mostly men, attended on a more causal basis and 1600 attended both schools between 1906–1914, while thousands attended local lectures and courses, largely held in restaurants and beer halls. Good speakers were quickly overworked, however, and others struggled to get attention of tired and emotional students. This was quite a serious blow to the educational ambitions of the SPD leaders who had hoped to achieve a cadre of disciplined and theoretically sound activists.

The trade unions meanwhile set about establishing a network of Workers' Libraries (*Arbeiterbibliotheken*) at first under local control but increasingly centralised after 1906. By 1914 there were 1147 libraries in 748 localities with collectively 833,857 volumes, a very substantial achievement. Seen as instruments for the workers' fight by Schulz rather than escapism, the libraries increasingly broadened their

173

scope as workers wanted. Some degree of political control and direction was nevertheless exercised by librarians and it appears that workers' choice of reading matter compared favourably to that of other Germans.

It is difficult not to suppose that, despite the high theoretical quality of the Marxist leadership, the educational programme of the SPD failed to meet its own expectations and Lidtke concludes:

> diversity held its own against total uniformity, the indigenous habits and preferences of workers often frustrated the lofty goal of Social Democratic reformers, ideological vagueness tended to win out over theoretical precision and traditions from various sections of the German *burgerlich* society and culture were carried over into the labor movement. At the same time the whole milieu, and the programs for political education in particular, spelled out the main principles of the alternative view of society and culture that so threatened many middle-class Germans (Ibid.: 191).

So, ironically, the fears of liberal intellectuals for the souls of the workers were probably misplaced. Or possibly the very fact that such official energy was put into popular adult education by charismatic educators like von Erdberg could not but nudge the SPD members in a similar educational direction. It was nevertheless a testament to the democratic nature of the SPD that discussion around the issue was not suppressed and that in the end the educational provision reflected what the workers wanted rather than what the leadership, for all its quality, prescribed. It foreshadowed the struggles between the WEA and the Labour Colleges and Plebs League for the souls of labour activists in Britain and with a similar outcome.

Science and Popular Education in Austria

Although it shared many of the aspects of the German cultural world that we have been describing, Austria differed in significant respects from the conventional narrative. What was for many historians a highly cosmopolitan entity, the Austro-Hungarian Empire, by the mid-nineteenth century was imploding from internal nationalist pressures.

174

Without a coherent constitutional structure, the territory governed by the Dual Monarchy lacked social, racial or geographical cohesion (Roberts, 2001: 157). Germans, Czechs, Magyars and Poles (as we noted in Chapter 2) fed by nationalist aspirations became increasingly impatient of imperial rule but were themselves barely tolerant of their own national minorities of Romanians, Croats, Serbs, Slavs and others. In the Austrian half of the monarchy unchecked executive power was complemented by what one Austrian Socialist leader called 'despotism tempered by slovenliness' (quoted in ibid.: 160).

The relationship of science and social reform begun in Josephine Vienna had faltered but as the century progressed and new social movements came to the fore, it once again revived. Its identity with masonry and philanthropy, though often illegal, remained strong. The celebrated philosopher Karl Popper, for example, remembered, during his childhood in the 1890s, his father Simon Siegfried Popper as a 'radical liberal in the school of John Stuart Mill' and that:

> as a freemason he was even a member of a society which at that time was declared illegal by the Austrian government, though not by the Hungarian government of Francis Joseph [...] He worked on two committees which were running homes for the homeless: a freemason's lodge of which he was for many years the Master ran a home for orphans (Popper, 1974: 9).

Popper's account of his childhood in Vienna furnishes a vivid account of the intellectual turmoil of the city which ran from masonic free thought through scientific empiricism and logical positivism to Marxism. The intellectual climate in which Popper junior grew up was heavily influenced by his father's concerns, which centred on the Monist movement of Ernst Mach and Wilhelm Oswald, especially their philosophy of science. Not surprisingly, perhaps, Einstein was his most significant influence, Popper claiming that, 'I had been brought up in an atmosphere in which Newton's mechanics and Maxwell's electrodynamics were accepted side by side as unquestionable truths' (Ibid.: 37).

As a student in Vienna, the philosopher of the 'Open Society' even had an early flirtation with Marxism. Having read the vigorous attack on nineteenth century capitalism, *Looking Backward* (1888) by the British socialist Edward Bellamy, Popper was briefly a Marxist convert:

for anti-Marxism in Austria was a worse thing than Marxism: since the social democrats were Marxists, anti-Marxism was very nearly identical with those authoritarian movements which were later called fascist (Ibid.: 35).

Popper went as far as to claim that 'The encounter with Marxism was one of the main events in my intellectual development' and he remained a kind of socialist even after rejecting Marxism concluding that although socialism was a beautiful dream, 'freedom is more important than equality' (Ibid.: 36).

Despite his misgivings about Marxist historicism, Popper had a great admiration for the workers of Vienna, popular education and the Social Democratic Party, maintaining that education was at the core of the success of the movement:

> Their leaders were able to inspire them with a marvellous faith in their mission, which was nothing less, they believed than the liberation of mankind. Although the social democratic movement was largely atheistic [...] the whole movement was inspired by what can only be described as an ardent religious and humanitarian faith. It was movement of workers to educate themselves in order to fulfil their historic mission; to emancipate themselves and thus to help liberate mankind: and above all, to end war. In their restricted spare time many workers, young and old, went to extension courses, or to one of the "People's Universities" (*Volkshochschulen*). They took a great interest not only in self-education but in the education of their children, and in improving housing conditions [...] This great movement and its tragic destruction by fascism made a deep impression (Ibid.).

Leading intellectuals became more closely associated with popular education in Vienna than in any other European city. For Dvorak (1994) Ernst Mach's work at the end of the nineteenth century signified a major change in the conception of science from a metaphysical discourse of the 'harmony of nature' (promoted by speculative masonry) to a strict empiricism and 'tool-like nature of theory'. By the time of Alfred Einstein, 'nature was no longer considered as an enormous mechanism with strict, immutable laws but as something disordered and chaotic' (Dvorak, 1994: 248). But in tune with the masonic forebears, Mach was passionate about an ethical world-order based on scientific insights, since for him the pursuit of science was not simply a matter of individual genius but very much a *collective* enterprise.

176

Friedrich Adler the leading theoretician of the unique version of Marxism with which Popper came into contact, Austro-Marxism, 'viewed Mach's conception of sciences as a major supplement to Marxian theory' (Ibid.: 248–9). In German academic circles, by contrast, the sciences were seen as divided between on the one hand the natural sciences which had immutable laws and on the other the human sciences dominated by 'genius'. This perspective was, as we have seen, unfortunately characterised by disdain towards manual work and placed and enormous emphasis on the spirit (*Geist*) and intellect and had little time for social relevance.

German academics expected the working classes to become assimilated into the 'German ethnic community' in direct contradiction to the Enlightenment scientific worldview, still affective in Vienna, which encouraged individual self-worth and alternative forms of collective identity. In contradistinction, the popular educational movement that grew up in the 1890s in Vienna provided a significant connection between the scientific worldview of which Mach was an exemplar and the growing working class movement. Although it was unable in the end to stem the tide of racial intolerance and nationalist fervour, the popular educational movement offered a robust alternative in tune with its early Enlightenment principles.

Another leading figure in the popular educational movement was the physicist and mathematician Edgar Zilsel (1891–1944) who also played an active role in modernist cultural activities in Vienna. Zilsel was a member of the highly progressive Vienna Circle which attempted to follow the trajectory set by Ernst Mach of uniting empiricism and logic whilst rejecting metaphysical interpretations. Deeply committed to popular education, he taught courses at a number of Viennese institutes of adult education during the early part of the twentieth century. He took up a teaching assignment in philosophy and physics at the remarkable *Volksheim Ottäkring*, 1922 until 1934 when he was forced to leave by the insurgent Austro-fascist regime. The same anti-enlightenment forces also refused his attempt to qualify as lecturer at the University of Vienna.

Zilsel's approach was characterised by his opposition to the holistic doctrines, idolisation of nature, the 'new' metaphysics and religiosity embraced by the political right. Instead he stressed the endemic *disorder* of nature, which could be structured only through

177

scientific approaches to nature and the possibility of rationalising the irrational. But Zilsel did not intend to enshrine yet another 'priestly' elite since he made no distinction between scientific behaviour and ordinary life. He was not disposed to segregate ideas into specialised disciplines and argued against compartmentalisation of the humanities, social sciences and natural sciences. His views on the role of intellectuals was not dissimilar from Gramsci's conception of 'organic intellectuals' in that he denied they were confined to a specific traditional class and that their role was instead determined by the scientific conception of the world.

The *Wiener Kreis* to which he belonged was wholly committed to bringing a scientific worldview to the lives of the masses in what Dvorak describes as a 'subversive attempt to democratise science' (Ibid.: 257). Its declaration in 1929 attempted to promote the unity of science and commonality of effort in order to form the intellectual tools of modern empiricism. The members of the circle saw the institutes of adult education in inter war years in Vienna as the primary educational vehicles:

> In the Viennese institutes of adult higher education progressive results of science which were controversial and banned in bourgeois academia (anything from the theory of relativity to psychoanalysis) found a stronghold, as did new models of scientific activity in education (Ibid.: 258).

And they were remarkably successful, particularly at the *Volksheim* Ottäkring at which we shall shortly look in more detail.

The Vienna Folk High School Movements

According the archivist of the Vienna movement Christian Stifter (1994) popular education in Austria evolved out of the liberal and workers' associations of the 1870s through a kind of hybrid of university extension and folk high schools that led to the terms *Volkshochschule* (misleadingly named as 'folk high schools' when popular universities is really more appropriate) and *Volksbildung* being used inclusively. Workers' educational organisations, *Arbeiter-bildungsvereine*, had been as elsewhere in Europe, frequently initiated by the liberal middle class as a form of compensatory education, largely in a response to the crisis occasioned by the 'social question' which dictated a ban on direct political activity. However with the gradual politicisation of the working class, as in Germany, and the eventual formation of the Social Democratic Party in 1888–1889 the liberal and workers' educational movements bifurcated and the labour movement concentrated on class struggle.

Although the first of the empire's popular educational associations was established in Prague in 1869 (largely because of the more relaxed approach to masonic activity in Bohemia), the movement spread through the provincial towns of Austria from 1870 and reached Vienna only in 1887 (Stifter, 1994). By 1893 however, the *Wiener Volksbildungsverein* formed the centrepiece of Austrian popular education. Popular university lectures followed in 1895 informally associated with the University of Vienna and initiated by individuals but nevertheless following the English model of university extension.

Vienna's second 'popular university' was the *Urania* founded in 1897 by industrialists concentrating on providing courses in the natural sciences and technical innovation, closer in style to the British Mechanics Institutes but characterised by popular and vivid lecturing, film shows and an observatory. But perhaps the most significant development, however, was the foundation of a *Volksuniversität* (which could loosely be translated as university settlement or popular university) in 1901 in the working class Ottäkring district, which had witnessed severe anti-Semitic riots during the 1890s. Four years later it was regarded as 'the first evening-class 'folk high school' (or more accurately 'popular university' in) of the kind in Europe' (Ibid.: 266). It was also the first time that an 'extra mural' function had its own independent existence. This Austrian version of the *Volkshochschule* (which became known as the *Volksheim*) became the most popular and successful adult educational institution in Austria, providing courses in all fields of modern knowledge from spelling to Kantian philosophical criticism, conducted in purpose-built accommodation and taught by academic experts. Stifter well-evokes the exciting atmosphere generated by this dramatically new kind of institution:

179

For the first time, these politically neutral schools for adults offered an opportunity for the ordinary citizen of Vienna to take advantage of a selection of systematic lectures and classes accessible to everyone, regardless of social origin, previous training, creed or sex. The courses covered a wide range of subjects from simple reading and writing classes to sophisticated scientific issues, art, philosophy, history, chemistry, physics, biology, mathematics, etc. The goal of this kind of education was not so much the satisfaction or short-term stimulation of educational interests but a more lasting effect, which, as Ludo Moritz Hartmann expressed it, was ultimately 'learning how to think' – a way of thinking free of false beliefs or superstitions, which bases itself exclusively on the authority of critical judgment and the objectivity of scientific knowledge. This rational approach, whose intention was a deeply democratic one – liberty, equality and fraternity were the focus of this idea – conflicted despite its 'neutrality' with the conservative and clerical organs and the authorities of the Habsburg Monarchy. This conflict proves how new and unknown the idea of such educational establishments actually was. In fact, the name 'Popular University', as these 'neutral' establishments came to be called in the First Republic, was once forbidden by the police authorities, who regarded the idea of a university for the 'common people' as immoral and offensive. (Hence the name 'Volksheim'). Yet, despite a number of financial and political obstacles, the adult education institutions survived and even flourished during the First Republic, which was not least due to wide-ranging support by scientists, middle-class liberal industrialists, the workers' movement and the labor unions (Stifter, 2005).

Although the members of the Vienna Circle later lent intellectual leadership to the *Volksheim*, initially many of the lecturers were grammar school teachers who had become stalled and frustrated by changes in the education system. Here they might advance their professional standing through cooperation with the 'university class' as well as their social and political idealism. For obvious reasons, however, political neutrality was essential. Ludo Moritz Hartmann, one of the most important initiators of the movement, insisted on the need for neutral education for both pedagogic and political reasons, affirming that:

> We want keep a distance from any kind of politics – not because we are opportunists, but because we believe strongly that politics should be a part neither of schools nor of the aims of popular education. We consider politics as belonging to parties and anything we aim at should be limited to the spreading of education and science (quoted in Stifter, 1994: 269).

Of course such neutrality also lubricated relations with the state and eased state subventions.

Who attended these classes? A survey in 1903–1904 of 1635 university extension students found interesting divergences in the nature and motivation of the actual student make up. Women made up forty per cent in classes, whose prime motivation was to widen their knowledge and increase their vocational skills but also to mix with higher classes. In terms of occupational mix up to 1914 some twenty-five to thirty-four per cent were mostly skilled workers rising to forty-four per cent in Ottäkring by 1932. The efforts of the folk high schools to attract a general public were much more successful than those of the politicised workers' associations and Social Democrat leaders appreciated the difference between their own workers' education for class-consciousness and the general education of the popular universities.[2] They were also well received by the left wing press and individuals like Ludo Hartmann, Reich and Leisching often wrote popular journalism. Support came from business associations such as chambers of trade and financial support from the Rothschild and Wittgenstein banking families.

Despite their attachment to political neutrality, they were fiercely attacked by the conservative-clerical press like *Vaterland* and the Deutsche *Volksblatt*, which, according to Stifter, either 'polemicized against freethinking-masonic-positivist scientific tendencies, or else invited readers to join the crusade against Jewish social-democratic influences, pointing out the incompatibility of such activities with the Christian-Catholic conception of the world' (Ibid.: 278). In reply, an article in the Social Democratic newspaper *Vorwärts* in 1922 entitled

2   Christian Stifter (personal communication) notes that the sociable side of the popular universities were just as important and that memoirs of those attending courses at *Volksheim Ottäkring* stress the social aspect of 'mixing the classes' was highly valued and there really was a *Gemeinschaftsgefühl*. There were summer-courses held in the countryside, which lasted for weeks and educational journeys both within Austria and abroad. Alfons Petzold (the famous working class poet) wrote about the *Volksheims* as the *Haus der hundert Lichter* (House of a hundred lights) which all members described as 'their own' – could popular enlightenment have a better figure?

'Von der Halbsbildung zur Volksbildung' affirmed the importance of the *Volksheim*'s work for creating citizenship:

> The authentic democratic state [...] requires a populace in which every single individual feels responsible for the whole and thus co-operates actively in order to make it successful – according to ability and capacity. The individual is not only seen as an economic cell in the narrow confines of an occupation, but – in addition – as a politically thinking and acting member of the unity' (quoted Ibid.: 279).

The *Volksheim Ottäkring* appears to be an exemplary model of scientific cooperation between intellectuals and general public. Inclusiveness, open access to lecture rooms and libraries and congress with scientists, artists and writers and great social-ideological diversity characterised the *Volksheim* whose scientific laboratories were in some cases better developed than those of the university. Between 1905 and 1932 no less than sixteen specialist groups (*Fachgruppen*) were established for the purpose of supporting intensive forms of education in the natural sciences and humanities which often led to members publishing articles in specialist journals.

The Austro-Hungarian Empire was finally defeated in World War One and the First Republic was declared. The Social Democratic Party elected to government (1919–1934), naturally encouraged and substantially funded the popular educational movement. The SPD's own educational apparatus also grew during this time but recognised that the work of the 'neutralist' folk high schools was not in competition with its cadre training. The decision of the Minister of Education under the Republic, Otto Glöckel, to make the task of adult education a responsibility of the Ministry for Education had a lasting administrative effect by creating an office for adult education which still exists (now as the Department for Adult Education) although voluntary adult education associations are still its main form of organisation.

The Viennese movement thus enabled a critically important expansion of public space for education and enquiry that created a radically new organ of science centred popular education. The *Volksheim* offered a challenging corrective to the traditionally authoritarian public schooling and elitist universities of the Austrian state. Stifter argues that the *Volkshochschulen* became part of a civic public realm, a 'democratic forum where heterogeneous elements came together to form a horizontal network of casual alliances', an inclusive public that had not previously existed (Ibid.: 271). As we saw in Chapter 2, Habermas might well have characterised this as a 'plebeian public' in contrast to the more oppositional and highly politicised social democratic 'proletarian public' of the labour movement. For Foucault these might even have been a kind of 'heterotopia' which he described as 'a realized utopia in which the real places in society are at the same time represented, contested and turned, so to speak outside all places, although they can actually be located' in contrast to traditional ensemble of political and cultural sites (quoted in ibid.: 272). Such fertile spaces of course may be seen by conservative opinion as profoundly unsettling and so it turned out.

The rise of Nazism and Austro–fascism during the early 1930s rapidly put an end to the *Volksheims* and *Volkschochschule*. Their members were dispersed and their leading lights forced into exile, were imprisoned and in some case killed. The post-war reconstruction in Austria, nevertheless, drew strength from the spirit of the popular educational movement which so valued enlightened tolerance and the scientific objective approach to social problems. Such values, although they may go out of fashion, never lose their currency and, as Stifter concludes:

> Even though the people's universities of the monarchy and the inter-war periods did not survive, today's people's universities continued the progressive and emancipatory educational tradition both in their principles and their concrete activities. In view of some reactionary and conservative thinking that prevailed for a long time both in the educational system and in society in general, the people's universities played an exemplary role. Facing a growing anti-democratic, rightist, conservative and even reactionary tendencies in society and politics, their role is undoubtedly a significant one (Stifter, 2005).

Chapter 8
The Nordic People's Enlightenment in Sweden, Finland and Norway

The Nordic countries have an enviable record of democratic participation, which has been achieved through early gaining universal suffrage and the rights of mass mobilisation for protests and demonstration, although each of the five countries Denmark, Sweden, Norway, Finland and Iceland differ in their historical paths taken to these rights. Located in the northernmost part of Europe and further isolated by means of the Baltic Sea and North Atlantic, the Nordic countries' extreme distance from Rome meant they were never subjected to the control of the Holy Roman Empire. They completely broke with the Roman Catholic Church in 1517 and, following Lutheran principles, created nationally distinctive cultural institutions (Rokkan, 1981). During the seventeenth century Sweden had emerged as the great power in the Baltic region with Denmark a serious rival. Both Finland and Estonia were under Swedish control and Eastern Baltic territories were seized from Russia and Poland by Gustavus Adolphus, turning the Baltic into a 'Swedish sea'. Further territories were seized from Denmark and on the southern coast of the Baltic. Swedish power, however, declined in the eighteenth century after the disastrous invasion of Russia and the battle of Poltava in 1709. The rising power of Russia and continued opposition from Denmark created serious problems.

Of the five countries two, Denmark and Sweden, had been politically independent for centuries while Iceland, Finland and Norway had been politically governed from elsewhere. Iceland was controlled from Copenhagen; Norway had shaken off Danish hegemony and Finland, once a Swedish conquest, was under Russian domination. The Napoleonic Wars had a significant constitutional impact on the region: Finland was ceded to Russia by Sweden in 1809 and in 1810 one of Napoleon's generals, was installed as king of Sweden. Norway declared its independence in 1814, only to be forcibly joined with Sweden a little later, a union that was not dissolved until 1905. With the notable exception of Sweden, the historically hegemonic power, the Baltic states as a consequence all underwent waves of cultural nationalism centring on language, folk culture, and the promotion of symbols of national difference like clothing and flags.

However, cutting across movements for national unity were elements of class conflict. This was especially the case in Finland where the Fennoman movement was sharply severed by conflicts between 'Old' and the 'Young' Finns who eventually engineered a socialist breakthrough in 1907 from which a civil war erupted. In other states class differences were managed through a process of constitutional reform which dramatically extended the franchise in Denmark in 1849 and more gradually in Sweden and Norway. Sweden and Denmark still harboured dynastic monarchies while Norway actually adopted one in 1814 but by the twentieth century all were constitutionally curtailed by parliamentary democracy. Predominantly rural at the start of our period, the Nordic countries already housed some large towns which nursed manufacturing industries and some civil government, although Copenhagen in Denmark was easily the largest metropolitan centre. Each had a substantial peasantry of varying degrees of wealth, a small but energetic bourgeoisie and a nascent working class.

As Rokken notes the national cultural revolutions in the Baltic states preceded their industrial revolutions, in some cases by decades, but persisted through the period and as we have seen in Denmark (Chapter 4) dramatically coloured the later-nineteenth century. Although Scandinavian cultural conflicts reflected those found elsewhere in Europe, the primary exception was the contest over religion. Because of the early and complete split with Rome, religious conflict centred on differences internal to Protestantism especially the role of the church in the state and the boundaries with secularism. Despite the often small linguistic differences between the Nordic countries (with the exception of Finland) language became a focus for cultural and national difference. The division between rural and urban interests frequently split the liberal alliances, or *Venstre*, which were compounded by religious affiliations and the usual pattern of a morally conservative, religiously fundamentalist countryside against a morally

186

permissive, secular and radical township was familiar as elsewhere in Europe, with the relative exception of Finland. An important difference was the role of the temperance movements in Norway and Sweden however, which played an exceptional role in popular educational movements. Rokkan accounts for this movement in two ways: the relatively small size of Swedish and Norwegian towns prohibited the growth of both a powerful middle class and organised working class and secondly, the returning migrants from the USA were less in evidence in Denmark. In Finland the countryside was remarkably radical possibly because the mobilising election of 1907 took place before any great waves of migration reduced rural class tensions (Ibid.: 70).

As urbanisation and industrialisation inevitably developed, the towns became more politically assertive through the emergence of the Socialist and Social Democratic parties, which became a defining feature of the remarkable Scandinavian 'middle way' for most of the twentieth century. For this national political formation the fault line was not so much between capitalism and socialism as between individualism and collectivism. It did not suffer the acute divisions between radicals and socialists as in France or liberals and socialists as in Britain because of the effective liberal socialist alliances before World War One especially in Sweden and Denmark (Levy, 1987).

Popular Education Movements in Sweden

Thirty years in advance of Britain, the Education Act of 1842 introduced compulsory schooling in Sweden which it is claimed all but eliminated illiteracy and moreover fed the desire for more learning, a consequence of which was the dynamic growth of public libraries. Founded in 1840, mostly by national and local associations, the public library system was a widespread and frequently itinerant institution which became the basis of popular education in Sweden (Torstensson, 1994). Swedish popular education (*folkbildning*) as a free and democratic education for adults emerged from the labour, temperance, Free

Church and cooperative movements which formed the motors for change in the nineteenth century. Popular education was organised through two main systems: the folk high schools (*Folkhögskolor*), which developed from Danish origins, and perhaps its own unique contribution to popular educational development, the 'study circle' organisations (*studieförbund*).

Strong local government and the extension of the franchise to farmers further spread popular education in the countryside. During the 1880s the rapid industrialisation of the towns created an urban working class and developed a flexible non-formal education to aid the transition from a largely rural population into an industrialised nation of concerned citizens. As in Denmark, popular education played a very important role in training and educating workers, farmers and others. Both the folk high schools and the study circle organisations provided for the free and voluntary study of human, social, scientific and cultural studies in order to strengthen democracy, community and offer specialist knowledge for adults beyond the ordinary schooling system. Jacobsen argues that because of a common tradition, there is greater diversity *within* each of the Nordic countries than between them. All share elements of the folk high school and study circle systems as well as some university extension type activities on the British model (Jacobsen, 1981). In all Nordic countries, the Temperance Movement played an instrumental role in founding popular education, quickly followed by and in some cases associated with social democratic movements and the activities of liberal university professors in offering university extension classes. While study circles date from around 1902, Workers' Educational Associations on the British model emerge in 1912 in Sweden, 1919 in Finland, 1924 in Denmark and 1932 in Norway. Although public authorities played no part in founding popular education, they robustly recognised their value and initiated funding (Jacobsen, 1981: 469). Importantly, public funding was dependent only on the ability of the voluntary organisations to demonstrate a demand for learning and public authorities made no demands as to content or political and religious affiliation.

The origins of Swedish popular education appear to owe not a little to the Scottish Enlightenment or at least the Swedish translation in 1832 of *Practical Observations upon the Education of the People*

(1825) by the leading Edinburgh Whig philosopher and politician, Henry Peter, Lord Brougham (1778–1868) (Rubenson, 1992). Brougham's most famous remark that 'Education makes a people easy to lead, but difficult to drive; easy to govern, but impossible to enslave' ensured him a prominent place in the annals of educational reform. Elected Lord Rector of Glasgow University in 1825, Brougham also played a vital part in founding London University in 1826, based on Scottish lines and severely secular. But, just as important for our purposes, he also helped to establish various mechanics' institutes and implemented a plan for the publication of cheap works by the formation of the Society for the Diffusion of Useful Knowledge (SDUK) in 1825. His *Practical Observations on the Education of the People* referred especially to the need of scientific education for the upper rather than lower classes. In 1833 Sweden founded its own Society for the Diffusion of Useful Knowledge with an accompanying journal that was largely moralistic and practical in tone. It played an important role part in promoting the formation of public libraries in Sweden and the moral tone of their work is aptly summed up in their introductory catalogue:

> Give joy to idle moments, counteract the inclination for bad company, public-life, drinking of alcohol and card-playing, diminish the circulation of indecent literature, ennoble home life, give practical knowledge that increases the work capability, strengthen the judgement in political and social matters and by this contribute to foster well-informed citizens, who understand to use their rights in central, regional and local politics to the general advantage (quoted in Torstensson, 1994: 2).

Study Circles, Folk High Schools and Workers' Institutes

The public availability of books made informal study increasingly possible and local interest groups, especially the temperance movement began to promote study circles. Possibly because of the simplicity and autonomy of their organisation, study circles were enormously popular. The founding of the study circle movement is largely ascribed to Oscar Olsson (1877–1950) an active member of the

Swedish branch of the International Order of Good Templars (IOGT), a Masonic-type body formed in 1894. As a young university student Olsson realised that conventional study methods were failing to inspire members and strove to make them more informal and participatory. He was inspired by a visit to America in 1893 and in particular the study circles promoted by the Chautauqua Literary and Scientific Society.[1]

Olsson contributed an informative outline of the theory and practice of the study circle movement to the *WAAE Handbook* in 1929. Since leaders from the old educated class could no longer be trusted, he claimed, its aims were to promote a culturally enlightened and socially educated citizenry to govern national affairs (WAAE, 1929: 412). The circles should emulate the 'spiritual dining clubs' of classical Sparta in which informed discussion should cement group solidarity. Previous reading of good books, he wrote, was essential to the conversation, the prime value of which was to correct the one-sided opinions of the individual by group learning through the Socratic method. In the early days, circles were led by group leaders elected from among themselves or occasionally invited teachers and academics but a time went on specialists were increasingly used. Nevertheless the practice of democratic elections and Socratic discussion continued to characterise the practice of the circles.

In the early twentieth century another leading temperance figure, Justus Elgeskog (1884–1975) formalised the work of study circles through articles in his journal *Ariel*. Elgeskog's long term approach to study was influenced by his appreciation of the WEA three-year tutorial class and he introduced correspondence methods for local circles. He also established closer links between the folk high schools and local study circles. Circle leaders, he believed, need not be professionally trained nor necessarily experts in their field but were

---

1   Curiously, while Olsson reinvented this system in Sweden, it declined in America to the point where it has been reintroduced only in recent years. Although Olsson did most to popularise the idea of the study circle it has been argued that it was in reality Edvard Wavrinsky (1848–1924) who actually introduced the idea (Arvidson, 1985). He too had visited Chautauqua in 1893 for the Swedish Temperance movement and was most impressed. The term 'study circle' appears to have been first used in the Templar's journal *Reformatorn* in 1894 and only subsequently picked up by Olsson.

responsible together with the group for ensuring that learning process took place. After its formation in 1912, study circles within the Swedish Workers' Educational Association (ABF), formed on British lines, were more likely to use specialists and teachers, especially in their longer course based on tutorial methods. For these circles some members would move onto 'higher' more specialised circles. Study circles were frequently used to complement the popular lectures offered by the IOGT and the lecture courses of the ABF so that by the 1920s they formed part of a more intensive form of adult education.

Increasingly the government was drawn into the provision of study circles and in 1922 its newly formed Adult Educational Committee proposed two year tutorial classes which from 1924 were directly funded, engaging the universities to take a leading role in association with the ABF. By the end of the twentieth century there were around eleven study organisations in Sweden alone catering for around three million participants per year, providing cultural events such as music concerts, art exhibitions, dance and theatre shows.

The other arm of the popular educational movement was based in the folk high schools, the first of which was opened in Sweden in 1868, following the 1866 constitution which enfranchised the farmers and raised their need to understand the principles of citizenship, as well as gaining practical knowledge. Although the Danish folk high schools were the direct inspiration for their Swedish counterparts they differed in important respects. Swedish folk high schools (*folk-högskola*) largely followed the Danish pattern of residential adult colleges but were never the property of the head teacher as in Denmark and were owned corporately. They shunned nationalist and religious 'Grundtvigianism' (in reality Kold's version) in favour of civic and cultural virtues. Although, as in Denmark, young adults from the countryside were the target group, the Swedes emphasised practical learning about local government and political work, book-keeping and surveying, and agricultural classes rather than the more 'spiritual' approach through poetry and music, emphasised in the Grundtvigian model, although they were certainly not absent. Typically the curriculum of the Swedish folk high schools was Swedish language and literature, history and sociology, geography, maths and science. As in Denmark, oral teaching was pre-eminent but book learning, abominated by true Grundtvigians, was also encouraged as a basis for independent study.

By 1900 the three most effective popular movements, those of labour, the Free Church and temperance, had all founded their own residential folk high schools. The battle to achieve non-interventionist funding from the state was won by the first Social Democratic folk high schools, Hola and Brunnsvik, against both the state governor and parliament, which had been reluctant to fund what they saw as the spreading of socialist ideas. Following this success it was permissible to teach courses from different ideological positions. But the folk high schools also provided general civic courses leading to a qualification of equal value to those from high school, which was acceptable for university entrance (in the early twentieth centuries many Swedish legislature members benefited from this alternative 'access' system). Inevitably, the state's role increased with its funding and eventually all came under the purview of the Board for Popular Education, which was allowed to inspect the schools periodically and could 'express an opinion' of the suitability of candidates for appointment, but as with the WEA in Britain, still allowing a substantial element of independence.

In the cities a related process was taking place but, as with other European urban popular education, it was based on presenting popularised science in newly founded Workers' Institutes. It was inspired by the work of Anton Nyström (1842–1931), an eminent dermatologist who practised in Stockholm and was widely travelled. Profoundly influenced by Auguste Comte's philosophy of positivism (see Chapter 6) which he was instrumental in introducing to Sweden, he founded the Positivist Society for the popularisation of science in 1879. The following year Nyström established the Stockholm Working Men's Institute (*Arbeturinstitut*) with a reading room and library, the first of its kind in Scandinavia, which from 1881 received a state grant and continued until the mid-1960s. Based on positivistic theory and his powerful belief in reason and knowledge as a means for the lower classes to ameliorate their own deprivation, it inevitably brought him into conflict with the church and political conservatives who feared insurrection. But its individualistic liberalism also offended the political labour movement led by August Palm, who insisted on 'food first, education afterwards' (Arvidson, 1985).

192

The popular lecture institutes which subsequently flourished were in reality a direct continuation of the educational circles of the liberal workers' unions which had come into existence in the 1850s and 1860s (Thompson, 1929: 407). They followed the same educational pattern of a series of lecture courses of one or more terms on natural science, medicine, mathematics or history. From the original institute, founded by Nyström in Stockholm, others followed in Malmo, Gavle, Norrkoping and Lund and from 1883 the *Riksdag* passed a bill to give regular grant-aiding to such institutes, which arranged courses for the working class in the larger towns. Initially the subvention granted was 15,000 kroner annually but by 1907 it had risen to 180,000 for the whole country (Koch, 1907). The bill was proposed by one of the originators of the Swedish folk high schools with the specific intention of offering an equivalent education for townspeople to that received in the country.

The educational movement in the towns grew substantially but, as elsewhere in Europe, although the grant-aiding was specifically for the 'working-class', the middle-classes soon became the net beneficiaries. Thompson suggests that this was because the modern working class, due to slow industrialisation in Sweden, had not yet made its appearance and the older working class was still based in the crafts. In the rural districts the lecture scheme faltered because finding lecturers for continuous courses was difficult and thus there was a marked tendency to move towards isolated lectures instead. Only in the larger towns were longer continuous courses retained. By 1904 grants were approved for at least 257 associations (Koch, 1907: 299). Popular lectures were however never seen as 'real knowledge' and in line with elsewhere in Europe, as we have seen, demands for more intensive education grew into a mass movement (Thompson, 1929: 395).

At the same time the labour movement began to establish its own educational centres but the argument about whether the education for its members should be 'class-conscious' or 'neutrally' objective also intensified. Gunnar Hirdman (1888–1963) one of the leaders of the Swedish Workers' Educational Association, the ABF, very much followed the path of an objective general education, claiming the outcome of education should be 'insights not opinions' (quoted in Thomas and Elsey, 1985: 264). For him adult education should resist the tendentialism of both the Church and Marxism and foster independent thinking: it should oppose dogma and absolute truths for the defence of 'humane values which are being threatened, both by ideologies of violence and by reactionary tendencies in Christian circles' (quoted in ibid.). Hirdman was also the first Director of the Arosgarden Institute which was also the most successful attempt to transfer the British settlement idea to Sweden. The neutralist position was also powerfully argued by Carl Cederblad (1886–1954) in his *Our Nation and Education* (1922) in which he proposed a single unified popular education organisation but despite founding the Popular Education Institute in Uppsala, lack of funding prevented it from becoming the research institute he saw as necessary.

University Extension

The attempt to introduce university extension on the British model could be seen as a way of reviving the ageing system of popular education by the direct involvement of the universities, the main element of which was the university summer school. Reports in the English extension journals at the time suggest that this was largely due to the activity of university intellectuals who had studied extension in England and America. One of the leading figures was Professor Harald Hjarne of Uppsala University, who following a visit to England in the summer of 1892, with the help of his professorial colleagues J.A. Lundell and Adolf Noreen, organised the first summer school in a Swedish University. The school ran for two weeks from 14 August and consisted of a demanding programme of five daily lectures from 9am–2pm and 4pm–7pm. While the courses largely reflected their scientific orientation especially in astronomy, physiology, botany and geology, they also included ancient history of Israel, Buddhism, Scandinavian history, psychology, philology and the Reformation (*OUEG*, Vol.IV, October 1893: 4).

As journal reports indicate, the summer school was in fact a very ambitious project comprising eighteen courses and 103 lectures with contributions from the organisers themselves and about a dozen members of the university. Students were expected to do serious academic work and carefully prepared syllabuses were distributed on the English model. The participants, consisting of 200 men and 130 women, were mainly young Board School teachers and pupils from the People's Academies (*folkhogskolorna*) from all parts of the country (*OUEG*, Vol.IV, No.46, 15 April 1894: 104). This initial summer school then initiated a four-year cycle which included the universities of Lund, Gothenburg and Stockholm and the Summer School, as such, became the main expression of university extension in Sweden.

While the predominance of teachers among the participants reflected the British experience, this is largely explained by the fact that Hjarne quite consciously addressed himself to this constituency. In 1892 on his return from England he had lectured enthusiastically to a congress of school masters on what he had learned (Picavet, 1901: 126). A report of the 1895 summer school notes that of the 470 members, 260 of whom were women, all but 100 were teachers from primary schools (*UEJ*, November 1895).

University extension did not however address the problem of workers' education and the relatively few skilled workers attending summer schools mirrored the English experience. However in an attempt to expand university extension from the base formed by the summer schools and establish relations with the Workers' Institutes, the four universities established 'mediation institutes', which published information on available lecturers. The Stockholm Institute, meanwhile, by 1907 had begun to dispatch lantern slides with explanatory texts to outlying districts where it was not possible to send lecturers in what appears to be one of the first technologically-inspired distance learning projects (Koch, 1907: 299).

As we have seen the subject matter of the summer schools was largely scientific following the pattern of positivistic and neutral education characteristic of liberal popular education. In this the organisers appeared to follow the common idea of popular science as a means to clear thought and problem solving that animated so many of the European intellectuals involved in extension. In his conclusion to the 1885 summer school, for example, Lundell asserted bluntly that the lines on which the work should proceed:

shall be scientific, directed towards the truth; its substance shall be up-to-date knowledge, consequently its imparters shall be exclusively such as are abreast of the times in their several subjects; its methods shall be critical, not dogmatic (UEJ, November 1895).

The summer schools were intended to arouse the powers latent in the inner consciousness, to widen the mental horizon and strengthen intellectual vision. In fact Lundell was taking his lead from Anton Nyström's practice and theory as published in his book *The Participation of the Workers in Contemporary Civilisation* which urged that 'the people should receive a systematic education by attending courses in all the sciences' (WAAE, 1929: 407). The syllabus of the 1895 summer school displayed a strong orientation to positivist 'objective knowledge' rather than speculative and creative thought or art, offering courses on Sweden in seventeenth century, organic life and modern languages, prehistoric Sweden, Swedish dialects and phonology, the early history of the Indo-Europeans, psychology of the will, education in England, and English colonies. In what was called 'the natural science section' (as opposed to the 'humanistic'), courses were offered in school hygiene, human anatomy and astronomy. There were also practical courses in beginners English, and 'ambulance' work. This interesting amalgam of national and racial history, psychology, language, Enlglish education, health and cosmology pointed to a common concern with social evolution, nationalism and modernisation.

Science was also complemented by philosophy. Lundell's colleague, Harald Hjärne was well-known for his contributions to corporatist state theory, in the conservative neo-Hegelian tradition, that stressed the obligation of the citizen toward the state. Political representation, Hjärne felt, ought to reflect the principle that the citizen derived his rights from the state in accordance with his personal contribution to the nation. Hjärne's book on English extension, published in 1893, proved widely influential and in 1895 at Stockholm he argued that university committees should choose lecturers, draw up programmes and make them available to workers' institutes and lecture associations. This proposal was first realised in Lund in 1897, Uppsala being more resistant, and invitations were sent out to those who had assisted at the summer schools to form an association for the promotion of university extension. The following year the Central Bureau for Popular Scientific Lectures in Lund was established, informally sponsored by the university. Unlike their counterparts in Britain, educational institutes in Sweden had a long history of receiving grant-aiding and this was extended to the Central Bureau in 1906 with the result that by 1914, 550 lecture institutes were subsidised (Thompson, 1929: 409–10). Extension in Sweden therefore came under the paternal eye of the state much earlier almost certainly because of the prior development of folk high schools and workers' institutes which had identified the importance of adult education at an earlier stage and by 1911 had acquired its own state inspector (Ibid.: 411).

Later developments in Swedish adult education included the 'field high school' from 1901 which was an attempt to humanise Swedish military service with high quality reading and stimulating lectures, proposed by the folk high schools. However this genuinely Swedish contribution to adult education may well have foundered on the lack of teachers to found in the officer corps. Another development was the *Studenter och Arbetare* enterprise related to English university settlements and French popular universities. The intention of this form of adult education was to effect a class rapprochement of students and manual workers through social and cultural events, which permitted free ranging discussion on controversial matters but remained politically neutral (Koch, 1907: 301).

Finland, Fennomania and the 'civic religion'

Following the pattern in the Nordic countries, Finland also borrowed the idea of Danish residential folk high school, the first of which opened in 1889. Such was the interest in all things Danish that Finnish university students were given scholarships by university student fraternities to visit Denmark and set up further schools. By 1926 there were fifty-four folk high schools of which forty were Finnish speaking and the others Swedish. They nevertheless differed in some ways from the Danish model; their curriculum was more like the Swedish, practically orientated rather than generally cultural and owned by dedicated corporations; they were also coeducational and generally housed in more spacious and technically better equipped buildings. Initially funded from voluntary contributions, by 1907 their revenue came from the state, a result of legislation that both permitted pluralistic values and took a non-interventionist stance.

Over the century 1889–1989, the number of residential folk high schools in Finland rose to ninety. About one third followed the Grundtvigian non-denominational humanistic model stressing communal unity while a further third were religiously or politically oriented and maintained a distinct ideologically orientated curriculum. A final group of folk high schools took a 'neutral' approach which supported individual growth without taking any particular moral, political or religious standpoint. The fact that these schools flourish over a century after the inception of he movement is a testament to their continuing value. They appear to operate as an important adjunct to the mainstream system sometimes in a 'deficit' repair role for what is seen as the state's inadequacies but equally important because they continue to identify and respond to new expressions of social and individual need.

But the expense of such a residential system stimulated the development of local evening classes on the lines of the Swedish Workers' Institutes. While the Swedish Institutes never developed into a major institution, after the idea was first introduced in Finland in the industrial city of Tampere in 1899, over the following seventy years the Finnish model developed into Finland's biggest single network of adult education institutes. This was due to very active local government support. Even so, although they were strongly supported by the Labour Party, their commitment to a 'scientifically neutral' approach and freedom from political and religious affiliation, as elsewhere, prompted the Left into viewing them as not sufficiently 'labour-oriented'. A Workers' Educational Association was therefore established in Finland in 1919, on Swedish lines which was the first to make use of study circle practice. Gradually, however, this form of adult education proved so useful that other popular movements and non-governmental organisations adopted it as a tool for educating their membership.

In this respect Finland seems to follow the Scandinavian pattern but it differed in significant respects. In the sixteenth century, Finland, like the other Scandinavian countries, joined the group of nations supporting the Lutheran Reformation, and adopted Lutheran doctrines. One of these doctrines meant that people had to learn to read in order to be able to study for themselves the word of God as revealed in the Bible and, as a consequence, the goal of nationwide literacy was possibly the most significant factor in creating a foundation for adult education in the mid-nineteenth century. Finnish identity however suffered from the twin imperialist ambitions of Sweden and Russia in the nineteenth century which created a specific tension in Finnish society. As consequence a strong body of Finnish folklore, almost mystical in intensity was fostered and eventually brought together in the 1835 collection the *Kalevala*. This collection formed an ideological core to nationalist ambitions and became a powerful stimulant to Finnish artists and musicians over the century.

Kantasalmi, argues that the period is marked by a continuation of the hegemonic enlightenment process begun in earlier Finnish popular education (Kantasalmi, 1996). He identifies two main stages in the emergence of popular education: firstly, the mid-nineteenth century *kansanvalistus* or 'people's enlightenment' which lasted until 1917 and secondly, *kansansivistys* or 'people's education'. This latter stage carries the same sense as the German *Volksbildung* in seeking the more intensive individual approach associated with the *Neue Richtung* (see Chapter 7). A dominant emphasis in popular education was national liberation, since Finland had been under Swedish rule until 1809 when it was incorporated into the Russian empire as the Duchy of Finland. As a consequence of the loosening of ties with Stockholm, the ruling Finnish élite, which was formerly Swedish–speaking, took the initiative to cultivate, perhaps even invent, a Finnish national identity. The Imperial Alexander University, which was established in Helsinki in 1828, marks this distinct Finnish turn (the Swedish-founded University of Turku dates from 1640).

The origins of popular education in Finland can be traced to the earlier nineteenth century. The Finnish Literature Society (SKS), established in 1831 by liberal elements in the small Finnish middle class, marked a major turning point. It aimed to reconcile the growing social conflict with the moral message of responsibility, diligence and submissiveness in the Christian fashion. As elsewhere in Scandinavia, the process was accompanied by a literary and cultural revival, in this case led by Johan Ludvig Runeberg (1802–1877) that idealised the peasantry and elevated the idea of 'the folk' to a semi-mystical status. Student corporations, for example, during the 1840s produced 'folk-booklets' celebrating folk wisdom which were widely distributed. Despite his Swedish-speaking background, Runeberg was adopted as the Finland's national poet and his poetry compared to that of the great European romantics, such as Hugo, Shelley, Keats, Lermontov and Petöfi.

Runeberg's first collection of poems, *Dikter* (1830) reflected his passion for Finland's landscape and the heroic inhabitants of the backwoods. One of the poems describes the peasant Paavo of Saari-järvi, who repeatedly loses his harvest to the frost, never complaining of his lot. When he has nothing else to eat, he nibbles hard bread, *pettu*, made from pine bark. 'The figure of Paavo has become one of the most enduring personifications of *"sisu"'* (or the dogged en-durance celebrated widely in other European literatures, such as Schweik in Czechoslovakia) (Anon, 2006). By the time of the Civil War (1917–1918) however, Runeberg's vision, in which common people in his works do not rebel against their fate, or against God, but understand instinctively their proper position, inevitably came to be seen as paternalistic and fatalistic.

At the University of Turku the dominant intellectual influence was German philosophical idealism while, significantly, the French Enlightenment gained no ground. Hegelian philosophy was widely espoused and its proponents, particularly J.V. Snellman (1806–1881) contributed strongly to founding the people's enlightenment project. Although it possessed significant common features, Snellman's 'national spirit' differed from Hegel's *Volksgeist* in claiming it as an inner property of the *individual* rather than the collective alone. It could be argued that this was also not dissimilar to Grundtvig's interpretation. He did not see the state as significantly separated from civil society, which drew charges of totalitarianism from liberal opponents. Nevertheless, the broad cultural movement embodying Hegelian ideas inspired students to disseminate popular literature and give lectures to rural audiences – the newly discovered 'Folk'. Universities played a (disputed) role in this, as did sections of the

Swedish educated élite. The movement which had been responsible for creating the educated middle class or *Bildungsburger* of the towns formed in the earlier half of the century, now moved towards an educated rural class or *Bildungsbauern*.

In the 1870s 'Fennomania' developed into an intellectual movement, pursuing Finnish cultural homogeneity and a nationalist cornerstone in opposition to Swedish hegemony (Liikanen, 1988). In 1874 the Fennomans founded the *Kansanvalistusseura* (KVS), the Society for People's Enlightenment, which was given the task of publishing and spreading instructive literature. The liberal press assumed KVS meetings would become platforms for Fenno agitation, aimed at mobilising the people against the Swedish-speaking upper class, although in fact it seems to have been rather conservative and, if anything, opposed to radical popular mobilisation. Fenno intellectuals were trying to create a Finnish-speaking élite rather than fomenting a movement of class struggle and centred their activities on cultural rather than political 'nation building'. By the following year the KVS had arranged meetings in over thirty-five localities in an atmosphere of nationalist enthusiasm and in 1876 held various festivities celebrating the ideological father of Finnish national movement J.V. Snellman, who remained aloof from such groupings, as a national hero.

Its educational organisation, which did not cast itself as a political vehicle 'but a new kind of civic religion of the national state', included intensive voluntary activity in Satakunta and other Finnish speaking rural areas (Ibid.: 428). The KVS became the largest civic organisation in Finland with around five thousand members and network of local agents throughout the country. Although the organisers opposed the old class distinctions between the different estates and appeared to open a channel of social mobility for Finnish-speaking peasants, in reality they also legitimated a new hierarchy. The KVS's educational programme adopted Snellman's political philosophy that the nation state should be based on its national culture (the Finnish term *sivistys* is closer to German *Bildung* than English 'education' or 'culture'). But it was by no means radically egalitarian and advanced the status of Finnish intellectuals in a movement that made 'education and knowledge the cornerstone of the social hierarchy' (Ibid.: 431). Agatho Meuron, president of the KVS summed up its aims succinctly, in 1881:

> There has been no shortage of voices wanting to regard the work done for popular education in this country as part of the world revolutionary movement. There has been talk of agitative demands that seek a kind of equality that would set aside dissimilarity born out of ability, education, knowledge and wealth, of demands for dragging all the people down to the lowest level of social stratification. We do not know where this kind of activity takes place and who is behind it. Concerning the Society for Popular Education, its aims are totally the opposite (quoted ibid.: 431).

The activities of the KVS peaked in the years around 1874–1876 when about 300 events in support of educational activities were organised and about 120 educational organisations and reading societies set up but, like the snow in summer, after a couple of years of intensive life they all but disappeared. Around Helsinki and Turku, the metropolitan Swedish language areas, little KVS Fennomania was evident and instead university students organised popular lectures on a voluntary basis, while in rural Swedish speaking areas there was in fact no popular education until the 1880s.

Educational activity in the countryside was thus rather patchy and inconclusive. In the province of Häme, while it led to a rise in self-esteem in the prosperous peasantry, increased class conflict with rural workers and crofters was manifest. Generally, the gentry began to speak Finnish instead of Swedish and the richer peasantry became increasingly gentrified. In Savo-Karelia (East Finland), educational meetings also had the effect of further polarising relations between the Swedish speaking gentry and Finnish peasants because it was a much poorer area. The poor peasantry created numerous disturbances but did not coalesce into a political movement at this stage.

For their part, Fenno intellectuals absolutely refused to undertake extra-parliamentary action or to mobilise the 'will of the people' or organise channels of public opinion, as happened elsewhere in Europe. Liikanen's conclusion was that:

> Still the educational activities of the 1870s had a substantial effect on the development of civic organisation in Finland. The decade witnessed a nationwide mobilisation closely controlled by a central leadership. Even though the mobilisation did not lead – and was not meant to lead – to a political mass

movement, by founding the SPE (KVS) an ideological and organisational centre of Fennomania was established and a permanent network of agents was created which connected the Fennoman intellectuals in the capital to the local élite in the rural areas (Ibid.: 438).

Fennomania's real significance lay in the profound cultural revival that produced a flowering of literature, the arts and especially music. In Helsinki, university student corporations dedicated to popular education in the Viipiri province held regular fund raising soirées in Helsinki to which the élite were invited, and featured the work of Fenno artists. It was for one of these in November 1893 that Jean Sibelius wrote a series of tableaux as a kind of musical diversion between acts. No one took the slightest notice, complained Sibelius in a letter to friend, since because of the loud babbling of the socialites, his music was inaudible. Such were the origins of his enchanting Karelia Suite which subsequently became identified throughout Europe with the folk soul of Finnish nationalism.

In the rural areas Fennomania was not aggressively anti-Swedish and it is not clear why its educational activities so abruptly declined. Possibly, the Fenno leadership stopped encouraging popular activities in the face of radical opposition from the very people it appeared ideologically, at least, to revere. There were clear contradictions in any programme that lacked an egalitarian political element and, despite its rhetoric of *Volksbildung*, Kantasalmi sees this as a failure to create an equal educated citizenry. The national movement, rather, served the ruling classes as 'civic religion' for the emerging state to enhance their rather fragile base (Kantasalmi, 1996). It ushered in a period of intensifying class conflict that comes to head with the civil war of 1917. The folk high schools and the nationalist Youth Associations eventually took over and formed the basis of the rural enlightenment project until the 1920s.

In the metropolitan urban centres the picture was somewhat different and led instead to a gender-based conflict. Some leading members of the KVS, though not all, had recognised the educational advantages of university extension to the movement and the universities of Turku and Helsinki introduced extension courses, initially for women from the upper class, in 1873. However the Women's Academy appeared to be aimed at female domestication and wholly ignored women's political issues. As a consequence, the issue of women's education stimulated the emergence of the women's movement in the 1880s, which was eventually to make Finland a pioneer of women's rights. This form of university extension, in practice, mainly meant popular lectures, summer lectures and continuing education of elementary school teachers, as in Sweden. A women-only folk high school was established by Sofia Hagman in the same year in 1889, which although criticised as insufficiently Grundtvigian, spawned a number of similar developments.

Workers' Associations and Institutes

While Fennomania was active in rural areas and affective among the cultural élite, radicalism was growing among the small urban working class. The first municipal workers' association was founded in Tampere in 1899, followed by a national Workers' Association on the Swedish model in Helsinki, by Viktor Julius von Wright (1856–1934) who specifically linked the struggle for political rights with *Bildung* and associational activity. The Workers' Assembly, which met in 1899, called for the creation of municipally owned and managed workers' institutes because its own poor resources could not support such a programme. Initially, and not unexpectedly, their efforts were frustrated by trenchant opposition from the Fennoman based KVS and the rural folk high schools. The General Strike of 1905 was a turning point and as a result of the relative electoral success of the Kautskyite SPD who introduced reforms, the idea of the folk lost some of its rural, romantic connotations and began to assume a more class-based political character. After the General Strike too, most of the Fennomen found themselves excluded from the leadership of the KVS and its educational policy subtly changed to embrace class-sensitive approaches – while abjuring militantly socialist ones. Hence, the renewed drive to create municipal workers' institutes, which had hitherto been resisted, was now largely motivated by the desire to guard workers against the revolutionary doctrines of the left wing workers' associations. Social studies were specifically excluded by municipal institutions and later a Civic College was set up in1918 to counter socialist doctrines and promote civic virtues.

Social conflict came to a head with the Civil War of 1917 when Finland declared independence from Russia, after which the left wing of the workers' movement was brutally eliminated, with over 8000 executions. Many more were imprisoned especially in the prison town of Tammisaari which became known as the 'University of Tamissaari' because of the intensity of its inmates' educational activity. Others went into exile and formed the Finnish Communist Party in the Soviet Union. The reformed SPD recovered to some extent and was allowed representation in parliament. It became increasingly active in education, fostering the Workers' Educational Union (TSL) in 1919, which was state-subsidised and based on Swedish practice. Its founder and first Director was Professor Väino Voionimaa who had become a (moderate) socialist in 1905. Voionimaa did not reject *Bildung* as such but wanted to complement it with 'self managed workers' education' and, influenced by the example of Ruskin College, Oxford, established a Workers' Academy in 1924.

During the 1920s Finnish popular adult education became substantially institutionalised and theorised largely due to the work of the philosopher Zachris Castrén (1868–1932) of the University of Helsinki. His report *The State and Liberal Adult Education* (1929) drew heavily on the British *1919 Report*, noting the value of state subsidies for liberal adult education but free from intervention or vocational training (Jukka, 1992). Also influenced by German *frei Volksbildungsarbeit*, he understood the term 'liberal' as referring to the autonomous self-organising nature of institutes and organisations with the freedom to define their own goals and programmes of education. His report therefore laid down the basis for the development of state-sponsorship and development for adult education. Castrén is also generally considered the pioneer of 'scientific' adult education in Finland and, like Nyström in Sweden, promoted the 'neutral' scientific attitude as the guiding principle of workers education. Impressed by the serious nature of study in WEA tutorial classes, he drew extensively on British workers' education experiences, believing he could further the project of national unity based on *Bildung*.

Thus, as Kantasalmi concludes, structurally, the forms of paternalistic popular education that characterised the early period of Finnish popular education eventually gave way to the social construction of the 'people's enlightenment project' as the result of the conjunction of a number of social movements activities, including nationalism, socialism and feminism (Kantasalmi, 1996). Although it drew confessedly on the Anglo-Saxon experience, its relation to English university extension was relatively slight and neither were popular universities of the French, Italian or Spanish kind set up. The 'civic religion' project eventually predominated but ensured continuity rather than rupture with previous folkish forms, seen notably in the persistence of Snellman's original project of Finnish cultural nationalism under the newly established state patronage. As a consequence 'right wing nationalist ideology continued to launch vitriolic attacks upon independent workers' education' while a centrist form of *Bildung* began to characterise the mainstream (Ibid.: 218).

Norwegian Lights

In Norway too, popular education is closely associated with nation building and modernisation. The Education Acts of 1889 introduced a common school for all Norwegian children, which followed the European pattern of establishing the school system as the most important institution of national integration. Popular educational projects appear to have been grounded in a number of social movements. The religious project, promoted by the Lutheran Church and revivalist movements, competed and interacted over a long historical period with the 'utilitarian' project supported by bureaucratic élites and the labour movement, and the national-democratic project supported by liberal educators.

Popular adult education in Norway also responded to the innovations of Sweden and Denmark. While Denmark furnished the folk high schools model, it was clear that Sweden had taken the lead in the Scandinavian countries in university involvement. Both Norwegian and Finnish students had attended the Swedish summer schools in a celebration of pan-Scandinavian fellowship and Norway like Sweden had developed a form of folk high school earlier in the century. Norway had also shadowed Sweden's developments in workers' institutes on the model of Nyström's in Stockholm and a similar association was formed in Christiana in 1884. However, there was evidence of municipal commitment to popular education in Norway dating from the 1860s which took the form of a Society for the Enlightenment of the People (*Selskabet for Folkeoplysningens Fremme*) followed a few years later by the Society for the Welfare of Christiania (*Selskabet foir Kristiania Bys Vel*) which gave weekly lectures for 'the young and old of the working and serving classes' (Gerrans, 1895).

University involvement in popular education dates from the formation of the Democratic Lecturers Association in 1892 and the summer course for non-members of the university held by the University of Christiania two years later. A contemporary reporter, A.E. Gerrans claimed that the Society for the Promotion of the Welfare of Christiania and the Democratic Lecturer's Association concerned themselves mostly with social and political questions, while only the summer courses and the workmen's associations had a definite educational goals, which corresponded roughly to British university extension (Ibid.). With a critical eye on immediate future, Gerrans looked forward to the full development of Norwegian extension and to the replacement of the isolated lecture in favour of a course of learning, as well as the growth of a better understanding between the lecturer and his audience.

Norwegian academics who had also attended British summer schools were especially enthusiastic about their potential for class rapprochement. Dr Mourley Vold's impressions of his attendance of the Oxford summer school of 1892 (while making some quaint observations on the nature of the English character, food, draughts under doors and the role of the small nation in global affairs) included the conclusion that the main value of extension was the elevating effect it had on the working classes. He believed it caused them to work together with their fellow citizens for ideal aims so that they felt themselves 'one part of a great culture-society' which he was tempted to compare with an old Greek festival (Hassel, 1894).

The Nordic people's enlightenment therefore was not dissimilar to the general European pattern of nation building and modernisation and also exhibits a tendency to isolate and massage out class conflict. The working classes through popular education were encouraged to see themselves as part of an emergent democratic nation in the process of throwing off ancestral imperialisms. The general defeat of revolutionary socialist ambitions around World War One however seems to have resulted in the success of reformist social democratic parties, which while contradictorily nursing constitutional monarchies in Sweden and Norway nevertheless presided over the extension of the franchise to working people and women. To this extent they have become models of relatively wealthy, egalitarian, tolerant and welfarist societies with a high degree of social harmony and educational achievement, in sharp contradistinction to the Anglo-Saxon neoliberal models of the late-twentieth century. The emphases of popular education on citizenship, general humanistic development and dialogic learning have without doubt been instrumental to this process, but the romantic evocation of the *Volk* that often inspired the earlier movements has left an ambiguous legacy. The positive side is that communality and respect for cultural tradition has created a powerful social bond between individuals, while the negative aspects of nationalistic xenophobia have at the same time been relatively successfully curtailed by a strong social democratic politics in which popular educational practices have received a high priority.

Chapter 9
Belgium and Holland: Anglo-Saxon Imperatives, the Rise and Fall of University Extension

In Belgium and Holland university extension on the English model underwent contrasting fortunes. While Belgium was a rising industrial power shaking off the shackles of Dutch hegemony and a conservative Catholic educational tradition, Holland had a long established popular education institution in the shape of the *Nut*, a well-bred schooling system and a sceptical university establishment. A three way cultural pull was exerted by Britain, France and Germany such that while English popular education was seen to offer a model of class rapprochement by many intellectuals, the left inclined to the more class conscious models of the French *universités populaires* while others looked to the German *Neue Richtung*. In Belgium university extension was adapted with enthusiasm as a vital tool of Flemish national independence, whereas in Holland it was contested both by conservatives and socialists as an appropriate model for popular education. In Belgium the domestic socialist party of Vanderveldt and Destrée closely followed the English university extension as a model of 'scientific' education while the Walloon, French speaking, territory, perceiving a lack of interest on the part of the working class, later adopted the French model. In Holland popular education was very much embedded in voluntary associations such as the *Nut*, which drew informal support for the universities but who were otherwise reluctant to become formally involved. Subsequently, Holland adopted a form of university extension while *universités populaires* were also established in some industrial areas. The Danish folk high school model, on the other hand, was resisted as too nationalistic for the Dutch situation, although the English religiously-inspired Woodbrooke type residential colleges were admired and to an extent emulated. Other forms of significant popular education were the Belgian masonic *Ligue de l'Enseignement*, which preceded the French *Ligue* by a year in 1864 and also the *Maison des Peuple* in Belgium and the

Volkshuisen in Holland which were forms of working men's clubs with largely sociable and mildly educational purposes and emulated elsewhere in Europe (see the Spanish *Casas del Pueblo* in Chapter 5).

Belgium: Flemish Nationalism, University Extension and *universités populaires*

Popular education in Belgium emerges during the mid-century when the council and liberal bourgeoisie in Ghent provided adult schools for workers (Frank and Van Damme, 1993). The municipalisation of Ghent at this time, through an accelerated programme of urbanisation, hygiene and domestication, public sanitation and spatial segregation, was rapidly advancing. Industrialisation doubled the population in the latter half of the nineteenth century to 200,000, the largest concentration of manual workers in Belgium. Syndicalist agitation began in the 1850s amongst textile workers and a broader labour movement emerged in the 1860s associated with the Workers' International and the founding of co-operative and mutual societies. By 1885 Ghent socialists were one of the most important pillars of the Belgian Labour Party but were more interested in social integration than revolution.

A forerunner of university extension was Francois Laurent, a celebrated professor of Civil Law at the University of Ghent, who had led a Protestant movement for the moralisation of the working classes in Ghent through the foundation of *Sociétés ouvriéres* in the 1870s. Tenaciously opposed to the Catholic domination of education in Belgium, he was anathematised, in return, for denying the divinity of Christ. He campaigned for the separation of state and religion but was frequently also at odds with other liberal social reformers. In Laurent's strongly Protestant ideology, man was called to a constant search for perfection, which led to individual and social progress but inequality was present from birth according to divine ordination. Everyone had their place including women, who were not encouraged to be educated. It followed that workers should become reconciled to their lot, they were uncivilised beings or *nouveaux barbares* who needed to be moralised to keep them away from the pernicious influence of workers' organisations and the socialist movement and, of course, their naturally base instincts. In his *Rapport sur la Société Callier* Laurent insisted: 'We are talking about the reform of a whole class of our society, left to itself for centuries, we are talking about the descendants of slaves and serfs. They carry crudeness in their blood, their reform will also take centuries' (quoted in ibid.: 80). Laurent had little interest in changing their material living conditions, housing or hygiene, however claiming that the tools for solving the social question and saving the working classes were education, savings and (bourgeois sponsored) workers' societies, thus: 'le foyer de la famille est constitué, l'ordre moral est fondé et, en même temps, le socialisme vaincu' (quoted in ibid.: 71).

For Laurent the function of education was to develop the God given capacities of reason and conscience. Hence the curriculum, he devised, focused on the practicalities of the prudent citizen and included constitutional law, elementary social economics – by which he meant the theory of savings – and active citizenship expressed as electoral participation. Backed by the small but active Liberal Protestant community, Laurent also emulated the traditional Catholic system of patronages operating in Ghent in order to create liberal patronages. Through annual membership fees and charitable donations he encouraged the spread of a Smilesian spirit of thrift and order among the labourers and contributed to the improvement of their material and moral condition.

Laurent's scheme was financed by the masonic society, *l'Avenir*, founded in 1875 to support secular education with Laurent as honorary president. It also financed the private *ecoles laïque* with the *Ligue de l'Enseignement* and ten workers' societies were established. Despite this backing, the years following 1887 saw the decline of the movement due to rift in Liberalism between 'progressives' (social radicals) and 'doctrinaires' (economic radicals). After the defeat of the Liberals in the 1890 election the progressive wing split and began working with the socialists. Although it was strongly denied by Laurent, the workers' societies were seen as breeding grounds for socialists but it seems likely that socialists were actively involved and pursued ends quite opposite to that of the founders. No less than thirty men were expelled from the 'Love of Freedom' association, some for

211

drunkenness and others for membership of the Workers International then based in Brussels and ideologically dominated by Marx himself.

Very much an eccentric talent, Laurent was immune to the influence of the circle around the radical republican Francois Huet, Professor of Philosophy at Ghent in 1840s. He also kept a distance from the radical liberal reformers of the masonic *Ligue de l'Enseignement* who were influential in other cities. Conservative in many aspects, his workers' societies rather too closely resembled Catholic patronages rather than radical liberal projects:

> His aspiration was not the cultural, intellectual or material uplifting of the lower classes but the construction of a closed and fully-supervised life-world in which the working class youngsters would be constantly exposed to moralizing incentives (Ibid.: 83).

Nevertheless, he was almost Jacobin in his view of state intervention in social relations and even private matters. The extent of the success of the societies on influencing the moral behaviour of the working classes in Ghent is unclear and as we have noted it seems that they used the societies for their own interests, including socialism. The societies failed to mobilise and integrate the working classes. Laurent's initiatives were part of a broader liberal strategy of 'pillarisation' (in which different ideological and political groups maintained their own cultural sectors) but liberals were much less successful than the Catholics and were never a substantial alternative to the emergent socialist organisations.

University Extension in Ghent and Brussels, a Political Rivalry

The emergence of university extension, meanwhile, was coterminous with the eruption of radical political movements associated both with the aspirations of Flemish nationalism and with workers' movements for socialism. Emile Waxweiler, a Belgian engineer wrote in 1893 that: 'The political and social crisis which the little kingdom is now

212

traversing and the sudden arising of an important labor movement under the leadership of the Socialists, have called the attention of the public to all kinds of social enterprises' (Waxweiler, 1893: 154). In a valuable study van Damme (1992) contrasted the two university extension movements in Belgium, formed in Ghent and Brussels respectively with each other and with the *universités populaires* in the French (Walloon) part. While university extension in Ghent originated under the leadership of Paul Frédericq very much in response to Flemish nationalist movements, in Brussels a more radical form later took shape. Both however were distrusted by, and distrusted, the initiatives to establish *universités populaires* on the French model.

In the large rapidly industrialising town of Ghent the movement for university extension was led by university-based liberals, and subsequently Catholics, with the largely conservative aim of permeating working classes with moralising influences. The movement to some extent rose on the back of previous popular education initiatives including the masonic *Ligue de l'Enseignement* founded in 1864 and the *Societé Franklin*. These organisations had already founded popular libraries, and had provided recreational activities in music, theatre and excursions intended 'to provide a civilizing alternative to unlicensed leisure and the popular culture of the public house and gaming' (van Damme, 1992: 13).

The movement for Flemish independence overlaid a nationalistic dimension to existing activities such as the *Willemsfonds* which was established in 1851 following the example of the Dutch Society for the Common Benefit (SCB) or *Nut*. This also had the effect of widening the internal rift between liberals and Catholics who in the 1870s founded their own confessional association, the *Davidsfonds*. '*Flamingant*' associations designed to strengthen the cultural confidence of the Flemish people flourished. They tried to create and intellectual enlightenment, which under the banner of a national movement attempted to overcome class antagonism and rediscover, though in practice virtually to create, its Flemish historical and cultural roots.

In the context of the national movement, interest in university extension grew further through dissatisfaction with traditional responses to 'the social question' especially universal suffrage and bourgeois concerns over social unrest and the socialist campaigns of 1886 and 1892–1893. Another leader of the new popular education,

213

Paul Leclere, insisted an educational campaign was needed to integrate the popular masses into the existing social order. Following his lead, Pieter Tack and Lodewijk de Raet, two students from Ghent, believed that inspiration could only come from 'the North', meaning Germanic Europe and England especially, the latter being 'the torch lighting Europe on the road that leads to the peaceful settlement of social conflicts' (quoted in ibid.: 15). For them this was exemplified in the London East End's Toynbee Hall, settlement work and especially university extension, which, in contrast with their contemporaries in Holland, was seen as a transferable educational practice and appeared to show that educational, cultural and personal contact was the only way out of class conflict. Frédericq saw the success of English university extension in incorporating working classes by voluntary and personal initiative with minimum of state interference as a preferred alternative to the French 'bureaucratic' approach.

Nevertheless there was some disagreement about how closely to follow the English model. Many valued what they perceived as a real social and geographical movement towards 'the masses' embodying recruitment of credible university personnel, decentralised administration, properly constructed courses, the didactic use of syllabuses, classes and written exercises, examinations and diplomas and representation of working people on local popular education committees. However, none of the new associations set up by the nationalists acquired a formal relationship with the universities but remained as voluntary enterprises on the fringe of university life.

Earlier forms of popular education in Belgium had shown only marginal interest in science, but increasingly belief in the understanding of science and its application for social progress was very strong, a kind of 'social technology'. van Damme notes that 'the reformist circle supporting university extension saw sciences as the ultimate confirmation of the efficiency and progress of bourgeois society' in which 'the workers would see that a harmonious relationship between the classes corresponded to the rationality of the natural world (Ibid.: 16). This perspective was also strongly supported by rationalist and positivist scientists at the University of Brussels such as Solvay and Waxweiler.

University extension in Ghent owed its origins to two primary sources: the first was the existing pattern of liberal non-formal adult education but secondly and more important was the political shift of nationalist intellectuals towards what was called *cultuurflamingant-isme* 'a cultural-political reformulation of the classic linguistic objectives of the movement' (Ibid.: 19). The aim of the movement was the restoration of the national energy and vitality of the Flemish people or *Volksracht*, as de Raet its most important ideologue called it, which was a form of class reconciliation for social and national progress. The extension committee was founded in 1892 by radical *flamingant* students and professors from the Dutch philology and literature department primarily to teach classes in Dutch, German and English literature and it received enthusiastic support from both the liberal and socialist press. Against what they saw as the 'paternalistic voluntarism' of Frédericq, Tack and de Raet insisted that charging fees for courses would move it away from 'old models of bourgeois missionary charity' (Ibid.: 20). Also more ambitious in their approach, they saw they saw it as spearhead for a future Dutch language university (which was eventually founded only in 1930). Not surprisingly local branches in small towns frequently generated conflict with the Catholic élite who, nevertheless, occasionally joined up.

There was also conflict with the radical extension movement in Brussels after 1895 when Ghent opposed the plan for a national organisation proposed by the socialist leader, Emile Vanderveldt. In return Hirsch from Brussels wrote a provocative book in which he criticised Ghent's provision as not genuine university extension since it lacked systematic elements of class tuition on the English model that included a prepared syllabus, written exercises and exams and non-student tutors. Frédericq responded by attacking Brussels for its lack of neutrality in favouring the rationalist and positivist thinking, associated with (implicitly masonic) anticlericalism. Ghent's refusal to deal with current social and political issues and Frédericq's refusal to include the socialist organisation *Vooruit* on the extension committee also antagonised local radicals and socialists, which Brussels capitalised on by attempting to set up its own operations in Ghent. Brussels also succeeded in other Flemish towns due to its greater resources, official backing by the university and, ironically, the expressed preference by most local élites for a French language initiative.

During the 1890s the university extension movement in Britain became very excited by what was taking place in Belgium and published regular reports in its journals. The first account of activities in Belgium in English, in the *Oxford University Extension Gazette*, (Vol.III, May 1893: 12) noted that there was a flourishing extension movement in Flanders, which appeared to have originated spontaneously and not to have been imitated from other countries' extension work. The report saw Tack (rather than Leclere) as the founder of the movement by means of pamphlets and addresses delivered in autumn 1892 in the national university in Ghent. Shortly, however, the founders resolved to organise lectures after the English extension pattern, open to all without payment initially, though later for a small cost. They intended that the courses should academic but popular and emphatically non-political in character. These resolutions, the report continued, led to the movement obtaining a lecture hall from the state and grants from the Council of Ghent for books and other expenses. The work appeared to have been markedly successful, the three courses already given attracting up to 170 members comprising teachers, including primary school mistresses, merchants and workmen. Lectures, on English, Dutch and German literature with botany to come in the summer, were avidly followed and notes taken. The correspondent believed that the early promise of success for extension work was likely to be extended throughout Belgium. Such was the enthusiasm of many in the English movement for the Flemish developments.

If the actual achievement was more modest, real progress was made. Of the ninety-six courses offered by Ghent between 1892–1913, a third were in English, Dutch and German literatures, which the organisers claimed was proof of a larger 'Germanic civilisation' in opposition to the Latin (an implicit critique of French hegemony). For Frédericq and his fellow nationalists 'class antagonisms and social struggle were seen as characteristic of a Southern European mentality with it roots in Jacobinism and revolutionary tradition' while Germany was the rising economic power and England was the cradle of social reform (Ibid.: 26). Not all those who attended saw it that way and average attendance fell sharply after the first year. Despite the nationalist rhetoric, the most popular parts of the programme were the many natural science classes celebrating triumphs of scientific dis-

216

covery. However, moralism still predominated and medical and hygienic issues 'were reduced to the supposed immorality and even bestiality of the industrial-working classes' (Ibid.: 28–9) – even so they were applauded by the socialist paper *Vooruit*.

Lectures were given mostly by the university members and teachers from local municipal secondary schools connected to the University of Ghent. They relied mostly on the demonstration 'to arouse feelings of wonder and admiration and respect for the wonders of nature' (Ibid.: 30). They attracted between twelve and 121 people and averaged around sixty. Unlike Britain, university extension does not appear to have been associated with the demand for higher education for women, who composed only thirty per cent of the audience, some primary school teachers and a few working women. Tack believed that the public for scientific higher education did not include industrial workers and that the middle-classes therefore had to play a mediating role in social change and they themselves had to be enlightened.

Worried by the longer-term political effects of the success of liberal associations, enlightened Catholic intellectuals also felt they should also become involved in popular education despite the Church hierarchy's viewing university extension as antithetical to Catholic traditions. Although there was considerable resistance among Catholics to the sacrilegious idea of 'scientific popularisation' eventually a Catholic-Flemish university extension committee was formed in Antwerp in 1898 and in Ghent in 1906 (Ibid.: 18).

By 1914 almost fifty university extension associations had been formed in Flemish Belgium but, with the notable exception of Brussels, less interest was shown in Wallonia. By this time a keen rivalry with the more radical *universités populaires* on the French model had grown up and in places enthusiasts would establish a university extension committee in opposition to an existing *université populaire*. The rivalry was largely political as *universités populaires* believed the cultural and political emancipation of the working classes depended on free education and democratic co-operation between workers and their sympathisers among the intellectuals (*éducation mutuelle*) as opposed to what they saw as the paternalism of the university based extension classes. Overall however this was a minority movement and the bulk of the newly organised labour movement settled for university extension. van Damme concludes that: 'The generally positive attitude of the socialists towards the extension project and the fact that they were not able to develop a truly oppositional, alternative cultural and educational tradition may help substantiate the argument that extension and comparable practices did contribute to the cultural incorporation of the working class into bourgeois society' (Ibid.: 38).

Brussels Free University: Extension and the Socialist Movement

While university extension in Ghent in 1892 was led by *flamingant* professors and students, in Brussels liberals, like Leon Leclere, set up the *Extension Universitaire de Bruxelles* in 1893. Leclere had studied extension in England and in 1892 published an appreciative account of English and American extension called *Les Universités Populaires dans Les Pays Anglo-Saxon*. An extract from Leclere's work which showed that he intended to copy the English model fairly closely was printed in the *Gazette* (Vol.iii, June 1893). Leclere believed that the system of extension in England could be adapted to Dutch conditions and was moreover necessary in order to embrace the spirit of the new democracy of the people which otherwise might turn to more violent pursuits. He noted the success of the Ghent initiative, now grandly called *l'Ecole superieure gantoise pour l'Enseignement du peuple*, and also the size, enthusiasm, social mix of the crowd and especially the number of school mistresses present, that overflowed the university hall in which the courses were held. But despite his enthusiasm for the English model and its Flemish application, Leclere did not think it was possible simply to transplant the English model unaltered, partly because Belgian secondary education already satisfied many of the needs to which English extension responded. He advocated a system of popular courses open to all, organised under the patronage of the universities and taught by members of the high schools.

Leclere's call to extension was driven by his near-apocalyptic vision of what otherwise might befall Belgian society as a result of the accession of democracy to political power which, he noted, was one of the undeniable phenomena of Western Europe. Through the power of numbers, democracy was becoming the absolute mistress of the destiny of the people who, if they remained ignorant, in the service of instinct and deaf to the education of science would misunderstand their true social interests. If this was allowed to happen the hour of their domination will mark the debut of an era of agitation, discord and possibly ruin. It was all the more essential therefore that the general culture that the popular classes lacked be given to them to prepare them for the tasks they wish to assume.

This grand, almost apocalyptic, rhetoric of the rise of mass democracy and the liberal academic's obligations to it was tinged with some degree of fear about the consequences of not doing so. Leclere's prose is punctuated by urgent summonses: the times press; the hour to renew the political is about to sound; they have to attend to education of adults without delay; if they are not taught the value of study and the role of thought they may not be delivered from those who dream of the brutality of force and the incoherence of numbers. It was, he said, necessary to adapt the education 'comme le font les Anglais' to political life in order to teach the people about history, science and most important, the 'law of progressive evolution'. The people would then come to the conclusion that to upset a society with a flick of the wrist would bring violent reaction and that it was as dangerous to overturn everything as it was to conserve it. Courses therefore must be planned which were at the same time practical, and general and tending to the moral and intellectual elevation of those who followed them. They could and ought to include artistic conferences, musical auditions and excursions to museums such as those already organised by the *Maison du Peuple* at Brussels. Thus, for Leclere there was no harm in grafting English extension onto native institutions of popular education.

Leclere believed that universities were best placed to coordinate, regulate and become missionaries for the existing popular education movements. He also commented on the perennial 'apathy and pessimism of young people'. If this was real, he says, there can be no more inspiring aim than university extension where teachers and students will march together toward the new dawn. Leclere's engaging pamphlet, as shown by this excerpt, exhibits both the enthusiasm and fears of the nineteenth century European liberal academic: the appeal to history, the moral burden of the proletariat, the Arnoldian terror of the mob, but also the duty of the educationist to be the guiding hand of the infant democracy.

His proposals were well-received and public approval for university extension in Brussels was forthcoming when the Minister for the Interior and Public Instruction, M. Schollaert, expressed sympathy in parliament in 1892. Although it was subsidised by the university council, the *Extension de l'Universite Libre* was not an official university body and had complete independence. It was composed of effective members (professors, course directors, *agreges*, doctors and university students) and associate members. The central committee had ten members, half of whom were from extension lecturers, while the others were from the professional core of the university faculties.

The committee organised programmes of courses in Brussels and the provinces through local committees, ultimately subject to Brussels sanctions. While these chose the courses and provided the material organisation, the central committee checked that the political composition was varied and that where possible the courses were given by a local scholar. The local committee covered the cost of the organisation including the lecturers' fees, copies of the course outline and so on with the central committee meeting any deficit. Each sent a delegate to the central Committee with a consultative role on all things which affected them directly. The financial resources were for the most part drawn from student fees, subscriptions, communal subsidies and literary and scientific societies (which again demonstrated the continuity from the older form of popular education). It was because of this decentralised organisation, Leclere held, that progress had been rapid and constant.[1]

Leclere specifically wanted extension courses in the most deprived educational areas and since he thought that localities of 5,000–

---

1   On its debut in 1894–1895, there were eleven Committees with nineteen courses and 3250 students, while in 1899/1890 there were twenty-five Committees with forty courses and 6000 students and also seven conferences and preparatory courses (Picavet, 41).

20,000 population provided the most numerous and fruitful students, he was aiming at a fairly urbanised and probably industrial population. He agreed with the distribution of syllabi to students and commented that many were bought by people who could not attend the courses but one feature of the English system he disagreed with was external assessment. 'Classes' and exams were considered but rejected at Brussels because Leclere held that in Britain '*auditeurs*' become students only because they lacked the education already supplied in the Belgian system (Picavet, 1901: 43). Belgians did not want certificates for practical advantage. Summer schools, however, were easily adapted to the local conditions and students from the provinces annually assembled in Brussels to visit scientific institutes and art museums with extension lecturers. Not least important were those essential items of the itinerant lecturer's impedimenta, a small travelling library left with the local secretary of a course and projectors (*des projections lumineuses*).

Waxweiler noted that the fledgling extension movement in Brussels had no special periodical of its own although accounts were given in the *Revue Sociale et Politique*, the organ of the *Societe d'etudes Sociales et Politiques of Brussels*. The English extension journal reports at the time confirm the general retrospective picture outlined by Leclere some years later. The *Gazette* reported that the Rector of the Free University of Brussels, Hector Denis had given his blessing to extension and thus offered relatively official status to what had been the voluntary work of the younger *professeurs* (Vol.IV, November 1893).

The *Gazette* also gave a list of courses to be followed in the academic year 1893–1894 as follows: at Andenne, Le transformisme (morphology) given by A. Lameere; at Anvers, Sociologies generale elementaire given by G. de Greef , Le systeme nerveux central given by L. Warnots at Brussels, Droit Constitutionel Belge given by P. Errera, Joseph II et la Revolution Brabanconne given by H. Pergameni, Le systeme nerveux central given by L. Warnots; at Hasselte, Le transformisme given by A. Lameere; at la Lourvriere Sociologies generale elementaire given by G. de Greef, Histoire des doctrines sociales des XIXe siecle given by E. Vendervelde; at Malines, Les grandes maladies infectieuses given by A. Bayet, Joseph II et la Revolution Brabanconne given by H. Pergameni; at Saint Josse Les

221

grandes maladies infectieuses given by A. Bayet, La philosophie del'art given by G. Dwelshauvers, L'origine del'univers given by M.E. Tassel.

This fascinating list of medical and scientific knowledge mixing with political history, sociology and art history illustrates both the intellectual milieu of extension work and the basic categories for decades to come.

Arthur Hirsch, a student of Law at Brussels, offered another account of the origins of the movement which included Leclere's own role and drew attention to the insurrectionary atmosphere that surrounded it (*UEJ*, 15 February 1894). He noted that there were special difficulties in the way of extension in Belgium not the least of which was that only two week previously the university had to be closed down because of political and religious 'tumults'. Hirsch reported that subsequent to publication of his article Leon Leclere, one of the young *professeurs*, had called a meeting of other university lecturers and established a society called the *Extension Universitaire de Bruxelles* in order to promote extension in Belgium especially in Brabant, Hainualt and Antwerp. On 21 March a general meeting was held chaired by Rector Hector Denis and attended by a hundred people on the basis of a manifesto drawn up at the initial meeting. Leclere drew up a series of rules of which the first was that extension consists in 'the promotion of scientific training based on free discussion'. Membership was confined to professors, doctors and graduates of the university and Leclere insisted that only university staff should be allowed to teach courses, thus maintaining the highest possible standards.[2]

But the movement faced serious political problems. It had not gained the approval of most academic authorities because its promoters were mainly socialists and 'determined radicals', moreover the Free University of Brussels had a strongly anti-clerical spirit which

---

2   The *Journal* however seemed more anxious to maintain a policing role over the fledgling institution and commented that: 'It will be seen from the above that M. Hirsch and his fellow workers have not quite thoroughly grasped the true idea of our method. The omission of Students paper-work from the scheme is a very serious matter, and must almost exclude the Belgian scheme from a claim to the title of "University Extension"'.

made it unacceptable to the Catholic masses, despite the fact that they needed the education most. More important though was the language problem the major popular language being Flemish, spoken in a variety of forms varying from village to village, whereas the middle and higher classes spoke French. Universities as a consequence teach in French and very few *professeurs* were capable of Flemish. Hirsch also thought the political problem could be overcome if a federation of University Extension could be achieved between the four main universities including the Catholic University at Louvain and the (Flemish) universities of Ghent and Liege but this was not possible.

The English Response

The English extension journals were keen to establish the Belgian continuities with extension's English origins whenever possible, rather than their significant differences. The *Gazette* noted that *La Flandre Liberale* had announced the forthcoming Oxford summer meeting with enthusiasm noting that, by a happy initiative, extension had been transported in its main effects to Belgium. The report also noted that the founders of University Extension did not restrict themselves to 'veritable Universitaires Populaires' but organised summer meetings for its students. It said that James Bryce 'le membre bien connu des Communes' would read the inaugural address and commented on how the ancient gothic aristocratic splendours of Oxford would be opened up for the democracy (*OUEG*, Vol.IV, May 1894).

The *Journal* contained an account by Mr E.A. Parkyn of the University Extension Congress held at Brussels in 1895 following the radical break and formation of the new university extension movement, which he attended the previous month as a delegate from Cambridge (*UEJ*, Vol.V, No.53, February 1895: 67). Parkyn properly claimed this was not strictly speaking an extension of the university since the authorities had opposed it (as prophesied by Hirsch) and had actually interdicted its professors from taking part. Because of this a number of enthusiasts proposed establishing a new university – which the system in Belgium permits so long as four base faculties could be formed. In Belgium the university system was 'free' and grant aid was obtained from the local authority not the state. But written work raised its head again and Parkyn continued: 'The meeting hardly seemed to appreciate the importance attributed to the written papers and Examination as essential factors of extension as understood in England' (Ibid.) Informally the question of an interchange between English and Belgian lecturers was suggested which Parkyn deemed desirable not so much on educational grounds as *l'entente cordiale*, though he did think some of the Belgian lecturers could give a good lecture in French on 'social and philosophical problems of the deepest interest and greatest importance'.

The following year the *Journal* sent congratulations to the *Université Libre de Brussels* which had, in the face of vehement hostility, attained noteworthy success commenting: 'Many of the syllabuses are perfect models of their kind, and the work is evidently being carried out with the utmost seriousness in all respects' (*UEJ*, Vol.II, No.2, November 1896: 19). A year later the *Journal* was reasonably content that extension had become well established in Belgium (*UEJ*, October 1897). It quoted extensively from the Annual report of the Central Committee for University Extension in connection with the *Université Libre of Brussels*. In 1896–1897 academic year sixteen local committees had arranged twenty-two courses attended by 4630 persons (or over 200 per course). The corresponding figures for the previous year were nine local committees, nineteen courses and 4150 *auditeurs* (this more passive term was preferred to '*etudients*'). Though the Brussels centre had arranged five courses less new centres had be set up in other towns and suburbs. The report noted that the centre at Namur had prevailed over much local opposition. However, the majority of students were middle class and teachers. Examinations played a smaller part than in England. Valuable contributions had come from the university and from the *Ligue de l'Enseignment* and from the *Union des Anciens Etudiants* and their work had been accorded a place in the Educational section of the Brussels Exhibition of 1897.

By 1901 the *Journal* confidently reported that Brussels had made the most successful attempt to introduce university extension on the English model (*UEJ*, Vol.VI, No.62, May 1901: 114). Provision had

224

grown to twenty-five local centres with forty courses and according to reports they attracted the devotion of its staff, the enthusiasm of the audiences and the growing sympathy from influential men and corporations throughout the country. The *Journal* again commented: 'It is satisfactory to note how closely the authorities have determined to follow the methods that have been developed in England' – educational efficiency and stringent regulations (Ibid.). Two years later the number of centres had risen to thirty and the courses to forty-five, of which two thirds were in natural science, nine in literature, six in history, two on political economy and one on constitutional law. It comments on the refreshing novelty of some of the Belgian courses which included, 'Why did the Egyptians make mummies?' and suggests local museums might imitate them. While natural science provision predominated, the social sciences were clearly not well established. Around half the courses are attended by workers, it was reported, some even giving up their winter national game of lacrosse to attend, but not at all in 'backward districts'.

This relative absence of social science from the curriculum was a concern to the radicals and socialists. Leclere later noted that the audience for extension was primarily middle class and in the majority women, many of whom were schoolteachers and observed that working class apathy may be accounted for because of socialist and Catholic Union's opposition to a liberal inspired idea (which may be a necessary correction to Waxweiler's account). As a consequence the university extension movement in Brussels split on political lines resulting in two new formations: *l'Extension Universitaire* in opposition to the official extension and the Socialist Party's own 'University Extension' classes.

The Brussels Schism

The crisis began when the council of administration of the Free University refused to allow Elisée Reclus, the celebrated French geographer, to hold courses at the university. The resultant uproar over academic freedom ended in the founding of the New University in which both Reclus and de Greef took part. Reclus was active in the international anarchist movement and had been exiled from France because of his militant involvement in the Paris Commune of 1871. He had refused to return to France despite the amnesty of 1879 given him because of his academic eminence, having received a gold medal from the Paris Geographical Society in 1891, until all former communards were welcome back and had arrived in Brussels at the invitation of his fellow masons

Initially, nominated by the Rector, Hector Denis, as a Fellow in the Faculty of Sciences, Reclus had been authorised to give a course in comparative geography in the School of Social Science. He accepted the nomination with enthusiasm but asked to postpone his course until early 1894 when his major work *La Nouvelle Geographie Universelle* would have been published (Fleming, 1979: 215). The Free University administrators however, fearful of Reclus's reported connection with terrorism and his exciting passions in Brussels, decided his postpone his courses *sine die*. The decision was widely reported and student agitation, scenting political repression, rose to such heights that many of them along with members of faculty were peremptorily expelled. Hector Denis himself resigned in sympathy with the students and the university was closed for several weeks. Reclus nevertheless went ahead with his lectures, at first in a large hall put at his disposal by the freemasons in association with the University Circle of Brussels and then in the break-away New University which offered a limited number of course in the academic year 1894–1895.

Meanwhile, having failed to prevent Reclus and de Greef from taking part in extension the original promoters of the movement, though probably not Leclere, themselves resigned and formed a new association called *l'Extension de l'Université*. This ran in parallel with

226

the existing extension association which had now shifted to the New University for some years, its courses, according to Destrée and Vandervelde, differing only in their philosophical or social tendency and the personality of the lecturers (Destrée and Vandervelde, 1903: 375).

Curiously, in their history of Belgian Socialism which contains an account of the schism, Destrée and Vandervelde refer to University Extension as the most interesting example of pure science, disengaged from politics and economics (Ibid.: 373). Nevertheless for the authors it deserved a place in a history of Belgian socialism because most of the lecturers involved in it were avowedly socialist and because of the support it received from democratic groups. Their account of the origins of extension differed somewhat from the official account and dates it from the founding in the *Maison du Peuple* in Brussels of a section on art and education by the *Cercle des Etudiants et Anciens Etudiants Socialistes*. Here, members of the workers' party were asked what provision they would like to see and a programme was drawn up which included courses on civil rights taught by Max Hallet, social economy, taught by Emile Vandervelde, maths, taught by Louis de Brouckere, Belgian history taught by Pinard and stenography taught by Merisse, a mixture of the practical and the political. Even so, these courses were not a great success because they were swamped by the volume of political meetings and other groups using the building. This, the authors claimed, was the immediate predecessor of the university's extension classes formed the following year. Once started though, they claim that large numbers of workers did attend classes particularly those held in industrial areas and that the most popular courses were in history and sociology. The teaching staff were drawn entirely from the Free University and included the Socialist senators, Eduard Picard and La Fontaine, Houzeau the Radical Senator, Demblon, Delbatee, van Kol, Toelstra, Destree and Vandervelde who were socialist deputies and Louis de Brouckere who was a socialist communal counsellor. Other assorted radicals and revolutionaries included G. de Greef, E. Vinek and L. Hennebicq and the brothers Elie and Elisée Reclus.

Despite the schismatic quality of extension in Brussels, Destrée and Vandervelde nevertheless affirmed that it diffused a 'scientific culture' based on the principles of free examination through popular

227

courses of higher education of an exclusively scientific character. They maintained, moreover, that when some years later the radical *université populaire* movement spread from Paris, it failed to take root in Belgium precisely because of the well-grounded existence of study circles and extension committees.

University extension in Belgium, in summary, shared a number of common European characteristics: a climate of popular opposition to a dominant clerical establishment, a radical liberal intelligentsia, an emergent but moderate socialist workers' movement, a nationalist regional movement and a receptive university establishment. The political conjuncture seems to have been overdetermined by the crisis in education itself. This was because the short-lived Liberal government had placed schools under state control and excluded religious instruction so that when the Catholics returned to power in 1884, as Benedetto Croce laconically remarked, 'they hastened at once to undo the labour of the liberals as to education' (Croce, 1934: 292). Thus the fact that the very meaning of education in Belgium was critically contested would have provided volatile fuel for the extension movement. These features led to the formation of coalitions of intellectuals and workers with the aim of achieving a democratic, secular and socialist society. University extension here was clearly part of, and may even have been the main site of, a larger political struggle over the social meanings and moral values. The close attention paid by English university extension journals to the correct application of the extension model seemed almost comically oblivious of the political context, yet nevertheless seems to have offered comforting reassurance to the founders that they were getting it right.

Holland: 'pillarisation' and Popular Education

The initiative in popular education in Holland (as we saw in Chapter 2) was associated with the radical but short lived Batavian Republic of 1785–1805. This was the Society for the Common Benefit (SBF) or *Nut* of the late eighteenth century formed largely by liberal businessmen for the moral improvement of the lower orders. Influenced by the economically progressive ideas of the English theorist, Jethro Tull, in agriculture and the Scot, Adam Smith in political economy the SBF was the first genuine attempt to provide organised popular education. As van Ghent noted:

> In addition to lectures to its own members on topics such as science, health and the upbringing of children, popular lectures were held in the optimistic hope that this would diffuse useful knowledge among a very broad audience from the lower orders and in this way put an end to the prevalence of massive poverty' (van Ghent, 1987: 284).

But it was clear that this hope was overoptimistic and that the SBF could not reach common people in other than the most marginal ways. Following the trauma of Belgian national independence from Holland in 1830 and the revolutionary upheavals of 1848, there was a significant growth of voluntary organisations, especially those concerned with popular education and enlightenment. In 1854 the Society for the Improvement of the Working Class was established by Hartmann a coffee shop owner in Amsterdam. Hartmann's subsequent proposal to the city authorities to form an association of artisans was however summarily rejected on the grounds that 'such an organisation would disturb the social order' (Ibid.: 285). Unabashed, Hartmann went on to establish what he called a Society for the Benefit of the Labouring Class devoted to popular education and after 1860 a variety of other organisations were established but, it seems, workers came mostly for the free beer.

Although there was significant religious tension between Protestants and Catholics in Holland, anticlericalism never reached the same intensity as in France, Belgium or Spain. Links with Britain had been reasonably fraternal especially after William of Orange had been established on the English throne. In return English speculative freemasonry had swiftly crossed the Channel and was popular among the business class as a bearer of liberal opinion and social harmony, and contributed to the formation of societies promoting enlightenment ideas (Jacob, 1981).

Nevertheless it was clear that little common agreement about social values and the nature of education could be found between progressive liberals and conservative Catholics. After the 1870 Paris

Commune, especially, the liberal and confessional establishment attempted to achieve social harmony by the policy of separate development or 'pillarisation'. Largely fostered by the confessional groups, power was devolved from the state to the interests groups of the 'pillars', each eventually with its own political parties, trade unions, education and communications. van Ghent notes:

> The practical consequences of all this was that the state and society no longer functioned autonomously but that there was a 'mutual penetration' although each interest group systematically ensured that its own organisations were in no way threatened (Ibid.: 286).

But there was of course another unstated agenda to this mutual process. Pillarisation was 'less a question of emancipation and the more unintended result of a policy to integrate the Catholic and Protestant workers within the denominational organisations in order to keep them away from socialist sympathies' (Ibid.: 287). In response the socialist organisations created their own 'red family' but it was only by 1910 that the socialist trade unions were able to establish a Committee for Workers' Education in Amsterdam for activists as the first step towards an Institute for Workers' Education. Workers' education was also not a priority for Catholics and Protestants until very late in the nineteenth century and it was 1909 before the first Christian trade union with educational activities was established.

To combat the particularities of religion and politics enshrined by pillarisation some liberals influenced by English university extension and settlement attempted to provide a form of 'neutral' education for workers. This initiative led to the establishment of Folk Houses (*Volkshuisen*) the first of which was in Leiden, for:

> raising the level of development, culture and happiness of the working, and comparable classes in Leiden and its surroundings by means of, among other things, the diffusion of useful knowledge, the encouragement of knowledge, arts and sense of community, through the provision of suitable relaxation and through stimulation of the social intercourse between all sections of society (quoted in ibid.: 288).

A second initiative gave rise to the Association for the Encouragement of Popular Scientific Knowledge in 1912 which marked the beginning of the many Popular Universities (*Volksuniversiteiten*). In 1930 a Radio Popular University was formed, perhaps the first to use electronic communication in this way. Belatedly following the German *Neue Richtung* (see Chapter 7) an Association for the Establishment of Folk High Schools was created in 1931, which in contrast to the extensive approach by means of lectures and course by the Folk Houses and in particular, the Popular Universities, were intended to achieve a more intensive approach based upon residential courses.

Unlike most of their Flemish equivalents, Dutch intellectuals took a very ambivalent attitude to English university extension which, they argued, was only a poor substitute for an effective secondary education system such as already existed in Holland. Speaking at the famous *Congres international d'Enseignement superieur* held in Paris in 1900, van Hamel of Groningen University maintained that the origins of extension in Holland were indeed not very 'popular'. This was because popular education circles, which built on the success of the secondary education, had been organised for many years in villages and towns on a voluntary basis. Since there were already widespread evening classes on literature, history and natural science, it did not seem necessary to take such a large step as to organise a general university extension movement and indeed the universities had not contributed (Picavet, 1901: 127). Nevertheless university extension was promoted by the anthropologist, Steinmetz at Leiden in face of his colleagues' and students' derision, to whom he replied simply: 'Those who sleep, are not bothered by darkness'. He went on to lead the Association for the Encouragement of Popular Scientific Education, formed in 1912 for university extension.

The official attitude was however changing and the Minister of the Interior invited the three state universities to consider becoming involved in extension work. In reply the university senates said that the universities would never refuse to be involved in popular education, so long as it did not detract from their main aim of advancing science and preparing students for their careers. Not exactly a ringing endorsement and following these inconclusive discussions between the government and the universities, it was in fact the voluntary society, the SBF that in the name of University Extension, began to organise scientific courses for adults, many of which were given by university staff. It was clear that this state-initiated attempt to involve the universities in popular education was still viewed with scepticism by the academic fraternity. van Hamel's Olympian perspective was that the strength of extension lay not so much the little knowledge that the university staff could pass on to the people but the penetration of the scientific spirit into the masses who, he said, lived their lives in more or less superstitious confusion.

Some university involvement in popular education, though, had dated from the early 1890s although the first folk house, the common term, probably owed its further origins to the Committee for the Discussion of the Social Question founded in 1870 (van Ghent, 1991). Although the male academic class was sceptical of university extension, the example of Samuel Barnett's Toynbee Hall in Whitechapel, established to raise the general level of society and not just that of the individual through a mingling of the classes, was very persuasive to liberal Dutch women. Significantly, the first Dutch settlement on Toynbee Hall lines in 1892 in Amsterdam was set up by the feminist writer, Helene Mercier. Called 'Our House' its aim was 'to promote interaction between different layers of society and to educate adults' with strict religious and political impartiality. Leiden Folk House followed in 1899 on the initiative of three law professors, 'to raise the level of education, culture, and happiness among the working, and comparable classes in Leiden and its surroundings' (Ibid.: 221). Largely a sociable venture, it included lectures, musical performances and exhibitions as well as legal advice and was led by another feminist pioneer of Dutch popular education, Emilie Knappert who said that 'the ideal of all settlements in our country is, or ought to be, to turn out happier and morally stronger and more efficient human beings, whatever their theological or political or social creed' (quoted in Yeaxlee, 1922: 71).

Though settlement work focused on the needs of children, adults were included in provision, which tended to be through such cultural means as concerts and drama. Whereas the earlier settlements had been coloured by middle-class paternalism, later ones became more consciously cooperative. Only the original Amsterdam settlement received any grant aiding from the municipality. In 1909 the Rotterdam Toynbee Association set up another 'Our House' mainly for young people, directed by A. de Koe a former minister, which took a more radical approach. However since few liberal intellectuals wanted

232

to live there and they had little contact with the poor, it is debatable how true these were to the Toynbee Hall model.

In the Netherlands the English model of university extension was adapted in two ways, neither of which perfectly followed the English model (de Vroom, 1992). It remained in the hands of a voluntary body, the *Nut* which kept control largely because universities either did not want, or were not advised, to take responsibility. Two reports to the *Nut* show why it was content to take a leading role. In a lecture to the *Nut* given in 1893 Dr H. Oort made it clear that because the Dutch education system was already more advanced than the English, its universities had other priorities. Whereas the *Nut*'s tradition of diffusing knowledge 'among the best and most talented of every class' made it the clear choice for such work (Ibid.: 47). He saw its role mainly in the training of administrators in health or poor relief also in providing working class people with a political education. The term 'university extension' was not in fact used by the *Nut* during 1898–1906 which preferred 'courses in scientific teaching for adults'.

Another report given six years later by J. Bruinwold Riedel, secretary of the *Nut*, in 1899 situated university extension as part of an historical continuum in Holland:

> as the most advance form of popular education, the culmination of a process which started with primary education, followed by libraries for juveniles, popular libraries, 'Toynbee' (settlement) work, and ending with popular lectures (Ibid.: 51).

He also thought that this was not university work: 'Furthermore, if the universities took charge, only professors, lecturers and assistants would be appointed as course leaders' whereas ministers, medical doctors, journalist and teachers should also be considered as course leaders' (Ibid.). Very much against the *spirit* of the English model (if not the practice) Reidel insisted that it should develop the middle class which 'is more or less neglected compared with all that is done for the lower classes' and that the courses were neither intended for nor suited to the working class (Ibid.). Hence the Society preferred the term *Hooger Onderrwijs buiten de Universiteiten* (Higher Education outside the university) to *Hooger Volksonderwijs*. (Higher Popular Education).

There were other issues of principle. Riedel opposed the fostering of independent enquiry in popular education because:

The distance between the intellectual development of men of science and of the lower classes [...] is too large to bridge in one noble, gigantic attempt. And yet a wave of light has to be extended from the universities to those men who are closer to the masses (quoted ibid.: 52).

The primary role for university extension was in waking up the middle classes to the importance of the social question and increasing social harmony. Poetically, he concluded: 'In these "scientific courses for adults" we can find the material from which different threads will be spun so that several circles will interweave with each other, and from which a cloak of social consciousness will develop' (quoted ibid: 52–3).

At the turn of the century the *Nut* saw the Law on Higher Education of 1905 as an opportunity to reactivate university extension and van Hamel, who was a theology professor from Groningen with anti-clerical and positivist views, was appointed to the new sub-committee on higher popular education. van Hamel wanted people to respect the scientific standpoint as the only way to arrive at the truth and 'to save the people from the power of superstition and to counter-balance the mere acceptance of authority' (Ibid.: 55). de Vroom notes that he attached greater importance to academic standards than vocational aspects and 'as an ethical modernist he paid tribute to the view that scholarly evidence was to be more highly valued in religious affairs than was revelation or tradition' (Ibid.).

The refusal of influential members of the *Nut* to reserve the society for the education of the middle classes and not deal directly with workers was of course hotly contested. Radical criticism came from the *Social Weekly*, a journal established in 1887 by Arnold Kerdijk, a radical liberal who previously had been the *Nut*'s secretary. He founded the journal in response to concerns that the society was not keeping up with the times and should adopt more 'social' position for 'improving the intellectual, moral and social condition of the people' (Ibid.: 235). Opposed both to 'Manchester' free trade liberalism and to revolutionary socialism, in what now can be seen as an international pattern, Kerdijk argued that 'the masses should be educated to make them fit for reforms' and to create social harmony between the classes (Ibid.: 238). He was forced to leave the *Nut* because it regarded his journal as too radical and he proposed to use it as a forum where 'those struggling for social progress from different bases could measure the strength of their weapons' (Ibid.: 239). A number of university professors were attracted to the editorial board including Pekelharing, a *katheder* socialist and there was also a small but significant women's involvement including Helene Mercier.

The *Social Weekly*'s role in promoting popular education was very important, largely through its coverage of educational innovations, reports of visits and reviews and summaries of books on university extension. Cornelie Huygens, a feminist novelist, for example, wrote on extension's capacity in England to bring higher education within the reach of all without distinction of rank, standing, capital or age. Convinced that low levels of intellectual development could pose a danger to society and given that it was impossible to provide the masses with access to the universities, she believed the universities should be brought to the people (Ibid.: 243).

There were also repercussions as a result of articles on Toynbee Hall from 1890 onwards. The journal noted that the workingmen's association in Amsterdam had taken the unheard of step of directly petitioning the university for courses. van Hamel, by now the Vice Chancellor of Amsterdam University and a regular contributor to the *Social Weekly*, reported on Sunday evening meetings 'for a couple of hundred workers and their wives where students provided free lectures' (Ibid.: 246). Other voices critical of university extension, however, repeated the claim that Dutch mainstream education was too well advanced to require it. Some noted the example of Germany's independent popular education which was seen as closer in spirit to the Netherlands and marked by a complete absence of university extension developments.

By the time of the World Association for Adult Education's conference in 1928, university extension, which had been urged on an apparently reluctant intelligentsia by the government's intervention had become rather confusingly identified with the French inspired *universités populaires* movement. In his contribution van Dugteren said that the popular universities had arrived in Holland only in 1913. The first was founded in Amsterdam and next year one in Groningen.

Progress was then interrupted by the war and then five new ones were begun in 1919 and five more in 1920 (WAAE, 1929: 216). van Dugteren saw the limitations of popular universities in their limitation to the large towns and in attempting to offer provision too extensive in character on only a small income from the local authorities.[3]

Because of their late development in Holland and the possible grafting of popular universities onto what there was of university extension, in her contribution to the conference, Jenny Kraft conflated both movements calling them 'The People's Universities (University Extension)' (Ibid.: 202). She was anyway quite dismissive, claiming that although they were aimed at the lower middle and working classes, they appealed mostly to the already well-educated. In her opinion, 'the Socialist Institute alone frankly acknowledges that its aim is to make the working classes ripe for socialisation and to found a new civilisation on socialistic principles' (Ibid.: 203). Nevertheless, Kraft keenly noted the evolutionary shift in popular education which had begun in Britain in 1903 with the formation of the WEA, what she called the 'Daltonisation' of the University Extension Movement, 'making the students become more than mere listeners and getting them to bear the work of their self-development on their own shoulders' (Ibid.: 206).

The Dutch experience of popular 'university' education may thus be interesting because, since there was no formal university involvement, elements of the English and French models appear to converge. It was, arguably, the example of the French *universités populaires* that had also provoked the English onto the path of democratic working class education and to insist that the universities provided tutorial classes under local study group control rather than the *données* of the extension class which led to the WEA tutorial movement. Kraft's

---

3   van Dugteren offered some useful statistics indicating considerable interest. Popular universities varied in size; the Hague was the largest with 8654 students in seventy-six courses, Rotterdam 5540 in forty courses, and Amsterdam 4630 in sixty-nine courses. At the other end of the scale Gouda had ninety-five and Arnhem sixty-five students. At Rotterdam the average attendance was 133 while at Amsterdam it was sixty-seven. Van Dugteren noted that eight popular universities ran 'tutorial classes' numbering forty-one, seventeen at Rotterdam with thirty-four students per class. Language classes were in particular demand.

inability or refusal to distinguish between university extension and popular universities and to assume the parentage of the tutorial class may be a clarifying moment in which it is clear the German *Neue Richtung* is also influential.

One otherwise powerful international influence that seems to be missing from Dutch popular education or was adapted in specific ways is that of the Danish folk high schools. While some residential adult education schools were established in the early twentieth century, they seem to have been influenced by English rather than Danish models (Hake and Both, 1991). One direct inspiration was the Woodbrooke Quaker settlement near Birmingham, established in 1903. A Christian Socialist Workers Community of Dutch 'Woodbrookers' was formed in 1919 and a residential college near Haarlem was established only in 1931. An association for the Encouragement of Folk Highs Schools was formed in the early 1930s which led to foundation of first folk high school in 1932 in Bakkeveen with the purpose of offering 'a moral-spiritual development for adults as a foundation for the renewal of folk culture and the strengthening of the sense of national community' (Ibid.: 184). The influence of Woodbrooke was evidenced in the many theology students who spent time there and returned often to prestigious posts at Leiden. One of them van Senden, a secretary of the Woodbrookers, became a humanist and later established the Community of Working Members for modern religious realisation, communion and culture, known as the 'Modernists'. Another Woodbrooker, Willem Banning, pioneered links with the Dutch Social Democratic Party (SDAP) and was later involved with the International Committee for Christian Socialism in 1928, a powerful cross-cultural association.

Banning was puzzled why 'there is such distance between continental and English culture' (Ibid.: 190). His scepticism of the Danish folk high school model was confirmed by Hermien van der Heide, the daughter of a 'Red Minister', who had studied it in depth. She concluded that folk high school work in Holland could *not* be based on a common sense of national identity which, in her opinion, did not exist and that it should be based instead on strong religious or political communities with a grounded identity such as the Woodbrookers (Ibid.: 191). Another pioneer of Dutch adult education, Emilie Knappert, who was also prominent in the International Association of

Settlements, took the same view. Initially involved in working class neighbourhood work in 1890s and then first director of the Folk House in Leiden in 1899, Knappert eventually became the Director of School for Social Work in Amsterdam 1915–1926. She too was inspired by English Christian Socialism, which was quite distinct from the Lutheran nationalism of Kold and Grundtvig.

A small association for the Promotion of Folk High Schools on the Danish model was nevertheless founded in 1931 by van der Wielen but this had no contact with van der Heide and other Woodbrookers and it developed only a tense relationship with social democratic organisations in what was classically a town and country split. While the SDAP promoted class-consciousness rather than national identity, van der Wielen preferred the opposite and it was no great surprise to them that under the Nazis, he became the secretary of the Dutch Union.

Although it could be argued that, except for the 'People's Houses' the Netherlands, Belgium and Holland, created no great innovations in popular education, the hybrids they produced are significant of specific national cultural developments. While in Belgium the social movements were fractured in a number of directions by for example Flemish nationalism, anticlericalism and then socialist class struggle in the more composed atmosphere of Dutch cultural life it was the older enlightenment voluntary society, the *Nut*, which took the lead and then renewed it in the controversy over university extension. In Belgium the contrast of Ghent-based and Brussels-based university extension was a good example of opposing nationalist and socialist pressures, while both attempted to confront the 'social question' by steering a middle way between laissez faire economics and revolutionary socialism. The masonically based anticlericalism of Belgium was of course intensified by the educational control exercised by Catholicism and its subsequent political organisation, which did not of course exist in Holland. Although both countries succumbed to a form of pillarisation, largely orchestrated for the benefit of the confessional groups, in Holland the role of the state as a 'neutral' arbiter and arguably its more developed civil society, proved more successful in educational terms. Holland too had a more highly developed educational system which, in the thought of its university intellectuals at least, precluded the need for university extension as a form of 'deficit' education – although there is no sense in which that was actually the case in England. The *Nut*'s frank view that it was in the end the middle class that needed higher education and not the masses was an admission few in England were prepared to concede.

Yet the political alignment of many of those involved appears in many ways to the left of that in Britain where the Labour Party was never able to organise a comparable educational wing to that of the Belgian or Dutch Social Democrats. It could be argued that the English WEA's close ties to the universities were both its strength and its weakness. Its strength lay in its ability to provide a very high quality of systematic higher education to working people while its weakness lay in its over-readiness to police its activities, which resulted in the fatal splitting off of what became known as 'Independent Working Class Education' (IWCE) and what was in effect an internal 'Cold War'. Belgian and Dutch Social Democracy also had their own enemies to the left but arguably the incorporation of educational movements within their political parties did much to raise the class and civic consciousness of their own working classes.

Chapter 10
Central and Eastern Europe: New Nations, New Humanity

Nationalist movements and popular education were more closely connected in Eastern and Central Europe than perhaps anywhere else. The struggle against the decaying empires of the Habsburgs and Romanovs and the doctrinal dominance of their respective clerical allies galvanised first the middle classes and then the lower orders into demands for enlightened reform and, at length frustrated by continued repression, revolution:

> The historical roots of adult education in Central and East Europe reach back to the mid-nineteenth century, the great period of national and linguistic awakening throughout the region. The national awakening movements, led by the growing intelligentsia and the struggle for ethnic survival and renewal in the face of foreign cultural domination were a significant motivating force for adult education throughout East Europe during the second half of the nineteenth century. A number of national associations and institutions for the enlightenment of the people were established by the intelligentsia, who saw it as one of their responsibilities to contribute to the education of their fellow citizens, particularly the working class (Kulich, 1985: 137).

Significant interest in university extension in Eastern Europe did not materialise until the latter half of the 1890s and as the nationalist and radical opposition to the Austro-Hungarian Empire increased, so popular education began to be espoused by both workers' associations and university intellectuals. Kulich claims that English style university extension was 'transplanted to several East European territories around 1900' including the Charles University, Prague and the University of Cluj, Romania while the Universities of Lvov and Krakow were popularising lectures from 1900 and the University of Belgrade from 1888 (Ibid.: 139). But, because of the success of the indigenous independent people's universities, it was never same 'magnitude and significance as in the Anglo-Saxon countries' (Ibid.: 140). The first popular university was founded in Moscow during the 1890s and societies of people's universities had developed by 1906 with a University for All in Poland in 1905. The Polish School Foundation also organised people's universities after 1906 and there was a Citizen's University of Zagreb in 1907. As elsewhere people's universities were mainly urban phenomena and in Poland and Hungary Danish type residential folk high schools were also established in rural areas. Movements in Hungary and Poland developed from popular science associations earlier in the century while in German Bohemia the dramatic influence of Masaryk, the nationalist leader and philosopher, introduced sophisticated social science discourses into worker-led associations. By the 1930s, with the exception of the Soviet Union, where they were discontinued in 1930s, Kulich sees people's universities as the major adult educational institutions in Eastern Europe.

Czechoslovakia and the Masaryk Effect

The emergence of scientific societies in Bohemia (as we saw in Chapter 2) and the 'new science' was implicitly bound up with national identity and opposition to Austro-Hungarian monarchy (Herman, 1988). Hence popular education was from the outset identified with nationalist aspirations which bound the enlightenment idea of scientific discovery to the political and cultural needs of the (newly discovered) 'People'. A vivid contemporary account of university extension in Czechoslovakia was given by Franz Drtina, a Professor of the Bohemian (alternatively Czech) University of Prague. Although he says little about the precursors to the introduction of extension Drtina makes it clear that during the Czech nationalist renaissance of the mid-nineteenth century politicians like Havlicek and Palacky had introduced cultural associations designed to educate the people about their national heritage (Drtina, 1907: 213). Palacky had stimulated the foundation of associations to publish and distribute didactic histories and encyclopaedias. Libraries were founded and movements for scientific knowledge formed, which by the 1880s in Prague had nurtured an association for popular education that organised systematic public lectures. There was also an association of Czech writers and artists and a workers' academy also formed to hold public lecture courses.

Drtina's commentary on extension in Czechoslovakia is significant for the way it discursively 'naturalises' it within what he calls the 'the tradition of the national cultural revival' (Ibid.: 222). University extension is a sign for cultural renewal and vitality within a modernising moment that is now nationalist but also, importantly, 'European'. He asks that the Czech people tread new cultural paths but stay in step with the broader cultural development of Europe. He believes that knowledge and life should be brought together as a contribution to both the moral development and humanising of mankind and bringing separate nations into a greater community. He invokes the names of two great Czech philosophers with international standing, Comenius and Leibniz, to indicate both the national and the universal ideal involved. The ideal community, for Drtina, is not only geographically horizontal but also socially vertical, in that it must include the working classes and notes the importance of the demand for extension from the workers' associations. Scientific knowledge must not simply remain the monopoly of the upper classes but, through the 'strength of education', be internalised by 'the individual' before the lot of the vast majority of mankind could be improved. He concluded that the Bohemian university's efforts were true to the slogan of 'Through enlightenment to Freedom'. Drtina's commentary here stands as one of the most humanely developed rhetorics of extension within the modernising discourse of popular education.

In this fertile soil general public interest in extension was stimulated by articles in journals and reviews during the mid-1890s. However the actual prime mover was not as might be expected the intellectual class but the Association of Czech Workers. It had petitioned Masaryk's Faculty of Philosophy at the Czech University, specifically for extension courses in 1896 (Picavet, 1901: 73; Drtina, 1907: 214). How far Masaryk himself actually stimulated the move is not documented but it would be hard not to draw conclusions. The faculty welcomed the petition and in turn sent a resolution to the Minister of Instruction to instigate a commission. In 1897 the minister approved but indicated that whole university or at least four of the faculties should be involved. The movement became statutory the following year along with a grant of 6000 kroner (Ibid.: 214).

The statute emphasised that lecture courses should be offered to those classes who had not hitherto had access to academic studies and permitted courses to held in Prague, it suburbs and the rest of Bohemia and with special authorisation the *Reichsrath*. However, it expressly excluded courses touching on contemporary religious, political and social conflicts. The courses were to be organised by a special commission of representatives from all Faculties, consisting of eleven members of which, four were to be elected by Senate and four by Faculty and to include a President and Vice-President (Picavet, 1901: 73). Apart from the government's own subvention, contributions were to come from corporations and individuals who would pay class fees of 1 kroner, Lecturers were to be paid and they would be expected to produce syllabi and use projectors where possible.

The first courses were inaugurated at a public meeting in the Prague Fruit-Exchange on 5 April 1899 in which the Rector J. Reinsteig gave a talk on the origins of university extension. The list of the impressive first series April–May 1899 was as follows:

1. Development of Socialism in the nineteenth Century – Prof. T.G. Masaryk – 443 students.
2. Light and Heat properties of Electricity – Prof. C. Stronhal – 107 students (which was limited by the capacity of the hall).
3. Theology in 3 parts – Profs. Sykona, Kaderavek and Solveicek – 54 students.
4. Infectious Diseases – Professor Illava – 81.
5. Francois Palacky and our National Development in the nineteenth Century – Docent Jos Paken – 85 students.
6. Air, Water and Carbon – Prof. B. Rayman – 92 students.
7. Composition of Bodily Nourishment – Dr. Formanek – 67 students.

Although 919 students attended this series almost half of them joined Masaryk's own course. The lectures were initially held at the university and in other official rooms and colleges but the intention was to decentralise subsequent courses to the suburbs. The following year, 1899–1900, a second series of courses was organised in Prague and also in the country, totalling 414 students (Drtina, 1907: 75). The third equally ambitious series held January–February 1900, included courses on Nervous and Psychic Illness by Dr L. Haskovec (250 students: 142 male, 108 female) part of which was devoted to the 'struggles and efforts of modern man' and Art and Society by Professor O. Hostinsky which dealt (in the town of Franz Kafka) with 'le signe, l'ecriture, l'image', which looked distinctly like a course on semiotics (109 male and 101 female students); total enrolment 759 students. The fourth series, held March–April 1900, included courses on China, Tuberculosis, French Poetry (164 students), Polar Regions, Children's Diet, and Intellectual Development in Europe, total students, 716. The composition of the course showed a steady rise in the number of workers and an initially high but decreasing number of women over the first three years.[1]

More courses were to be organised outside Prague including a special library. Reflecting developments in Scandinavia and Britain, secondary school teachers were much more involved in the movement in the provinces and there was a demand for special primary education courses. From 1900 local associations took a greater initiative in organising courses which included reading circles, gymnastic societies and teachers' associations, some working under the aegis of town councils. In 1903–1904 the university committee supervised ninety-five lecture courses in twenty-five towns in Bohemia and Moravia outside Prague with a remarkable average attendance of 295 in each lecture. The demand from teachers for continuing education courses was met by Masaryk's faculty of Philosophy, perhaps signifying an (inevitable) shift of emphasis from the workers' associations that initiated the movement to the group whose professional and vocational, in the wider sense, interests would most benefit from it. Teachers' education was not formally provided by the state but both the Austrian and Moravian governments financially supported the new courses (Drtina, 1907: 220).

One reason why Bohemian University appears to have developed one of the most sophisticated programmes of extension in Europe,

---

1   Drtina also thoughtfully supplied the 1900 Paris Conference with the occupational statistics of students. Workers, artisans and tradesman comprised in the 2nd series – 19.63%, 3rd series – 26.14%, and 4th series – 21.71%. Of Women – (usually not precisely indicated) – school teachers comprised 47.6%, diminishing over the three series 46.1% of the whole to 31%.

may lie in the charismatic presence of T.G. Masaryk (1850–1937), the Professor of Philosophy who later became the first president of the liberated Czechoslovakia. Described as a 'philosopher-king', Masaryk was responsible for bringing together the movements of nationalism and socialism in the unhappily named Czech National Socialist Party. Even while he was president of the republic he refused to give up his chair of philosophy. He was also one of the founders of social science as an academic discipline and when he arrived at the university in 1882, he gave what were the first courses in sociology in any university, European or American (Kolger, 1968). Masaryk was also probably a freemason (Fejto, 1998).

Masaryk was responsible for challenging the hegemony of German intellectual life over Czechoslovakia by introducing new discourses into the academy. He clashed with the conservative leadership of Prague University 1879 where his public lectures on humanism and Pascal challenged the previous monopoly of German philosophy; he was denounced as a traitor, a nihilist and worst of all a cosmopolitan (Skilling, 1992: 2). These lectures were drawn largely from Anglo-Saxon and French sources, particularly Mill, Spencer and Comtean sociology which were, in a sense, the wedge of 'scientific' positivism driven into the metaphysical side of German idealism – although it was not without its tragic aspects: like Durkheim he produced a study of suicide. The belief in the application of science to society was for him, as for many popular intellectuals, a key to social progress.

Masaryk's involvement in workers' education was central to his conception of adult education. When the trade unions founded the Workers' Academy (*Delnicka Akademie*) as we have seen, he supported it and later created the Higher School for Workers. The Masaryk Institute was named after him in 1920 in recognition of his devotion to popular education. Strong on democracy and love and virulently opposed to anti-Semitism, Masaryk was married to and greatly influenced by an American feminist, Charlotte Garigue, who translated Mill's the *Subjection of Women* into Czech and as a unregenerate cosmopolitan intellectual, she found Czech nationalism intensely parochial. But it was also in America, among the Czech exiles, that the nationalist movement had found one of its earliest expressions. Thus, as for Dvorak, so for Masaryk 'modernity' was recruited from the New World to assault the crumbling ruins of 'Old Europe' in the shape of the Habsburg Empire.

Masaryk nevertheless drew heavily on Czech sources, especially Karel Havlicek (1821–1856), for much of his political thought, when nationalism was changing from a primarily cultural to a political phenomenon (Reinfeld, 1991). Against the flow of German folkish tendencies, Havlicek had linked Czech nationalism to Western liberalism, a tendency that Masaryk closely emulated. Although not a nationalist as such, while a student in Vienna he was an active member of Czech clubs and founded the Athenaeum (1883–1889) to broaden the perspectives of Czech intellectuals and improve scholarship. Masaryk discovered Havlicek's work in 1890s, having resigned as a delegate of the Realist faction from the Czech parliament and returned to university life. Increasingly drawn to the nationalist cause, he was impressed by the universal humanism of Jan Hus and the Czech Reformation of the fifteenth century that had in many respects anticipated the eighteenth century Enlightenment. Appalled by what he learned of the violence of the counter-reformation of the sixteenth century, Masaryk converted to Protestantism and became involved with the radical masonic network. Increasingly anticlerical, he found Catholicism an 'oppressive, outdated institution' and became a 'strong advocate of freedom of scholarship against Catholic clericalism and censorship in the schools' (Reinfeld, 1991: 311; Skilling, 16).

He was dismayed also by the Catholic Church's obsession with political power and theocratic absolutism, which gave no lead on moral progress and, unsurprisingly, the Catholic clergy hotly opposed his election to parliament, where he campaigned against clericalism and in favour of freedom of conscience (Skilling, 1992: 106). Skilling noted his 'conviction that there was an absolute conflict between the science and scholarship pursued at universities, based on reason and experience, and requiring freedom and criticism, and the spiritual work of theology and the Church, based on authority and revelation (Ibid.). In what could be an encomium for the popular education movement, Masaryk maintained that:

> We in the world of learning have accustomed ourselves to recognize the existence of universal laws at work, not only in nature, but also in history and

society. We eliminate every miracle; while the theologian desire miracles [...] Our methods are different. On the one side the idea of revelation, on the other, the custom of using experience and generalisation: there authority, here the individual, subjective understanding and conscious criticism; there tradition, the past, the ancient, if possible the oldest, here criticism of tradition, progress, the present and the future, the freeing of the modern working man; on the one hand infallibility, on the other relativity, criticism; there, exclusiveness and ortho-doxy, here, tolerance; there, belief, trust, obedience, here conviction and criticism (without criticism we cannot believe) (quoted in ibid.: 108).

But he was not inflexibly atheistic and his concern for social justice was not unlike the Christian love for one's neighbour. Religion, too, was not incompatible with science, if it was based on reason and conviction rather than faith and authority (Ibid.: 113). However the Church's opposition to the emancipation of women, for which he held the Virgin cult responsible, and its resistance to equality in all spheres including income and insistence on celibacy for official posts, only increased his opposition. Masaryk strongly agreed with Havlicek's ideas on political inclusiveness and he advocated universal suffrage alongside the educational and legal equality for women. Like Hav-licek, he resisted the Russophilism that appealed to pan-Slavists and saw Czechs and Slovaks as one nation, subordinating the so-called 'historic' rights of nations to rationally derived natural rights, saying: 'Humanity is our final national and historical objective; it is our Czech programme' (quoted in Skilling, 1992: 6).

Masaryk established his 'Realist' movement, which he described as 'a small circle of educators' that had gathered around him and drew on his political ideas for a evolutionary, anti-revolutionary approach (Ibid.: 314). Inasmuch as he embraced the idea of revolution it was one of the 'head and common sense' subordinated to the power of education since, for him, an informed citizenry could not be held in bonds indefinitely (Ibid.: 315). Political change should embrace a grass roots democracy and self-help to develop a strong communal sense and like Havlicek he believed that all labour done with deter-mination humanised the world. He admired Proudhon's anarchist dictum, 'property is theft' but rejected the Marxism of the Czech SPD as too materialistic. Ultimately, for him, the social question was an ethical question that relied on raising sensitivity to social justice throughout society, which he saw as primarily an educational task. Thus popular education was a political necessity, as Skilling argues:

> In particular, workers' education should be promoted through a Workers' Academy which would provide industrial workers with two or three years of schooling: the emphasis should be on general and theoretical not practical training. There should be extension lectures courses for popular education at high schools and at the university [...] Women should have equal facilities' (Skilling, 1992: 16).

Masaryk's humble origins as the son of a Slovak coachman with no clear idea of his future, who stumbled into his career as a university teacher, only reinforced this conviction and he remains one of the beacons of enlightened popular education.

Hungarian Culturalism

In Hungary popular education took a different course as a result of earlier government intervention but cross cultural influence was still a important factor. Until 1919 Hungary was an independent kingdom within the Austro-Hungarian monarchy linked to Austria by the common institutions of the army, foreign affairs, diplomatic relations and financial affairs. Although nominally equal, Hungary was actually a junior partner in the joint monarchy and patriots had long held a desire for independence. Hungary had also been the bulwark against Ottoman ambitions in Europe and was the site of many a bloody battle. As a consequence its population was ethnically very diverse and although the Magyar identity was proudly projected, it did in practice jostle uncomfortably with claims from Slavs, Rumans, Poles and a host of Balkan nationalities.

A succession of largely paternalistic institutions for advancing popular education had existed since the days of its great nationalist leader Louis Kossuth. The eruption of national consciousness in the early nineteenth century was exemplified by the formation of clubs and 'casinos' debating political issues, the first of which was established in 1827 in Pest by Count Istvan Szechenyi on the basis of what he had learned from England about political debate and cultural development. In 1841 a Natural Science Society had been founded to propagate scientific achievements with rural reading societies and libraries. In 1847 a society to publish 'good cheap books' was set up by philanthropists but the development was suspended during the revolutionary upsurge of the following years (Maroti, 1993).

As early as 1867, however, the government took the initiative in coordinating popular adult education under the Minister for Public Instruction, Baron Joseph Eötvös, who in the 1870s created popular, especially workers', circles for popular science under the name of Popular Cultural Associations. These developed into weekly, well attended, popular courses centred in Budapest which ran for twenty-five years. Significantly, the government initiative was energetically promoted by Istvan Türr, one of Garibaldi's generals, who had been in exile in France since the War of Independence of 1849. Impressed by the Masonic popular educational network the French *Ligue de L'Enseignement* (see Chapter 6), Türr was commissioned by Eötvös to organise such movement in Hungary beginning with a Centre for the Education of the People (*Központi Népoktatási Kör*) in Budapest and branches in provincial towns (WAAE, 1929: 236). Little came of it however since state funding was not forthcoming although a single centre in Pest did continue. Worker's Association were formed at the end of 1860s for 'intellectual training' of members and lectures popularising science assisted by middle class intellectuals, libraries, choirs and drama groups which recognised that 'culture' was indispensable to the workers' movement. Towards the end of the century provincial Cultural Societies were founded and, although not specifically for adult education, encouraged Sunday workers' educational circles. These received a significant state subvention and claimed to have instructed over 30,000 industrial workers annually (Picavet, 1901: 79–83).

The agrarian socialist movement of the late nineteenth century was also linked to the peasant cultural societies established in the villages. Fabry and Soós claim that 'the first actions of the workers took place within the frameworks of the cultural associations in the 1860s' so that in the 1890s peasant reading circles grew and some became militantly class conscious (Fabry and Soós, 1986). The role of workers' associations was eventually taken over by the Social Democratic Party (SPD), formed in 1890 and the trade unions under the leadership of Ervin Szabó (Ibid.). These initiatives were eventually given state support by the short-lived 1919 Hungarian Soviet Republic policy but were forced underground by the repressive Horthy government.

University Extension

Because of this existing tradition of popular cultural education Professor Emile de Grosz of the University of Budapest maintained that university extension in Hungary was implanted into an already well-prepared soil (Picavet, 1901). But by the 1890s, however, the universities were still not as yet involved and instead another institution stepped in. This was the 'Free Lyceum' (*Szabad Lyceum*), which de Grosz argued, in reality played the role of university extension (like the *Nut* in Holland, see previous chapter). Founded in 1893, it also aimed at popularising of science through courses of education but it also promoted the 'general raising of things of the spirit' through art and intellectual culture in general. The Lyceum was supported largely by the middle-classes, although periodic attempts were made to recruit workers.[2] It became the focus of extension activities partly because it was so well-endowed in the first place, with for example a large hall, reading rooms and a library although the first course did not in fact begin until 1902 (Schultze and Hamdorff, 1907: 223–47). What was offered was six-meeting courses on subjects already taught in the university and polytechnic for those unable to receive a university education. As in England summaries were circulated before the lec-

2   In 1899–1900, a report notes that there were twenty-eight courses with 2680 students or nearly 100 students per course; thirteen special industrial circles with 1210 students and for the more educated public, 105 courses with 4438 students. Its income was raised from members subscriptions and entry fees, which were supported by public subventions from Budapest and the Ministry of Culture and Public Instruction.

tures to the audience and a discussion was held afterwards. The lecturers were for the most part from higher education, although other specialists were employed, on a payment by results system (a fee of 33 Marks plus thirty per cent of admission fees). It survived the great political upheavals following World War One and in 1928 its chairman the Marxist philosopher, George Lukacs, was able to give a moving historical account of its progress (WAAE, 1929: 238).

The transition to more formal university extension relied on Jules Wlassics, the Minister for Education, who himself had given classes in science, and took the initiative in 1897. The universities responded positively and created a commission consisting of men who had already been involved in the popular education movement, such as Bela Foldes, Elienne Hegedus, Eugene Gaal, Edmond Jonas, Elienne Schneller and Charles Lechner, who submitted a plan to the Minister proposing special extension committees for the principal centres, Budapest and Kolozsvar. In the provincial centres many existing societies such as the Society of the Museum of Transylvania were also encompassed by the name of 'extension'. The Hungarian parliament warmly received the plan and voted 4000 crowns for it. The state's funding was apparently at arm's length which allowed the universities to supply the bulk of the committee and to furnish and monitor the quality of the courses. Like Masaryk in Czechoslovakia and his predecessor Eötvös, Wlassics saw university extension was a key element in an overall programme of national cultural unity through a unified education system (Ibid.: 238). Magyardom was being threatened by both the Slavs to the north and the Romanians in the east who were colonising Transylvania and the role of the cultural associations was to promote a deep sense of national identity.

Beyond Budapest the ministry pursued extension by continuing to involve cultural associations in founding extension committees. Thus unlike the English and Dutch models, Hungarian extension was both already deeply nationalist in its inspiration and also much more closely integrated into the state. Significantly perhaps, in towns where there were no higher education institutions and continuing education was in the hand of schoolteachers, who preferred to work only with existing learned and literary societies, there was some opposition to the state-funded initiatives. Also in response to courses explicitly held to counter the growth of agrarian socialism during a period of unrest,

252

by Catholic agencies, the Minister of Agriculture, Daranyi, set up a kind of rural 'extension' on Sunday afternoons for agricultural workers with the landowners' cooperation. With Wlassics's involvement and state funding this scheme then developed along the lines of the Danish Folk high schools into regular training, under military discipline, for farm workers and included domestic science for girls (Ibid.: 247).

Extension in Hungary therefore was fairly highly politicised from the outset, enjoying a high level of state support and direction which corralled voluntary sector agencies into the system. It appears to have responded to perceived political threats both from without and within the polity though perhaps the extreme fluidity and sensitivity of its boundaries encouraged this. Hungarian nationalism was still a relatively labile and disputed entity. And because state supported initiatives appeared to be saturated by government policy, rival progressive enterprises were launched by free-thinking intellectuals. The 'Workers Training Courses', the 'Free High School of Social Sciences', the 'Cultural Circle' and later the 'Galilei Circle' organised by Budapest University students represented 'a steadfast leftist, free thinking, even revolutionary type of university adult education' (Soós, 1988: 23). Under Bela Khun's short lived Hungarian Soviet Republic of 1919, in which George Lukacs was prominent, special workers' universities with lectures given by university teachers, were organised but these were swiftly repressed by the counter-revolutionary Horthy regime of 1919–1944.

However, new progressive developments arose more or less spontaneously in regional university towns, for example: The Arts College of Szeged Young People was founded in the 1920s by university students; The Summer University developed from summer courses by Professor Janos Hankiss at Debrecen University in 1927 and a later Debrecen initiative was the 'March Front' movement of 1936–1938 which although mostly communist in character, was also educational. The Conferences of Balatonszarszo, organised by the Protestant organisation Soli deo Gloria between 1928–1943, were open air events which attracted mainly students but also workers and peasants.

With the assumption of the Communist government after World War Two, the state was once more politically directly engaged in adult education through the People's College movement, 1945–1949, but these were eventually closed by the repressive Rakosi government. The new period of university adult education, 1956–1968, which was organised by the Society for the Popularisation of Scientific Knowledge held summer schools specialising in particular disciplines. There were also various 'free universities' such as the Jozsef Attila Free University in Budapest which ran three month courses mostly in languages but increasingly in history, the arts and social sciences. It could be argued therefore that, despite the changing political character of its governing regimes, extension activities in Hungary have maintained an interesting continuity by repeated absorption by the state of civil sector popular education into the state apparatus.

The Hungarian Folk High Schools

In the rural areas radical university-based popular education was not welcomed by all and a Catholic Country Association was launched in 1893 to promote religious belief. However, as elsewhere in central and Eastern Europe, it was Grundtvig's ideas that were found to be most inspirational. Danish folk high schools were first mentioned in 1895 by Mor Karman. Pal Guttenberg noted the prerequisites of well-equipped designated facilities, well-prepared teaching staff and curriculum, which were supported by the Hungarian Smallholders Association and the Catholic Education Council from 1910.

But the movement did not really gain ground until the late 1930s when a visit by some Finnish Lutheran clergy in 1937 stimulated a movement to form the first Lutheran folk high school. This was established by Gabor Szthelo in 1938 and was opened by the Finnish ambassador, offering five month residential courses for both tutors and students in a 'symbolic village' (Toth, 1998: 52). While some claimed the Hungarian folk high schools were modelled on Grundtvig's to promote a Christian world view and national consciousness, for others the derivative Catholic folk high schools were a means to religious education and character formation. Some of the 119, largely men only, folk high schools prepared students for leadership and local government roles, which had been Grundtvig's original intention in Denmark (see Chapter 4). Courses lasted for ten months and attracted young students in autonomous self-governing and village-like societies. Permanent bonds were formed among students, many joining the Farmers' Party and later playing an important role in public life.

While there was a common belief among the folk high schools leadership in the social emancipation of the peasantry, there were marked differences between the schools in which right wing anti-communism existed side by side with anti-fascism. The most left wing insisted on radical political transformation of political system, land reform and voluntary cooperative movements shared by all. Most schools, however, formulated contemporary ideals of state and administrative reform and aimed at training a stratum of citizens and people's leaders capable of developing self-governance. But 'regarding intellectual values, one of the most decisive features of the alternative status of folk high schools was their attitude to traditional peasant culture, which was in the course of disintegration' (Toth, 1999: 260). Reading circles expanded in villages, fostering communal life and there was a growing interest in peasantry and cultural traditions. Folksong collecting, folklore groups and traditions grew and led to the musical renaissance exemplified by the remarkable work of Bela Bartok and Zoltán Kodály.

At the movement's peak, between 1936–1948, Toth claims that of the 119 folk high schools fifty-one were Protestant, thirty were under the control of the local authority, twenty were Catholic, fourteen were operated by the Cultural Association and four by *Levente* a semi-military youth organisation. This curiously inverts the actual denominational proportions which were sixty-five per cent Catholic and twenty-one per cent Calvinist, six per cent Lutheran, five per cent Jewish and three per cent other. Toth claims that while the Catholic Church, which was more closely integrated into the State, wanted a universal social church, the Calvinists tapped into traditions of Hungarian popular radicalism and developed contacts with the political left such as the SPD. The deepening crisis of the semi-feudal agrarian society split the church between higher and lower clergy who, like many intellectuals, were especially influenced by the movement of people's writers (Toth, 1999: 259).

As Maroti (1986) concludes, around the turn of the century the Hungarian intelligentsia saw it as their duty to propagate culture and raise the living standards of the peasantry, but it failed because while the peasantry was not interested in cultural viewpoints of the intellectuals, the intelligentsia was unable to identify with the peasantry's more practical needs. The Horthy regime (1920–1944), moreover, successfully drove a wedge between the peasants and workers internationalism through nationalist indoctrination – a tactic, ironically, later emulated by the Communist regime after 1948 (Maroti, 1986). Thus, following the 1920 peace treaty and fragmentation of Hungary, adult education lost its radical liberal character and became trenchantly nationalist (and eventually porous to Nazism). Maroti's epitaph on it was that:

> The state expected education to raise the national consciousness and inculcate religion to counteract the internationalism and atheistic views current in the workers' movement and amongst middle class radicals. Adult education was largely at primary level for literacy, general utility 'refining the spirit and forming character' (Maroti, 1993: 29).

Poland: Nationalism and the 'Woman's Question'

Poland nurtured a strong national tradition of scientific education (as we saw in Chapter 2), which refused to be extinguished completely during the years of foreign occupation and partition. Modern Polish popular education can be dated from the formation of the Society of Friends of Science of Warsaw (1800–1831) (Trzeciakowski, 1988). But during the nineteenth century, conditions for the promotion of popular education could hardly have been worse. Partitioned and dominated by three imperialist powers, Russia, Austria and Germany, Polish identity found itself confronted by hostile hegemonic forces bent on suppressing it. Poles had suffered from rival imperialist ambitions for decades. During the years of the partition of Poland in eighteenth century, Germany and Russia actively used education as a tool of denationalisation. Following the defeat of Napoleon, a quasi-independent Kingdom of Poland was brought into being by the 'Great Powers' at the Congress of Vienna in 1815 but manacled to Russian despotism, it was finally suffocated after the January Insurrection of 1863 (Miaso, 1981). The introduction and rapid development of a capitalist system of production coupled with agrarian reform of 1864 created new industrial centres and removed the crippling feudal dependence of peasants who at last were given land of their own.

Following the defeat of revolutionary ambitions in 1863, young intellectuals turned away from direct political action towards the project of cultural and educational reform. Similar new societies based in university towns and in non-violent nationalist groups were formed in which: 'scholars and writers who had previously been sucked into the turmoil of political life returned to the serenity of their studies, where they considered how best to concentrate their energies' (Ibid.: 293). Strenuous efforts were made to popularise the understanding of science, but with political connotations so as to awaken national pride in Polish achievements – one lecture called on young Poles 'not to yield to anyone primacy in virtues, work and science' (Ibid.: 294).

In this vibrant oppositionist atmosphere in which institutional forms of education were still under largely foreign political control, self-education flourished. Self-education was encouraged by journals and newspapers and self-help books like the widely influential *The Self-Teaching Handbook* published in 1896, was widely read. From the culturally resistant texture of Polish society, courses of a popular scientific character, often of a high standard, as well as reading rooms and libraries began to emerge. Miaso notes:

> Systematic adult education was for the most part of a clandestine nature and it was conducted by underground associations, as well as by socialist organisations such as the Circle of Workers' Education. The socialist movement was in fact from its very beginning, and to a high degree an educational movement' (Miaso, 1981: 108).

Such societies, fostered by the intelligentsia, stimulated social awareness and served the hunger for knowledge fed by illegal workers' libraries. Despite their clandestine nature, centres of popularisation of knowledge began to emerge and by the beginning of the twentieth century a range of workers' educational organisations, concerned with literacy and the popularisation of science and art were catering for tens of thousands of workers.

Despite the engagement of intellectuals with the work of popular education the relatively weakly developed middle-class contributed little to cultural progress compared with other European countries and there was little educational sponsorship by the wealthy. Hobsbawm notes that despite the various parties dedicated to Polish independence it was in fact the leadership of the Polish Socialist party that was most responsible (Hobsbawm, 1987: 162). So limited was the enthusiasm of the Polish bourgeoisie for nationalism that Rosa Luxembourg thought that there was no basis for it at all in that class. Although the number of schools increased as a result of legislation, their net effect actually reinforced the existing social structure and prevented rather than encouraged social mobility. The backwardness of the Russian czarist system, in particular, both preserved undesirable feudal elements and imposed an oppressive Russian cultural hegemony.

Polish emancipatory aspirations could never be entirely quenched however and popular education reignited into a national awakening which brought to life many cultural and educational societies such as: The Society for Popular Education, the Secret Society for National Education, the secret Warsaw Popular Education Circle, the illegal Women's Educational Circle and the 'Flying University' so called because it had frequently to flee its location to escape Russian persecution. In the later years of the nineteenth century the slogan of those carrying the flame became, 'Through education to freedom' (WAAE, 1929: 331).

Women and the Folk High School Movement in Poland

One of Polish popular education's most important cultural borrowings was the Danish folk high school model. Because of the more acute national and social forces at play, most interest in Grundtvig was felt in the Russian third of the partition, while in the less repressive German third Poles already attended some agricultural schools. In

1888 newspapers carried articles about the role of Danish folk high schools after the Danish defeat by Prussia in 1864 and Swedish folk high schools were publicly noted in 1891 – which may suggest that, outside the Nordic countries, Poland probably took the most intense interest in Grundtvig.

Polish folk high schools began to be established a few years later the first near Warsaw by the first of a number of remarkable women popular educators, Jadwiga Dziubinska (1831–1937). Dziubinska came from a Polish intellectual family, attended agricultural school and became the head of the first residential agricultural school for men in 1899 (Thomas and Elsey, 1985: 160). For most of 1903, in visits to Denmark, Sweden and Belgium and agricultural schools in Germany and Czechoslovakia, she studied folk high schools at first hand. She decided she must emulate them in Poland but to carry out her work it was necessary to obtain permits from Russian authorities and they had to be called simply 'agricultural courses'. In reality, as well as farming and husbandry, they illegally taught courses in the Polish language, literature and history as well as geography, hygiene, social sciences and ethics. Her aim was 'to spread education and culture amongst the peasants, to fight underdevelopment and old-fashioned ways of the country, to promote this social consciousness of the peasants, and to struggle for national independence' (Kulich, 2002: 55). Despite the weakness of the middle class, the small Polish intellectual elite became very active in the educational field and by 1917 there were seven of these schools in Russian Poland. Because the Russian authorities had banned general education in Polish including note taking and the use of books, tutors therefore had two sets of curriculum plans, the legal and the illegal; books were hidden in the cellars and guards posted to warn of inspections. Despite the heroic foundations of the schools, Dziubinska's curriculum later came under fire from both the populist left, as dominated by bourgeois ideology and by the Roman Catholic episcopate, which attacked the schools as 'hotbeds of socialism' (Kulich, 2002: 56).

The very prominent role of women in these schools is re-markable. A prominent authority Robert Blobaum has eloquently noted the pioneering scale of their activities:

Populists, many of whom were elite women, aimed to modernise the village and bring 'civilization' to the peasantry. Consequently, they tended to view peasant wives as sources of rural 'backwardness' and 'superstition,' the remedy for which they saw in 'enlightenment,' or the secular education of peasant daughters [...] By 1914, the populist movement, in its various conservative, nationalist and 'progressive' shades, had created some thirteen 'agronomy schools' for girls in the Congress Kingdom in its effort to propagate a new vision of the woman in the peasant family and rural economy (Blobaum, 2002: 48–9).

The so-called 'Women Question' in Poland so shaped the dominant political discourse that it came to dominate that of the 'nation'. Women from the intellectual elite were already organised in clandestine groups such as the Women's Circle of Popular Education or *Kobiece Kolo Oswiaty Ludowej* (KKOL) which included Dziubinska, Helena Radlinska and Irena Kosmowska who is credited with creating the trademark populist slogan of *sami sobie* 'we ourselves' (Ibid.: 51). For Blobaum:

The Polish nationalist movement (a coalition of organisations eventually grouped under the National Democratic Alliance or Endecja), whose response to the 'woman question' would ultimately prove the most influential as it came to dominate the larger political discourse on the Polish 'nation,' viewed women as bearers and nurturers of peculiarly Polish values and equated patriotic duties with those of motherhood and child-rearing. In its secularisation of Roman Catholic teachings of women's obligations to faith and family, nationalists charged women with no less a task than preserving and nourishing the nation, and the movement was prepared to supply them with the means of modern cultural, social, and political organisation in order to do so (Ibid.: 52).

The leading role of women in Poland is remarkable and perhaps unique. It is also significant that women associated with the nationalist movement before the Revolution of 1905 were drawn largely from those who had campaigned for popular education and eventually joined the nationalist umbrella educational organisation, the Society of National Education, *Towarzystwo Oswiaty Narodowej* (TON), as well as its women's organisation, the Circle of Women of the Crownland and Lithuania (*Kolo Kobiet Korony i Litwy*) (Ibid.: 53).

Not surprisingly the Catholic Church became very anxious about the progressive tendencies exhibited by Poland's educated and militant young women and tried to 'defend' them from spiritual and moral degeneration:

> For this reason, the Catholic press railed against the migration and emigration of single women and engaged in heated polemics with liberals, socialists and feminists who advocated civil marriage and divorce [...] Moreover, the boundaries drawn by the Church, from its view, could only be upheld by patriarchy – in society, in the family, and in the Church itself. Its concerted assault on Jadwiga Dziubinska's school for village girls in 1910 is only one indication of the lengths the Church would go to preserve the traditional patriarchal order and its own vision of women's proper role in the family [...] It is also true, however, that the Church was a major promoter of female literacy among the lower classes as it developed its own industry of moralistic and devotional literature to advance the faith (Ibid.: 57–9).

Just as nationalists targeted the Polish mother as the inculcator of national values, so too the Church viewed women in their maternal capacity as preservers and nurturers of religion in the family and in the community. Concerned with the breakdown of community as a consequence of social change, the Church increasingly identified women as its bonding element.

It did not entirely prevent their growing radicalisation, however, and the folk high schools operated under principle of a high degree of self governance and genuine community. Students took considerable risk in attending and were often persecuted when they returned to their villages:

> Through the work (what we would now call *community development*) of the young peasant men and women, who attended them the first Polish folk high schools contributed significantly to the awakening of the rural population in the Russian part of Poland (Kulich, 2002: 56).

Students acted as models and innovators of agricultural practices but sadly all the schools were destroyed by World War One, creating ten year hiatus in popular education in the countryside.

National Unity Following World War One

Poland finally gained its territorial unity and national independence only at the end of hostilities in 1918. Now the initiative shifted from the women's movement to the newly formed Polish state in which, sadly for the women who had led the movement for popular education, the Church was elevated to prominence. It created a new department, significantly entitled, the Ministry of *Religious* and Public Education in which priests were prominent. In 1921 Antonin Ludwiczak, a Catholic priest and Director of the Association of Folk Reading Rooms (TCL), addressed a conference held by the ministry. Like Dziubinska, a generation earlier, Ludwiczak was impressed by the economic and moral development of the Danish peasantry through education received at their folk high schools and advocated repeating the experiment in Poland. Despite opposition from the conference, TCL founded its first folk high school in Dalki in 1921, with a wide ranging curriculum including religion, literature, science and agricultural skills. Two short lived Catholic folk high schools followed in 1926 and 1927 but both closed two years later and the Catholic Action group opened five folk high schools giving religion a major role in the 1930s but with mixed results.

Despite this inauspicious start, another leading role in the folk high schools movement was taken by Ignacy Solarz (1891–1940) an agricultural engineer who attained near legendary status, despite being fiercely attacked by Catholic Church for his political stance and was eventually killed by the Nazis. Described as 'a Polish Grundtvig and Kold combined' Solarz studied in Denmark for six months in 1922 and opened his first school in 1924. Like Grundtvig, Solarz saw folk high schools as 'schools for life', using the living word as its didactic basis. The school he established at Szyce, sponsored by the Elementary School Teachers Association, aimed at enabling peasants to become social and cultural leaders in their own communities, but it was dogged by political difficulties with his sponsors and temporarily closed in 1931. Solarz open new school in Gac Przeworska in 1932 supported by the Cooperative Society of Rural Universities and the Association of Rural Youth or *Wici*, a left wing arm of the peasant political movement. The school centred on three primary aspects: the spiritual culture of the common people, the cultural traditions of the peasantry and progressive popular movements. Although a member of the Peasant Party, Solarz was sceptical of political parties in general and was more interested in the 'moral renaissance of the nation' and believed in 'the courage and the ability of the masses to create their own culture' (Ibid.: 61). Under pressure from Marshal Pilsudski's reactionary regime, Solarz was forced to moderate his views and he turned his attention to dissolving the boundaries between peasants, workers and intellectuals, during which time he was instrumental in establishing health cooperatives and other productive forms of co-operation.

In adapting Grundtvig's ideas to the Polish context, Solarz diverged from his mentor in a number of ways (Ibid.). His approach was characterised by three elements, firstly an emphasis on historicity to reveal historical roots and antecedents; secondly the role of the 'common folk' in the development of mankind and the life of society – similar to Grundtvig's concept of *folkelighed* and thirdly, an insistence on 'actuality' so that learning could be effectively applied here and now. But although he emphasised the importance of discussion, observation and experience rather than theory, he was critical of the one-sidedness of the 'living word' approach, fearing it could exclude artistic and emotional expression (as did his artist wife Zofia). He also advocated scientific learning for fostering moral values.

During the inter-war period Kulich estimates that twenty-six folk high schools were established in Poland catering for around 5000 students. They were of three types: firstly, Catholic religious based instruction, secondly Solarz's left-wing peasant schools and thirdly government educational policy schools largely set up to counteract those of Solarz (Kulich, 2002). The actual influence of the folk high schools is highly contested. While it was claimed that former students of folk high schools in this period played a leading social, economic and political role out of all proportion to their numbers, this is disputed. Solarz's schools were acknowledged as the most progressive educationally and were the most popular (Thomas and Elsey, 1985: 551). However, there was frequently conflict with the traditional village hierarchy, which meant in practice that the folk high schools were often isolated from the local villages. All were destroyed by

World War Two and although they were revived by the Communists following the war, they were not allowed to remain politically neutral and state apparatchiks waged an ideological campaign to overcome the 'false Grundtvig spirit' (Ibid.: 66). In turn they too were liquidated during the Stalinisation of the early 1950s, although due to the strength of peasant resistance some were actually re-established but under Stalinist ideology they had little in common with either Grundtvig's or Solarz's ideas. The mantle of conservative opposition to progressive popular education thus passed from the Catholic Church to the Communist regime, apparently, seamlessly.

University Extension or Popular Universities?

Meanwhile in the larger cities the university extension idea was also taking root, despite considerable ideological repression from Poland's imperial masters and the Church. In his address to the International Conference on Adult Education in 1900 Paris, W.M. Koslowski, Vice President of the Krakow Popular University reported that, due to Russian and Prussian domination, conditions for founding a university for the people were, to say the least, not favourable (Picavet, 1901). In Galicia (Austrian Poland) however, there were two Polish universities but even here the movement for popular education received no state backing and had been initiated privately. The prime mover had been the Society for Primary Education, which introduced the first courses in popular education in Krakow in 1894. The curriculum consisted of various branches of science and the arts, including physics, chemistry, biology, literature, and history which were taught in courses of six to eight weeks and although initially very popular, attendance declined.

Urban popular education was then revived by members of the Workers' Party when in 1898, in the centenary of the patriotic poet Mickiewicz, a society for the special extension of science to the working class was formed, the *Societe de l'Universite Populaire du nom Mickiewicz*, at Krakow and Leopol. Though founded by a political party it was not sectarian in spirit and included a number of university lecturers on its administrative council. The society was self-financing with each society member paying a small quarterly fee for which he obtained free entry to all classes. Non-members paid ten centimes per class and tickets for the series at reduced prices were distributed to workers.

Classes were well supported. Koslowski claimed that in Krakow 1899–1900 there were 123 classes with 16,860 students, averaging 136 per class, with 600 maximum and twenty-eight minimum attendance. He also instanced a course at Krakow on the French Revolution that attracted 600 members (Ibid.: 840). 'Objective knowledge' however, was equally important and an instrument known as the 'sciopticon' was used for classes in physics and chemistry. Generally, discussion classes were arranged after the course had finished. The society also held a number of musical concerts, which attracted 600 people. In Leopol the activity matched that of Krakow except more classes took place in outlying areas. Leopol introduced 'Cors Universels' in the evenings, on the same lines as the popular university, a year after the society was formed. In smaller towns local committees were established to run similar courses; these dealt with technical matters and sent delegates to the committees at Krakow and Leopol. In 1898 Posnanie founded a similar association called the *Societe des conferences populaires du nom de Mickiewicz*, to which there was free entrance on Sunday afternoons and lectures were given voluntarily (Picavet, 1901: 86). At Varsorie infrequent classes were held at the museum but had to pass the censorship of police and the Russian Minister of Public Instruction at St Petersburg.

The Krakow committee produced a bulletin to direct the lectures and facilitate instruction called 'Conception du Monde' which contained the theoretical underpinnings and practical principles of Polish popular education, the whole forming, says Koslowski, a philosophy of life. Here then was a kind of non-formal university extension, which was politically based in the workers' movement and perhaps closer in spirit to the French *universités populaires*. The socialist movement perhaps ignored the name of extension chose instead the cultural name of Mickiewicz to indicate its patriotic orientation. Koslowski's account however fails to mention that in the Russian sector secret educational circles for women had begun as early as 1883. From these came the (already noted) engagingly named 'Flying

265

University' in 1886, which in 1906 became the Association for Scientific Courses (ASC) (Stelmaszuk, 1994).

From these underground organisations emerged another remarkable woman, Helena Radlinska (1879–1954) who later pioneered the understanding of the history and theory of adult education. Like Dziubinska, Radlinska was from the small Polish intellectual elite and her parents lived in Paris. She was widely travelled and participated in various international adult education and social work conferences including the WAAE. She admired the Danish folk high schools and campaigned for them to be established in Poland but much of her experience was gained in Peoples' University in Krakow. In Warsaw she joined with other academics including Ludwik Krzywicki the sociologist in forming the Free University of Poland (FUP) in 1919 which emerged from the ASC. This had a 'spiritual' connection to other free universities in Europe such as those in Belgium, France and Germany which were largely Protestant, Masonic or anarchist (or all three) in origin and like them aimed at students from rural and working class families.

The FUP established the first Polish School of Adult Education and Social Work in 1924 of which Radlinska was appointed head, remaining in post until 1944. The School was notably secular in character in which Radlinska created a well-theorised concept of adult education and, it was claimed, was instrumental in shaping new generation of Polish intelligentsia. Krzywicki lectured on social development at a time when sociology was only just receiving academic recognition and offered Sunday lectures from 1919, which were especially popular with teachers who lacked the necessary academic qualifications for university. Kornilowicz studied voluntary educational circles among industrial workers following the examples of self-improvement movement based on co-operatives in England and became a founder of the Polish section of the World Association for Adult Education (WAAE). As for the participants in the School they were young, mostly in their late twenties, the men were from the rural districts and the women largely from the intelligentsia: 484 students completed their studies by 1936.

Radlinska went on to hold the first chair of Theory and History of Adult Education in 1927. For her, 'adult education' meant the dissemination of cultural values which should serve as the basis for personal and social development, aiming at the formation of creative and active dispositions among students. Although interested in Grundtvig, unlike him she was convinced of the value of book learning, the habit of reading and especially libraries, which she saw as 'schools of citizenship' (Thomas and Elsey, 1985: 503). But she also maintained that adult education could not in itself remedy all social ills and had to be founded on a basis of universal, free primary education and a developed system of social welfare that could sustain the minimum conditions for individuals to develop.

Polish popular education was therefore uniquely progressive in number of ways. The leading role played by women from the intellectual elite significantly mediated the patriarchal tone of traditional Polish society. Similarly the leading role taken by the workers' movements in establishing a form of university extension gave nationalism a distinct class basis. The popular universities developed the idea of social science as a progressive popular mode of analysis which in turn contributed to the high reputation of Polish academic sociology (whose best know current representative is probably the increasingly respected public intellectual, Zigmund Bauman). However the rural folk high schools movement was seriously limited by its friction with the conservative Catholicism of the villages, which it was ultimately unsuccessful in challenging for local hegemony.

Russia and the Baltic States

No clearer example of the fear of popular education as a threat to the old regime exists, than in the case of Czarist Russia. Political suspicion of educational 'subversion' was so widespread that voluntary associations of all persuasions were closely scrutinised and universities were forbidden to undertake anything under the name of 'extension'.

A contemporary account of the political difficulties facing popular educators in Russia was given by Vinogradoff, formerly Professor of History at Moscow University, in the *University Extension Journal* of 1902 (p.19). Despite some brave early attempts, he wrote, extension as practised in England was quickly suppressed by the authorities. Instead university intellectuals had created a 'Home Reading Organisation' in which a form of extension was smuggled in by the back door. Although many professors were keen to be involved, formal connection with the university was forbidden and: 'even detached lectures are considered by the ruling bureaucracy as a kind of violent poison' (Ibid.). Nevertheless the most energetic of the university liberals persisted, 'in spite of endless worry and obstruction on the part of educational and police authorities' (Ibid.). One example was a scheme started in St. Petersburg to supplement the deficiencies of the secondary system by lectures and a number of centres were opened in the capital but, although the work was immensely successful, it was abruptly terminated by order of the Ministry of Public Instruction. Similarly when a new Pedagogical Society connected with the University of Moscow petitioned for leave to carry on extension work, it was refused. Vinogradoff commented: 'This policy of the government in regard to one of the most self-evident needs of the people would alone be sufficient to show what part it is playing in Russia and in what state it is trying to keep the country' (Ibid.). With such inflexibility on the part of the authorities, the modest demands of university extension, in which the intellectuals may well have played a mediating role of class rapprochement, gave way to more energetic means of political modernisation shortly leading to the revolutionary movement of 1905.

Other popular educational activities in Russia noted in the English extension journals included the Sunday School movement of which M.Y. Abramoff had written two interesting pamphlets: *Sunday Schools in Russia* and *The Book for Adults*, both translated into English. The schools were designed for both adults and children who were unable to attend school during the week, to combat widespread rural illiteracy, the first of which were established in 1859, growing to 200 by 1860 and 1500 by 1905 with 89,000 students.

In the mid-1890s the universities had made tentative steps towards extension-type activities through a movement for 'objective knowledge'. It was led by Professor Protopoff from Odessa University who had visited England in 1894 to study extension methods. His report was approved by his university at the suggestion of the South

Russian Society for Scientific Research and a formal start was made in the autumn of 1895 (Protopoff, 1896). The programme followed the English model with two three month terms and lectures open to all ages and sexes and syllabuses were provided. The courses were mostly scientific in character and included physics, maths, chemistry, botany, bacteriology, zoology and anatomy, no doubt reflecting the Society's interests but also perhaps with an eye to the political situation. The committee had also hoped to offer courses in philosophy but they were a step too far. Fees were twenty roubles per term but teachers could attend for half-price and those who could not afford it were let in free. Anatomy, attracting over 350 students, was apparently the most popular subject, while average attendance in all subjects was over 200.

In his report on Russia to the 1900 Paris International Conference, Professor A. Vassilieff of the University of Kasan claimed that the first university extension courses in Russia of the English type were held in Kasan in 1895 by the Physical-Mathematics Society (Picavet, 1901: 87). These too were of the positivist, objective knowledge type centring on the subjects of philosophy of science, mechanics, astronomy, chemistry and meteorology. Vassilieff also emphasised their close modelling on English university extension, with six-lesson courses and printed syllabi. The courses attracted 765 students (from a population of 120,000) and a second equally successful series was organised in Spring 1896 and the following year the Society of Medicine of Kasan University organised courses on medicine over three semesters. Vassilieff also confirmed that in 1895 the Societies of Naturalists in Odessa and Kiev organised university courses for the public and added that 'higher' science courses had been given in St. Petersburg in 1896–1898. No doubt because of their isolated situation, the Russian extensionists were keen to see an International University Extension Bureau established in London or Paris to advise and encourage the cause in Europe.

Following the 1905 Revolution popular education managed to gain a foothold and national associations were formed including an all-Russia Congress of People's Universities in 1908 and the first all-Russian Congress of Popular Education in 1912. There is no evidence of interest in Grundtvig preceding 1917 and Danish folk high schools were not mentioned at either of these conferences. But the 'people's universities' bore no relation to Danish folk high schools. They seem to have fulfilled a dual function of, on the one hand, teaching general cultural education and natural sciences and on the other of Marxist political propaganda, causing constant conflicts with Czarist officials and all were destroyed by World War One. Following the Soviet Revolution of 1917, Holmann's important book on Danish folk high schools was translated and published in Russian in 1918 (under the name of Khol'man). But, after brief period of freedom, all non-Party educational institutions were outlawed until the 1980s. State institutions then concentrated on utilitarian programmes of literacy and academic upgrading of working class and vocational education.

The Baltic States and Popular Resistance to Russification

Strategically placed on the Baltic coast, Estonia suffered from intense pressure for Russification by the Czarist authorities. As in Poland oppression gave rise to many voluntary cultural and educational associations fostering the Estonian language and national culture. Folk high schools were first mentioned publicly by Jaan Tonisson in 1897, who suggested that such schools were established in rural areas for the preservation of language and culture, which confirms the pattern that the historic role of folk high schools in northern Europe was to rescue a traditional culture in the face of threats of modernisation and imperialism. After visiting Nordic countries, Tonisson published a book on folk high schools in 1910. Because of the historic Baltic Sea shipping routes, Estonia had long standing contacts with Nordic countries which were much visited by teachers, clergymen, writers and others and Estonian Nordic cooperation was developed through conferences in 1909 and 1917. Closest contact was with Sweden and Estonia's first folk high schools were established for its Swedish minority from where it spread to other regions. The first Swedish minority folk high school was opened in Birkas in 1920 followed by the first wholly *Virumaa* folk high school in Junda in 1925 and then in Ravila in 1930. Estonia's extensive popular education network, built up between the wars was, however, destroyed by the Soviet invasion and incorporation into the USSR.

Modern popular adult education begins in Latvia in the early nineteenth century, then also under imperial Russian rule. There was a much higher literacy rate than Russia and a thriving periodical and book publishing industry which combined with voluntary educational circles, clubs and associations for an adult population eager to learn its own language and culture. Latvia had long standing relations with Denmark and many Danish works were translated. Discussions about Danish folk high schools as well as English university extension took place between liberal intellectuals before World War One with the English model gaining predominance after the war, when Latvia gained independence. In 1911 the Latvian Educational Association proposed establishing two folk high schools but the Russian authorities refused to accept their curriculum. The first 'people's university' was established in Riga only in 1920 along English university extension lines followed by others set up by legislation in Liepaja, Valmiera, Valka and Jelgava. All were banned in 1939 following the Soviet occupation.

The first Grundtvig-inspired folk high school, the Murmuiza Folk University was established, later, in response to flight of young people from villages to cities post 1920, in 1930 by Paul Peterson (who also greatly admired the Indian poet and educator, Rabindranath Tagore). Murmuiza was not however residential and operated on a daily basis, housing a large library and lecture hall which held 200 students. Although there was some state subsidy, it depended largely on voluntary tuition. This included lectures by Zenta Muarina, the first Latvian doctor of philology, who although confined to a wheelchair through polio, gave lectures on literature, ethics and aesthetics over ten years and introduced many prominent artists to the students. Other subjects on the curriculum included gardening, housekeeping, geography and education. It was closed in 1940, although students continued to meet privately and Peterson was deported to Siberia for ten years. Under *perestroika* it was gloriously opened in 1988. Karlis Ulmanis, the first President of the newly independent Latvia took up the slogan 'Back to the Soil!' and his national appeal went: 'Father and mothers, if you want to keep your children at home, send them to the People's University where they will learn what is good and what is

271

not, what is beautiful and what makes them healthy' (quoted in Kulich, 2002b: 132).

Despite bans on Lithuanian schools and native language publishing by the Russian authorities, secret societies continued with educational projects. These were legalised after 1904 when the publishing ban was lifted and Lithuanian was allowed to be taught. Some liberal intellectuals also established evening and Sunday schools for workers and tradesmen but it was only after independence in 1918 that popular education expanded with state support. Grundtvig's ideas had been made know by J. Gabrys in his book *Education of youth abroad and in our country* (1906) and people's universities were established between the wars, based more on the Austrian and German *Volkshochschule* model than English university extension. Again all were closed or turned into propaganda vehicles after 1940 when Lithuania's brief independence was terminated and the country was incorporated into the Soviet Union.

The Balkan States

Popular education in the Balkans during the nineteenth century suffered from both widespread poverty and instability caused by endemic war and Ottoman expansion. As elsewhere groups of liberal university intellectuals attempted to provide popular lectures and schools for workers and rural movements themselves created educational provision. The Bulgarian National Revival had begun during the eighteenth century with the establishment of secular school under school boards, the development of natural and social sciences, books and newspapers and reading clubs. The role of exiles in the formation of Bulgarian cultural centres especially those in Constantinople and Prague was most important. The Bulgarian Learned Society (BLS) was formed at end of Turkish rule in 1869 until 1911 when it was reorganised and transformed into the Bulgarian Academy of Sciences. It was initiated by Vassil Soyanov and Marin Drinov after study in Prague and contact with Czech scientific and cultural societies originally in Braila, Romania, with the object of spreading 'universal enlightenment among the Bulgarian people through language literature and history' and 'dissemination of general enlightenment among the people', mainly through the periodical journal of the BLS and other publications (Hristov, 1988: 336). It was supported by voluntary contributions from widely different classes and covered a broad range of scientific educational and practical issues but its activities were forcibly discontinued in 1876 and it moved to Sofia in 1878.

Reports of university extension type activity in the English journals are minimal. In Germany, Keilhacker noted that extension-type courses were introduced into Sofia, Bulgaria during the second half of the 1914–1918 war with the specific, if not especially laudable, intention of making Austrian and Hungarian culture better known and thus strengthening the military alliance (Keilhacker, 1929: 111–12). M. Demchevsky's contribution to the WAAE *International Handbook* claimed the origins of adult education were in associations called *Chitalishta* which sought political liberation from the Turks and religious liberation from Greek Orthodoxy. They were voluntary and spontaneous origin and growth and 1984 of these institutions by 1929 existed. In what appears to be a form of university extension, the Free University for Political and Economic subjects was founded in 1920–1921 for men and women over twenty-one with Gymnasium education but no other institution was mentioned (WAAE, 1929: 41–5).

In Romania popular adult education opens up during the period of modern cultural awakening in the early nineteenth century, largely through French educated intellectuals who returned home with enlightenment ideas. The Romanian Academy, established in 1867, was preceded by several literary and cultural societies aimed at national cultural development such as the *Soceitatea Literaria* in Wallachia 1821 while the leader of the Wallachian national movement, Ioan Campineau, had established the *Soietatea pentru Invatatura Poporului Roman* in the late 1830s for 'the cultural advancement of the Romanian people as a whole' (Bodea, 1988: 341). Romanian students educated in Paris had attempted to set up a Society for the Cultural Advancement of the Romanian People but were forcibly prevented by Russian and Austrian authorities.

Nicolae Balcescu's leadership of liberal youth marked a new phase in Romanian national movements. In 1843 he founded a new

Literary Society, with the published aim of promoting the advancement of language and history, but actually as a cover for the underground 'Brotherhood'. This evolved into the Romanian Academy, the first all Romanian institution, in 1879. Cultural associations, such the Transylvanian Association for the Advancement and Culture of the Romanian People, *Astra* in 1861, the *Junimea* and *Fratia* in Moldavia and *Valahia* and *Athenee*, developed significant educational activities. These sponsored grants for students and publications but were rather conservative in tone and hardly popular, favouring the Latinist etymological trend over the vernacular. They were encouraged by the leading enlightenment figure, Spiru Haret, who was Minster of Education at various times after unification in 1859. Haret also understood, 'like Grundtvig, that formal academic education is not enough and that a large process of "popular education" should also be realised if a country was supposed to make progress' (quoted in Kulich, 2002b). As a result, especially in the villages, he used the priests and the teachers to initiate popular education. The Romanian Athenaeum Society, formed in 1865 for further basic education and cultural and scientific dissemination created in turn the Society for the Education of the Romanian People with various types of basic, vocational, commercial and teacher training schools. The *Casa Scoalelor* (1896) was the first specifically adult education institution, which set up village libraries and recruited leading literary figures and cultural circles that researched ethnography and folklore.

The Romanian Social Institute (RSI) led to the Bucharest School of Sociology, founded by Dimitire Gusti, which developed a flourishing school of empirical sociology and was centred on activities at the village and peasant's cultural level. Gusti assumed, in the spirit of positivist enquiry we have widely noted, that empirical study should precede all reforms. He was also familiar with Grundtvig's ideas and wondered:

> whether in Romania such higher schools for peasants could be created, according to Grundtvig's model, without blindly imitating the latter but turning it into a specific Romanian schools, adapted to the real needs of the Romanian peasants and villages, designed to meet national and state demands characteristic only of Romanian rural society' (quoted in Paun, 1985: 101).

Gusti is also reported to have remarked, somewhat quirkily, 'Here I am to create a new breed of people, like me, looking like me' (Ibid.). Practically, he organised teams of students to work among the peasants in 1935 and inspired or founded peasant's higher schools, which were usually residential with small farms attached for practical instruction, spiritual, scientific and artistic education. Some also trained leaders for village clubs, librarians, projectionists and lecturers, taking their theoretical underpinning from the work of Leon Topa, whose book based on research into rural needs, called *The Peasant University Theory and Practice* was published in 1935 in Cernauti (Thomas and Elsey, 1985: 606).

In his only contribution to the 1900 Paris conference, M. Xenapol, Rector of Jassy University, Romania, echoed Gusti's approach claiming that university extension took the ideas formed by the elite to the masses and raised the masses up to civilisation (Picavet, 1901: 135). This one-sided, if apparently assured, reading of extension pedagogy certainly missed out any dialogic qualities it may have been developing but may well have reflected the views of its more conservative members. The first people's university was founded in 1908 at Valenii de Munte, the moving force being Nicolae Iorga a professor at the university of Bucharest who was well-aware of Grundtvig, although this was an evening adult education institute rather than a folk high school. Later People's Universities evolved from the former institutes which practised a more systematic from of adult education, the best known of which was the summer university at Valenii de Munte (county of Prahova) in 1922. Paun makes the important theoretical observation that:

> in most cases practices (i.e. institutional) in the field of adult education preceded theoretical conceptualisations. Ideas about adult education were most often implicit, being stated in the practical activities of the respective institutions. Most of these ideas were closely linked to the assertion of national, cultural and egalitarian ideals' (and) 'a more rigorous psycho-pedagogical perspective crystallised later on' (Paun, 1992: 98).

As we have seen this understanding could well apply to the rest of Eastern and Central Europe, if not more widely.

In the former Yugoslavia, the total absence of universities made extension impossible until the twentieth century. However, in 1907

The People's University of Zagreb was founded on the initiative of Dr Albert Bazala, an assistant professor at the University of Zagreb (Jug, 1994). This was intended as a reflection of the English university extension movement in 'science outside the walls'. Because of problems in obtaining a permit from the authorities, courses did not begin until 1912 and were then interrupted in 1916 by the onset of World War One. Several series of six week courses along English lines were held and following the 1918 armistice, Bazala was once again able to recommence provision. He also published the first journal devoted to 'folk universities and high school extension', an interesting mingling of the forms of the two predominant European streams. The People's University of Zagreb thrived between the world wars as the centre of educational and cultural life of Zagreb, receiving many distinguished international lecturers. It continued to hold courses, on a much reduced but still independent basis, even into World War Two but eventually seems to have been absorbed into the Tito government's educational structures in 1954. There appear to have been other 'people's universities' but, except for the Belgrade 'extension', they are not named. Jug suggests that ideas of university extension were probably introduced into the former Yugoslav states by students who had, in the absence of domestic universities, studied in Vienna, Prague and Graz (Jug, 1992) – the first university in Slovenia itself was not opened until after World War One. Thus university extension in the Balkan states was almost certainly inflected by its German expression, although as in the case of Czechoslovakia exiles returning from the United States may have added a New World experience.

Jug also shows that Slovenia had a tradition of adult education which was coterminous with the rise of Slovenian nationalism in the eighteenth and nineteenth centuries (Ibid.). He notes three kinds of popular adult educational activities, although these are perhaps loosely defined. The first was the literary salon of Baron Zig Zois a patron of artistic and scientific activities which appears to have been central to establishing Slovenian as a literary language. There was also 'a completely utilitarian trend' of professional schools for adults, for example, miners, surgeons, metal workers and farmers. The third stream is what Jug describes as 'autochthonous folk creations of predominantly anonymous authors', the *Bukovniks*, who wrote dialect stories from the oral tradition for the rural population. Jug presents this interesting melange of the elite, professional and folk elements of an adult educational tradition as a site of class collaboration in the national interest.

Long traditions of adult education, which assumed more modern forms in the late nineteenth century, are also reported in other Balkan states including Montenegro (Delibasic, 1991). Here, in the absence of universities, the Montenegrin government held courses of people's education and professional training. Institutions mentioned as involved in adult education between the world wars included, political parties, welfare organisations, cultural-artistic societies, libraries and bookstores, civic centres and people's universities. The state's role in this was limited to making proclamations and financing teachers for certain schools, then as in other parts of the former Yugoslavia, Tito's government incorporated much independent adult education into a formal state structure in order, 'to overcome the people's cultural and educational backwardness and to awaken its spirituality on new foundations' (Ibid.). Despite the rhetoric, a very substantial system of adult education, which included people's and workers' universities, was formed under the Communist state which in Montenegro, at least, had engaged nearly one third of the population in one form or another.

The glories of its classical civilisation long buried under Ottoman occupation, modern Greece had to fight for its independence, a conflict that took the lives of many of its young people and, intoxicated by its heroic struggle, that of the British Romantic poet Lord Byron. It evolved piecemeal over the century and the driving force in popular education was the desire to 'heal a broken nation' (Boucouvalas, 1988). A National Library was founded in 1828 and by the mid-nineteenth century further cultural and educational societies were created by voluntary and private activity aiming to 're-Hellenise' the Greek population from Ottoman rule. Learned Societies especially those concerned with archaeology also developed during this period. The Society of Friends of Education did the same for 'free' Greece in 1836 and the Parnassus Literary Society in 1865 was founded 'to raise the people's standard of culture and civilisation' (Ibid.). A further Society of the Friends of the People was established in Athens in 1862 with a library, courses and a publishing company to give the working classes a grounding in the sciences, by Aristidis Economou a Greek (probably masonic) positivist influenced by Fourier and Mazzini

(Vergidis, 1992). This was followed by the Society for the Promotion of Greek Education in 1869.

The position of women and workers also received some attention. A Women's Cultural Association in 1871 promoted education for working women and a Poor Women's Workshop developed 'home industries' such as dressmaking and sewing. The Greek Woman's Cultural Association in 1910 aimed to raise the cultural level of women, with lectures and discussions, cultural excursions, exhibitions, concerts and literary gatherings and included evening classes for illiterate mothers. The Association for the Dissemination of Useful Books in 1899 included lectures for women from the 'leisured class'. An Industrial and Artisan Society of Athens for technical education was established in 1892 and the Greek Labour and Socialist Movement, formed in 1870 only later attempted more systematic education for its members. In 1909 in Thessaloniki, the Socialist Federation and Socialist Youth Association held evening classes in science, literature and socialism. The Labour Centre Sunday School in Athens in 1911 organised classes for workers in the sociology of work, religion, hygiene, social economy, labour history and physics and held literacy classes for women.

Boucouvalas summarises Greek popular education during this period as consisting of three tendencies: firstly the promotion of libraries; secondly, efforts to raise the social, cultural and intellectual knowledge of masses and thirdly, learned societies and special interest groups. Nevertheless, the problems of rural poverty, the lack of industrialisation and the country's halting recovery from centuries of foreign occupation contributed to inhibiting the overall national popular development.

Chapter 11
Conclusion: The Fall and Rise of Popular Educational Movements

If the examples of the Balkans, can be taken as characteristic of the region as a whole, popular adult education was clearly closely tied to national, cultural and professional aspirations. A national language and literature and concern for history were frequently constructed within élite groups to articulate unity while the professional training for the rising middle-class gave functional skills. Simultaneously, the notion of the *Volk* complete with its own rural wisdom and learning was constructed, significantly, at precisely the moment the folk oral tradition was collapsing. The *Volk* was then largely a production of educated patriots who poured the volatile material of peasant life, folk story and legend into the written mould, where it was cast solid under the name of the 'nation' in much the same way as in other European countries. Although this is not 'extension as we know it', perhaps, the willingness of scholars to stretch the net of 'adult education' to incorporate these phenomena in such an unorthodox way reveals the usually hidden narrative of more orthodox accounts. Seen from this angle, 'adult education', although analytically separable, is actually a sign within the system of European nationalism. It appears to denote a series of activities which construct a form of national selfhood within a modern polity in which, though some separation of the estates is visible – the folk to their 'wisdom', the intellectual élite to their 'literature' and the middle class to their 'professions' – a new state of affairs based on geographic boundaries and linguistic identity and with some degree of democracy and justice (more marked in northern Europe) is desirable. The creation of a triad of subject areas in extension-type popular education supports this: science and 'objective knowledge' – which in some of the more progressive courses becomes social science; history, which becomes the narrative of the 'nation' and of rupture; and literature, which becomes the 'genius' of the language and the 'expression' of the people, exclusively conceived.

Beyond this triad lurks the functional and vocational education of the emergent professional classes, especially the crucial mediators of the new articulations, the teachers.

Finally there are the aspirations of the organised working class to political power, or at least some form of just and democratic incorporation of its most skilled sections into the new form of nation state. This, the most potentially dangerous element of popular education, is closely monitored and fostered by the university intellectuals themselves. This is not so much an interpretation of workers' inchoate demands as perhaps a recasting of the language of proletarian liberation into more 'realistic' objectives linked to the intellectuals own vocational aspirations as a group (Gouldner, 1985). Nor is it simply manipulation of workers' aspirations, though it is partly that, but a close system of negotiations in specific circumstances in which apparently differing objectives surface according to locality and time. In much of European extension workers and intellectuals aspirations appear occasionally to fuse into a system of liberatory knowledges out of which new political initiatives emerge and become materialised. This may be overstating the case. However the relationship is cast, it is clear that in many European states extension was viewed, and occasionally feared, as a reforming if not revolutionary alliance between the intellectuals and the 'people' which led to the modernising of the political state.

By the World War Two, the fate of much popular education was to be absorbed into state regulated provision such as the Responsible Body status in Britain and the various state funded provision in Europe, or captured (and frequently) closed by political movements such as Communism and Nazism. It has been argued that the expansion of education at all levels, primary, secondary and now higher, has made popular educational movements redundant. However the emergence of new social movements over the last three decades involved in issues such as feminism, ecology, peace, disability and currently Third World debt, anti-globalisation and anti-war have questioned this. Equally the functionalist and vocationalist spin put on much state-sponsored adult education has evacuated it of the meaningful personal, cultural development and radical social purpose, which is sorely needed. How far then might reflection on the radical traditions of popular education between the revolutions of 1848 and

World War Two inform the new social movements and contain potential for a renewed radical, critical and above all popular adult education?

Old Europe and New World: Citizenship and Globalisation

Perhaps we should begin by looking at where we are now. Hardt and Negri's book *Empire* (2000) caused a stir on the jaundiced Left when it was published in the millennium year. Indeed it was millenarian in its implications. For Hardt and Negri, this is the golden age of the Left, not its defeat. Despite the unravelling of nation-state systems of power, globalisation is not just about deregulating markets, but is actually a supranational order of interlocking regulations or 'empire'. It is an epochally original phenomenon, a Foucaldian, diffuse and anonymous network that cannot be monitored from metropolitan control centres, for which conventional Marxist analyses are wholly anachronistic. The old dichotomies of ruling class/proletariat, core/periphery are now broken down into an intricate pattern of inequality, a volatile totality that transgresses inherited divisions of political thought.

This new historical order, for Hardt and Negri is based on the classical tripartite order of the 'monarchy' of US nuclear supremacy, the 'aristocracy' of G7 wealth and the 'democracy' of the Internet. The iconoclasm of their approach rests on the proposition that Empire rose *not* through the defeat of systemic challenges to capital, but because of the success of heroic mass struggles that shattered the old Eurocentric regime of national states and colonialism. Now the increasing importance of intellectual labour in high value added sectors is shaping a new collective labourer, in the Marxist sense, with acutely potential subversiveness. This new productive force displays a plebeian desire for emancipation through increasing malleability of social relations and permeability of borders. But conservative forces frustrate this desire: the functioning ideology of Empire is a supple, multicultural aesthetic that actually deactivates revolutionary potential.

Hardt and Negri argue that academic theorists of multiculturalism, far from subverting hegemonic relations as they imagine, actually serve the interests of hegemonic inclusion. Similarly NGOs, the white hope of liberalism, are not necessarily the resistance agencies of civil society, but mobilise support for 'humanitarian' intervention. But is Empire a coherent legal structure or a permanent state of emergency? Balakrishnan (2000) argues that Hardt and Negri seem to want it both ways. They deny it is a specifically American empire because sovereignty has no purchase, any power or decision-making centre. Empire, on the contrary, is brought about by the 'multitude', a collective subject (but not yet 'for itself' in the Hegelian sense).

Negri's position seems to be derived from his 1970s autonomist position when he abandoned the working class as revolutionary agent but turned, via a reading of Marx's *Grundrisse,* to the 'dispossessed' and 'disaffected'. There is, he argues, a new collective worker taking shape that rejects politics as a strategic field for a pervasive, diffuse, popular desire for liberation. Although local rebellions may not connect globally or strategically, they can become immediate media events and attack the virtual centre vertically, making Empire permanently vulnerable to marginal but highly publicised events. Empire is Debord's 'society of the spectacle', seemingly powered by the pursuit of happiness, but actually based on mobilisation of desires that are intimately related to fear of failure, exclusion and loneliness. The masses no longer need Machiavelli's Prince or *any* leader but immediate, if episodic, empowerment. They are hostile to borders and restrictions on cosmopolitan freedom: 'the general right to control its own movement is the multitude's ultimate demand for global citizenship'. But who will guarantee this right if there are no global or international regulatory institutions?

But others argue there are reasons to view Empire as simply a new form of the old American imperialism. Under the new National Security Strategy announced in September 2002, no comparable power to the US is now tolerated, which is supported by the doctrine of 'pre-emptive war', of which Iraq is the first 'beneficiary'. The consequences of the new doctrine are far reaching. Key to this, as Chomsky has maintained frequently, is that the US public is kept on permanent alert to potential threats, real or imagined by the 'War on

Terror' (Chomsky, 2006). Its definition however, only causes problems:

> To take one of these official definitions, terrorism is 'the calculated use of violence or threat of violence to attain goals that are political, religious, or ideological in nature [...] through intimidation, coercion, or instilling fear,' typically targeting civilians. The British government's definition is about the same: 'Terrorism is the use, or threat, of action which is violent, damaging or disrupting, and is intended to influence the government or intimidate the public and is for the purpose of advancing a political, religious, or ideological cause.' These definitions seem fairly clear and close to ordinary usage. There also seems to be general agreement that they are appropriate when discussing the terrorism of enemies [...] But a problem at once arises. These definitions yield an entirely unacceptable consequence: it follows that the US is a leading terrorist state (Ibid.).

America's huge new Department of Homeland Security threatens domestic civil liberties and recasts citizenship in authoritarian ways around patriotic obedience rather than individual or group freedoms, although, cynically, protection of the latter is given as the reason for suspending them. Suppression of dissent is achieved also by ideological massification, the 'War on Terror' serving as a blanket for invasion of privacy and silencing criticism.

The external complement to this policy of internal containment was already signalled by the Bush government's readiness to withdraw from international agreements when they do not suit US strategic interests and strategic retreat from Internationalism. Already the signs of this change are obvious: the downgrading of the UN as a forum for the solution of international problems and international peacekeeper; the promotion of generic American commercial interests over internationally agreed ecological treaties, such as the Kyoto Protocol; the refusal to submit to key aspects of International Law (one of the great post-World War Two signs of progress that energised Habermas's generation) that limited power of states and immunity from prosecution. The threats to global citizenship of these changes are also clear: a reassertion of national interest over global agreements, weakening of moves toward global rule of law and the reassertion of brute force as solution for international disagreement. These are hardly the messages of optimism that the young Habermas and his fellow students found in the American-supported advances to international regulation that succeeded World War Two.

US foreign policy is enormously unpopular. This is the natural consequence of economic policies that impoverish 'developing' countries through the enormous debts generated by the Neoliberal reconstruction of failing economies through the American dominated International Monetary Fund. The US is also widely perceived as propping up unpopular regimes, in Asia and Latin America, and siding in ethnic and religious conflicts, as crucially with Israel in Palestine (the two state solution merely confirming the dispossession of the Palestinian people).

The New(ish) Social Movements

American exceptionalism in global terms is as major concern as the impact of various kinds of religious fundamentalism (some of which also emanate from the US). The paradox of the global dominance of American corporate capitalism is that the liberal values of the Constitution and the democratic impulse of the Puritan Founding Fathers are also rhetorically present as justification. The Bush regime can defend its invasion and destruction of other sovereign nations through the language of democracy and an appeal to 'the People' despite the fact the intention is to promote American strategic interests.

However, the US has also been the source of many of the radical movements that have altered the texture of everyday life: the women's movement, the black consciousness movement, the gay pride movement and disability groups have all developed into significant social forces and created global popular literatures in the US. Despite the enormous ideological leverage that neoconservative regimes are able to mobilise through the popular media, there is clearly a radical *otherness* in American society, which has its roots in the freedoms guaranteed by the Constitution. The same freedoms, particularly of the press and of information, can also question the massive corporate corruption that funds the regime, such as Enron for example. The speed of global communications, especially through the Internet, again originated in the US, does imply, as Hardt and Negri have maintained, the potential for truly global democratic movements, even if, as Habermas says, it is pervaded by digital parochialism.

Arguably, a commercially driven popular culture is also fuelling a demand for democracy in traditional or ethno-religious societies. A global youth culture fuelled by cheap cultural consumption goods such as fast food, clothes and music, subverts local patriarchal traditions and authoritarian norms. Liberal humanism and secular civil rights are carried by non-governmental organisations (NGOs) and movements to otherwise isolated and oppressed groups. Even the global prevalence of the English language means an unprecedented amount of information and, perhaps more importantly, radical democratic ideas are available.

As a consequence, anti-globalisation currents have flourished, of which the most acute are the growth of ethnicity and religion. Religious revivalism in the global South has replaced socialism as the leading anti-capitalist movement, but from an anti-progressive perspective. Islam is now the cutting edge of the fault line, due to historic resistance to Western imperialism and the warrior sect tradition of puritanical fundamentalism. As Mann notes, 'Combat Fundamentalism' is epitomised in the Palestine/Israel conflict where the poor South (and East) meet the affluent North (and West) and thrives on the consequences of Western economic exploitation (Mann, 2001). Ironically, regional fights against corrupt and authoritarian regimes are imaged as part of a global struggle of the faithful against the infidel, thereby giving cosmic significance to what are in fact local conflicts.

Such fundamentalisms may be already on the wane. Terrorist movements like al-Qaeda, Anderson maintains, are not so much the expression of the vigour of Islamic fundamentalism but a sign of its popular decline and marginalisation (Anderson, 2003: 13). If so, non-fundamentalist forms of cultural identity may emerge that are more conducive to democratic citizenship. Then the case for a separation of *ethnos* from *demos* in a form of representative government free from religious, ethnic or gender discrimination, but respecting local traditions, may be possible. The collective rights that Habermas talks about will have to be enshrined in a way that leaves individual freedom from group oppression unharmed (Habermas, 1999). Even the 'multitude' so dramatically interpellated by Hardt and Negri will need formal procedures and structures, if goodwill, neighbourliness and brotherhood are to be projected into global solidarity. If so, then social movements must embed many of the popular educational paradigms se have been reviewing.

Cosmopolitanism Revisited

It is an interesting paradox that America creates both the greatest threat to world citizenship, through its hyper power exceptionalism, yet produces some of the most creative thinking about it. Martha Nussbaum, a celebrated feminist theorist and Aristotelian philosopher from the Chicago School, over the past decade has strongly defended the liberal humanistic tradition in education in the face of pluralistic attacks upon it. She is not opposed to pluralism; on the contrary she believes that classical liberal humanism is *per se* pluralistic. But against extreme relativist tendencies she insists that all particular forms of humanity are underpinned by a *common humanity* which can itself be discovered through dialogue and analysis. Her fundamental position is that cultural traditions are not monolithic and unitary, but are subject to internal as well as external rational criticism:

> Since any living tradition is already a plurality and contains within itself aspects of resistance, criticism and contestation, the appeal to reason frequently does not require us to take a stand outside of the culture from which we begin. The Stoics are correct to find in all human beings the world over a capacity for critical searching and a love of truth [...] In this sense any and every human tradition is a tradition of reason (Nussbaum, 1997, 63).

To this extent we are 'fellow citizens in a community of reason', a community that the enlightened popular educators we have been investigating would have championed. Nussbaum recognises that we are necessarily historically and culturally located, but that if norms are human and historical and not immutable or eternal, then the search for rational justification of moral norms is not futile. She seems to operate with a kind of qualified universalism that shares neither the absolutist certainty of religious transcendentalism that believes in divinely given truth nor the absolute relativism of some versions of post-modernist identity politics that insist on the incommensurability of cultures.

Nussbaum takes the Enlightenment view that ethical enquiry requires encouraging a critical attitude to habits and conventions rather than unqualified acceptance of authority. This is enhanced by cross-cultural understanding, which removes the false air of naturalness and inevitability of our practices. The true basis for human association she finds in Aristotle is not any pre-existing cultural or religious 'identity', but what can be defended as 'good for human beings'. Hence the Stoics developed from Diogenes a critique of conventions and cross-cultural study to generate the idea of 'World Citizen' or *Kosmoi polités* as the centre of their educational program. They held that national, cultural and religious identities are for the most part an accident of birth and should not be seen as boundaries between people. The true moral community is humanity itself with its fundamental ingredients of reason and moral capacity (which becomes the source of Kant's 'kingdom of ends'). While loyalties based on non-rational cultural or religious identity are more open to manipulation by traditional (usually male) elites, nevertheless some form of local identity may be more desirable. The special love of nearest and dearest, for the Stoic emperor Marcus Aurelius, was preferable to an abstract equality of love. Even though locatedness or roots seems to be important for humanity, *closest* is not necessarily *best*. Hence Nussbaum recommends the project of the 'examined life', which can distinguish between what is merely parochial and what can be recommended to all.

Nussbaum insists that it is possible to recognise the virtuous life in all cultures and hence a common humanity. But local group loyalties frustrate world citizenship by neglecting commonalities and prioritising the identity of the group. While it is desirable that oppressed groups should find pride in their identity and deny the representations of them by the hegemonic culture, this cannot take an inflexible supremacist form which merely mirror images that of the oppressing group, a stance that makes it impossible to evaluate other groups with fairness and justice. The world citizen therefore has to be a 'sensitive and empathetic interpreter' cultivated through education.

World Citizenship Education

Nussbaum's recommendations, as a result of a wide scale survey of programs of multicultural education in American liberal arts colleges and universities, fit well into popular adult educational parameters. Firstly, education must be multicultural in the sense that it examines the fundamentals of all major religions and cultural groups. Secondly, it should demonstrate awareness of cultural difference accompanied by a critical understanding of one's own traditions, habits and conventions, with the capacity to question the 'inevitable naturalness' of our own ways. Thirdly, local identity should be explored through regional or group history, but in a global context. Finally, education should start early with stories of or from other traditions so that, by the time they encounter higher education, students are well equipped for the study of diversity, not simply as way of confirming the superiority of their own identity.

Not surprisingly, Nussbaum is suspicious of programs of multicultural education limited to uncritical recognition or celebration of differences, as if all cultural practices were morally neutral or legitimate. She prefers the term 'interculturalism' by contrast, which connotes a comparative searching for common human needs across cultures and of dissonance and critical dialogue within cultures. Such 'interculturalist' programs embrace a number of principles. First, they resist the impression of a 'marketplace' of cultures, each asserting its own claim. Second they emphasise the importance of imagination in crossing cultural boundaries and thinking oneself into the place of the other. Third, they acknowledge certain common human needs and last, they doubt the unqualified goodness of one's own ways through structured encounters with other cultures. Programs of education that attempt to enter into other cultures and seek their human core are an essential part of the 'examined life'.

Nussbaum here has contributed an important defence of liberal education that reflects many of the rational priorities articulated by older forms of while counteracting the problems of non-differential cultural unity. She recognises the strength of religious, national and local identities but appeals to the classically argued paradigm of cosmopolitanism. The insoluble problem of cultural identity is that while it may properly strengthen oppressed communities in their struggle with hegemonic forces, it may not protect individuals or minority groups within. As Bauman also notes, in a very rewarding short study of the idea of 'community', cultural distinction can often take more malignant forms than language, dress or ritual expression and may include practices such as female humiliation that cannot be made palatable simply because they are 'traditional'. Bauman comments:

> [W]e (western intellectuals) may be readier to accept that, as much as we should respect the right of a community to protection against assimilatory or atomizing forces administered by the state or the dominant culture, we must respect the right of individuals to protection against choice-denying or choice-preventing communal pressures (Bauman, 2001: 138).

Bauman, Habermas and Nussbaum all inhabit conceptual frameworks derived from classical, Enlightenment and to an extent Marxist thought, and in Nussbaum's case, feminist theory. Their engagement with current politics reflects a pessimistic distance from revolutionary socialism and a more or less qualified embrace of Western liberal traditions allied to the social-justice project of socialism and a post-colonial sensitivity to cultural difference.

Third World Popular Education Movements

But, the activist will argue it is fine for Western intellectuals to promote a pluralist liberal education from the security of their ivory towers, but what about those at the sharp end working with the desperate dispossessed? Here the post-war history of Third World liberation and especially Latin American popular educational movements may give some leads.

The struggles of colonialised countries for independence following World War Two were a defining feature of the history of the second half of the twentieth century. Many took their inspiration from the European national struggles we have been charting, indeed many of the nationalist leaders of the Indian and African movements were educated in Western institutions, Mahatma Gandhi in London and Julius Nyrere at Ruskin College, Oxford for example. Gandhi's Basic Education programme or *Nai telim* was one of the first authentic community development programmes that based itself in the life of the rural villages rather than the educational institutions of the towns (Steele and Taylor, 1995). Following Indian independence Gandhi became a beacon for the progressive young in the west and his ideas taken up with enthusiasm. Although community development could be viewed as another kind of 'deficit' educational perspective, it had the virtue of taking the needs of communities themselves seriously, rather than simply imposing ready-made educational packages. Even so, some of the newly independent nations rejected the paternalism implied and in Tanzania, for example, this led to its Ruskin College educated, Marxist president, Julius Nyrere, introducing the policy of *Ujamaa*, a kind of community-based approach to 'nation building' and rejection of imperialist imposed notions of community. Young adult educators from Britain and America flocked to the newly independent countries of Africa to be involved in these projects and returned, radicalised, to see how the ideas could be applied to their own inner city 'Hearts of Darkness'.

But without doubt the most influential popular educator has been Paulo Freire. Popular education in Latin America has for several decades been a source of inspiration for radicals. Because it is based on the transformational pedagogy of Paulo Freire, it is transparently political in its aims and has emanated from grass roots organisations. It is characterised by 'horizontal relationships' between educators and participants and is usually a response to a need expressed by organised groups as opposed to an off-the-shelf institutional programme. It involves the group in the organisation and training and desired political outcomes and places heavy reliance on the community and personal knowledge. At its best this process helps a community understand the nature of the oppression it is suffering and form strategies to overcome it using its own resources. John Hurst (1995) notes:

> Popular education is, at root, the empowerment of adults through democratically structured cooperative study and action, directed toward achieving more just and peaceful societies within a life sustaining global environment. Its

priority is ordinary people – the poor, the oppressed, and the disenfranchised people of the world – who comprise a majority of the world's population (Hurst, 1995).

The publication of Paulo Freire's two works the *Pedagogy of the Oppressed* (1972) and *Cultural Action for Freedom* (1972) in English and Spanish was a formative moment in global adult education. His approach drew on both Marxist and Christian traditions particularly the existentialist and humanist Marxism of Sartre and Fromm and the radical Christian humanism of Martin Büber. His attack on what he named 'banking' education of the schools in favour of a strategy of 'conscientization' literacy work that drew out and built on the learner's experience of oppression, introduced a radically new model and set of relations between educator and educated. This form of dialogism was to an extent familiar to those from the Mutual Improvement and IWCE traditions in Europe, where collective learning was uppermost and tutors were frequently drawn from the class members. However it created a new political terminology for framing literacy work within poor communities. Freire's pedagogical approach probably owed more to John Dewey's experimental pragmatism than Marxist dialectics and also to a profound Christian belief in (an almost mystical) personal transformation. But unlike most educational theorists, Freire's ideas were developed from his practical work as an adult educator, particularly in Brazil in the 1950s and early 1960s and later in exile in Guinea Bissau.

Smith picks out five especially significant aspects of his work: his emphasis on dialogue and collaboration in an informal educational situation; the need for education to enable oppressed people to change the world through their own actions or 'praxis' (a Marxist term); developing a transformed understanding of the nature of social and political oppression or 'conscientization'; centring on the experience of the learners rather than a standard book-led curriculum; lastly, Christian metaphors of redemption and transformation (Smith, 2005). One of the most engaging introductions to this process is Liam Kane's book *Popular Education and Social Change in America* (2002) which includes an in-depth look at one of the most successful social movements to use popular education, the Movements of Landless Rural Workers (MST) in Brazil, as well as wide-ranging theoretical and practical analyses. Freire has been so influential that even the CIA uses his methodology in its training manuals and 'empowerment' has become a term no government bureaucrat can fail to mouth with enthusiasm.

Despite this incorporation and political blunting, Freirean type popular education still has an important resonance. It says with absolute clarity that education begins with the needs of ordinary people both to understand and change their situation, that this process has to be seen to engage in political action and that it begins as did the popular education of the nineteenth century with a reconceptualisation of the self and community as agents for liberation through which the world can be changed for the better. The Enlightenment ideals of justice, equality and citizenship that animated nineteenth century radicals are as pertinent now as never before. The difference is that the forces that oppose them now also use the same language.

Bibliography

Abbreviations

UEJ is *University Extension Journal* (published by Cambridge University)
OUEG is *Oxford University Extension Gazette*

Unpublished Sources

Benchimol, Alex (2001) unpublished doctoral thesis, *Intellectual Formations in the Romantic Period: A Comparative Study of Cultural Politics and Social Criticism in the British Public Sphere, 1802–1832*. University of Glasgow.
Caldwell, T.B. (1962) unpublished doctoral thesis, *Workers' Education in France, 1890–1914*, University of Leeds.

Published Sources

Ahonen, Sirkka and Rantala, Jukka (eds) (2001) *Nordic Lights: Education for Nation and Civic Society in the Nordic Countries, 1850–2000*. Studia Fennica Historica, No.1. Helsinki: Finnish Literature Society.
Allardt, Erik, Friis, Erik J. and Wisti, Folmer (eds) (1981) *Nordic democracy: ideas, issues, and institutions in politics, economy, education, social and cultural affairs of Denmark, Finland, Iceland, Norway and Sweden.* Copenhagen: Det Danske Selskab
Allchin, A.M., Jasper, D., Schjorring, J.H., Stevenson, K. (eds) (1993) *Heritage and Prophecy Grundtvig and the English-Speaking World.* Aaarhus: Aarhus University Press.
Anderson, Benedict (1989) *Imagined Communities.* London: Verso.
Anderson, Perry (2002) Internationalism: a Breviary in *New Left Review* 14, second series March–April 2002, pp.5–25.

—— (2003) The Casuistries of War in *London Review of Books*, 25(5) 6 March 2003, pp.12–13.

Anon (2006) Johan Ludvig Runeberg. http://www.kirjasto.sci.fi/runeberg.htm, [Accessed July 2006].

Arvidson, Lars (1985) Anton Nyström in Thomas and Elsey (eds) *International Biography of Adult Education*, pp.467–8.

Auspitz, K. (1982) *The Radical Bourgeoisie The Ligue de l'enseignement and the Origins of the Third Republic 1866–1885*. London: Cambridge University Press.

Bacevich, A. (2002) *American Empire; The Realities and Consequences of US Diplomacy*. Cambridge, MA: Harvard University Press.

Balakrishnan, Gopal (2000) review of Hardt and Negri's *Empire* in *New Left Review*, 5, September/October 2000, pp.142–8.

Bauman, Zigmund (2001) *Community, Seeking Safety in an Insecure World*. Oxford: Polity Press.

Blobaum, Robert E. (2002) The 'woman question' in Russian Poland, 1900–1914, *Journal of Social History*, Summer, 2002 Available from: http://www.find articles.com/cf_dls/m2005/4_35/88583555/p10/article.jhtml?term=) [Accessed 3 June 2003].

Blom, J.C.H. and Lamberts, E. (eds) (1999) *History of the Low Countries*. translated by James C. Kennedy. New York; Oxford: Berghahn Books.

Bodea, Cornelia (1988) Precursors of the Romanian Academy (1867) in *East European Quarterly*, XXII, No.3 September 1988, pp.341–9.

Bookchin, Murray (1977) *The Spanish Anarchists: the Heroic Years, 1868–1936*. New York: Free Life; London: Wildwood House. Available from: http://www.english.uiuc.edu/maps/scw/ferrer.htm [Accessed 16 June 2005].

Boucouvalas, Marcie (1988) *Adult Education Greece*. Monographs on Comparative and Area Studies in Adult Education, Vancouver, Centre for Continuing Education, U.B.C.

Bowen, James (1981) *A History of Western Education Volume Three: The Modern West: Europe and the New World*. London: Methuen and Co Ltd.

Boyd, Carolyn P. (1976) The Anarchists and Education Spain, 1868–1909 in *Journal of Modern History*, Vol.48, No.4, On Demand Supplement (December 1976), pp.125–70.

—— (1997) *Historia Patria Politics, History and National Identity in Spain, 1875–1975*. Princeton, NJ: Princeton University Press.

Bugge, K.E. (1983) Grundtvig's Educational Ideas in (eds) Christian Thodberg and Anders Pontoppidan Thyssen (1983) *Tradition and Renewal*. Copenhagen: Det Dankse Selskab.

Calhoun, Craig (ed.) (1992) *Habermas and the Public Sphere*. Cambridge, MA: M.I.T. Press.

Chevallier, P. (1975) *Histoire de la Franc-Maçonnerie Française – La Maçonnerie: Église de la République (1877–1944)*. Paris: Fayard.

Chomsky, Noam (2006) War on Terror, Amnesty International Annual Lecture Hosted by Trinity College, Cambridge, 13 February 2006. Available at: http://www.zmag.org/content/showarticle.cfm?ItemID=9718 [Accessed 7 July 2006].

Condorcet, Jean-Antoine-Nicolas de Caritat, marquis de (1804) *Œoeuvres complètes de Condorcet*. Brunswick: chez Vieweg, chez Henrichs.

Croce, Benedetto (1934) *History of Europe in the Nineteenth Century*. London: George Allen and Unwin.

Davenport, Allen (1997) *The Life and Literary Pursuits of Allen Davenport*. Aldershot: Scolar Press.

Davie, G.E. (1964) *The Democratic Intellect*. Edinburgh: Edinburgh University Press.

de Vroom, Xandra (1992) Adaptation of an Educational Innovation: the introduction of university extension into the Netherlands, 1890–1920 in Hake and Marriott (eds), *Adult Education Between Cultures*, pp.43–60.

de Vroom, Xandra and Hake, Barry J. (1991) University extension in the Netherlands: The role of the 'Social Weekly' in the dissemination and adoption of ideas and practices in Friedenthal-Haase, et al. (eds) *British-Dutch-German Relationships*, pp.227–55.

Delibasic, Rade (1991) resumé, '100th Anniversary of Adult Education in Montenegro', Belgrade.

Destrée, Jules and Vandervelde, Emile (1903) *Le Socialisme en Belgique* (2nd edition). Paris: Giard & Brieve.

Donzelot, J. (1991) The Mobilization of Society in Graham Burchell et al. (eds) *The Foucault Effect*. London: Harvester, pp.169–79.

Drtina, Franz (1907) 'Die volkstumlichen Vortrage der bomischen Universitat in Prag', in Schultze and Hamdorff, *Archiv.*

Eley, Geoffrey (1992) Nations, Public and Political Cultures: Placing Habermas in the Nineteenth Century in Calhoun, Craig (1992) *Habermas and the Public Sphere*, Cambridge: M.I.T. Press, pp.290–339.

—— (2002) *Forging Democracy The History of the Left in Europe 1850–2000*. New York: Oxford University Press.

Elsdon, Konrad (2003) *Crisis of Opportunity Perspectives on Adult Education and Humanism*. Leicester: NIACE.

Elwitt, Sandford (1982) Education and the Social Question: The *Universités Populaires* in Late Nineteenth Century France, *History of Education Quarterly*, Spring, 1982, pp.55–69.

—— (1986) *The Third Republic Defended Bourgeois Reform in France, 1880–1914*. Baton Rouge and London: Louisiana State University Press.

Esdaile, Charles J. (2000) *Spain in the Liberal Age: from Constitution to Civil War, 1808–1939*. Oxford: Malden, MA: Blackwell Publishers.

Fabry, Katalin and Soós Pál (1986) Some Problems of the history and cultural policy of voluntarism in Katus and Toth (eds), *On Voluntary Organizations in Hungary and the Netherlands*, pp.67–73.

Fejto, François (1998) *Requiem für eine Monarchie*, Die Zaerschlagung Österreich–Ungarns: ÖBV.

Fidler, Geoffrey C. (1985) the *Escuela Moderna* Movement of Francis Ferrer in *History of Education Quarterly*, Vol.25, Nos.1 & 2, pp.103–32.

Filla, W., Gruber, E. and Jug, J. (1999) *Erwachsenenbildung in der Zwischenkriegszeit*. Wien: Studienverlag.

Flecha, Ramon (1990) Spanish Society and Adult Education in *International Journal of Lifelong Education* Vol.9, No.2, pp.99–108.

—— (1992) Spain in Jarvis (ed.) *Perspectives in Adult Education and Training in Europe*, pp.190–202.

Fleming, Marie (1979) *The Anarchist Way to Socialism, Elisée Reclus and Nineteenth Century European Anarchism*. New Jersey: Croom Helm.

Forchhammer, Henni (1900) University Extension in Demark, *UEJ*, March 1900, Vol.V, No.42, p.84.

Francis, Mark (1985) *The Viennese Enlightenment*. London: Croom Helm.

Friedenthal-Haase, Martha, Hake, Barry J., Marriott, Stuart (eds) (1991) *British-Dutch-German Relationships in Adult Education*. Leeds: Leeds Studies in Continuing Education, Cross-Cultural Studies in the Education of Adults, No.1.

Gerrans, A.E. (1895) A Norwegian on University Extension, *OUEG*, Vol.V, August 1895, p.113.

Gott, Richard (2003) *Cuba: a New History*. New Haven and London: Yale University Press.

Gouldner, Alvin W. (1985) *Against Fragmentation: the Origins of Marxism and the Sociology of Intellectuals*. New York; Oxford: Oxford University Press.

Great Britain, Ministry of Reconstruction, Adult Education Committee (1980) *The 1919 Report the Final and Interim Reports of the Adult Education Committee of the Ministry of Reconstruction*. Reprinted with introductory essays by Harold Wiltshire (et al.). Nottingham: Department of Adult Education, University of Nottingham.

Guereña, Jean-Louis (1996) Socialism and Education at the Beginning of the Twentieth Century: The Spanish *Casas del Pueblo* in a European perspective in Hake, Steele and Tiana (eds) *Masters, Missionaries and Militants*, pp.39–60.

Habermas, Jürgen (1989) *The Structural Transformation of the Public Sphere: an Inquiry into a Category of Bourgeois Society*. Translated by Thomas Burger with the assistance of Frederick Lawrence. Oxford: Polity.

—— (1999) The *Inclusion of the Other Studies in Political Theory*. Oxford: Polity Press.

Hake, Barry J. and Morgan, W. John (eds) (1989) *Adult Education, Public Information and Ideology: British-Dutch Perspectives on Theory, History and Practice*. Nottingham: Department of Adult Education, University of Nottingham.

Hake, Barry J. and Marriott, Stuart (eds) (1992) *Adult Education Between Cultures, Encounters and Identities in European Adult Education since 1890*. Leeds:

Leeds Studies in Continuing Education, Cross-Cultural Studies in the Education of Adults, No. 2.

Hake, Barry J., Steele, Tom and Tiana-Ferrer, Alexandro (eds) (1996) *Masters, Missionaries and Militants, Studies of Social Movements and Popular Education in Europe 1890–1939*. Leeds: Leeds Studies in Continuing Education, Cross–Cultural Studies in the Education of Adults, No. 4.

Hake, Barry J. and Steele, Tom (eds) (1998) *Intellectuals, Activists and Reformers: Studies of Social, Cultural and Educational Reform Movements 1890–1930*. Leeds: Leeds Studies in Continuing Education, Cross-Cultural Studies in the Education of Adults, No.5.

Hake, Barry J. and Both, Heili (1991) Cross-cultural influences and the origin of residential Adult Education in the Netherlands: The British and Scandinavian connections in Friedenthal-Haase, et al. *British-Dutch-German Relationships*, pp.177–209.

Hardt, M. and Negri, A. (2000) *Empire*. Cambridge, MA: Harvard University Press.

Hassel, Olga (1894) A Norwegian Account of University Extension, *OUEG*, Vol.IV, February 1894, p.63.

Hayward, J.E.S. (1961) The Cooperative Origins, Rise and Collapse of the *Universités populaires*, *Archive Internationale de Sociologie e la Cooperation*, January/June 1961, Vol.9, pp.3–17.

—— (1963) Educational Pressure Groups and the Indoctrination of the radical Ideology of Solidarism, 1895–1914, *International Review of Social History*, Vol.VIII, 1963, pp.1–17.

Headings, Muriel (1949) *French Freemasonry under the Third Republic*. Baltimore: John Hopkins Press.

Hennessy, Alistair (2005) Cuba's Longue Durée in *New Left Review* 31 Jan/Feb 2005, pp.145–52.

Herman, Arthur (2003) *The Scottish Enlightenment The Scots' Invention of the Modern World*. London: Fourth Estate.

Herman, Karel (1988) The Activities of the Scientific Societies of Bohemia and Slovakia in the Nineteenth Century and up to 1914 in *East European Quarterly*, Vol.XXII, No.3, September 1988, pp.321–31.

Hernandez Diaz, José María (1996) Social Catholicism and Education in Spain, 1891–1936, in Hake, Steele and Tiana (eds) *Masters, Missionaries and Militants*, pp.81–92.

Hill, Christopher (1965) *The Intellectual Origins of the English Revolution*. Oxford: Oxford University Press.

—— (1975) *The World Turned Upside Down*. Harmondsworth: Penguin Books.

—— (1979) *Milton and the English Revolution*. London: Faber and Faber Ltd.

Hirschkop, Ken (1999) *Mikhail Bakhtin an Aesthetic for Democracy*. Oxford: Oxford University Press.

Hobsbawm, Eric (1985) *The Age of Capital 1848–1875*. London: Abacus.

297

—— (1989) *The Age of Empire 1875–1914*. London: Abacus.

Hristov, Hristo (1988) Foundation and Activity of the Bulgarian Learned Society (1869–1911) in *East European Quarterly*, Vol.XXII, No.3, September 1988, pp.333–9.

Jacob, Margaret C. (1981) *The Radical Enlightenment Pantheists, Freemasons and Republicans*. London: George Allen and Unwin.

Jacobsen, Kim Morch (1981) Adult Education in the Nordic Countries in Allardt et al. (eds) *Nordic Democracy*, pp.465–94.

Jarvis, Peter (ed.) (1992) *Perspectives in Adult Education and Training in Europe*, Leicester: NIACE.

Jug, J. (1992) Personal correspondence, 6 March 1992 including 'Adult Education in Slovene Ethnic Territory 1750–1800', Belgrade 1991 (Dr Juri Jug of Maribor University, Slovenia cites two sources on university extension in the former Yugoslav territories: *80 godina Puckog–narodnod sveucilista grada Zagreba* (80 Years of People's national University in Zagreb Town), no author or date and Ranko N. Bulatovic, *Univerziteti za sve* (Universities for all) Belgrade, 1980).

Junco, José Alvarez and Shubert, Adrian (eds) (2000) *Spanish History since 1808*. London: Arnold.

Kane, Liam (2001) *Popular Education and Social Change in Latin America*. London: Latin America Bureau.

Kantasalmi, Kari (1996) The University and Popular Adult Education in Finland 1890–1930: A revisionist interpretation in Hake, Steele and Tiana (eds) *Masters, Missionaries and Militants*, pp.191–222.

Katus, J. and Toth, J. (eds) (1986) *On Voluntary Organizations in Hungary and the Netherlands*, Budapest: National Centre for Culture.

Keane, John (1995) *Tom Paine A Political Life*. London: Bloomsbury.

Keilhacker, Martin (1929) *Das Universitäts-Ausdehnungsproblem in Deutschland und Deutsch Österreich, dargestellt aufgrund der bisherigen Entwicklung*. Stuttgart.

Kolger, Ferdinand (1968) T.G. Masaryk's Contribution to Sociology in Rechcigl (ed.) *Czechoslovakia Past and Present*, pp.1526–39.

Korsgaard, Ove (2000) The Struggle for Enlightenment: Danish Adult Education during 500 years (English summary of *Kampen om Lyset, Dansk Voksen-oplysning Gennem 500 Ar*. (1997) Gyldendalske Boghandel og Nordisk Forlag A/S).

Kulich, Jindra (1985) University Level Adult education in East Europe in *International Journal of University Adult Education*, Vol.24, Nos.1–3, pp.135–52.

Kulich, Jindra (1997) Christen Kold, founder of the Danish folk high school: myth and reality in *International Journal of Lifelong Learning*, Vol.16, No.5, pp.439–53.

Kulich, Jindra (2002) *Grundtvig's Educational Ideas in Central and Eastern Europe and the Baltic States*, Copenhagen: Forlaget Vartov.

Lambert, P. (1963) *Studies in the Social Philosophy of Co-operation.* translated from French by Joseph Létargez and D Flanagan, Manchester: Co-operative Union Ltd, Manchester.

Lee, D.C. (1988) *The People's Universities of the USSR,* New York, Greenwood.

Levy, Carl (ed.) (1987) *Socialism and the Intelligentsia 1880–1914.* London and New York: Routledge & Kegan Paul.

Li, Solomon (1962) Francisco Giner de los Rios. Modern Educator of Spain in *History of Education Quarterly,* Vol.2, Issue 3 (September 1962), pp.168–81.

Liddington, Jill (2006) *Rebel Girls Their Fight for the Vote.* London: Virago.

Liddington, Jill and Norris, Jill (2000) *One Hand Tied Behind Us: The Rise of the Women's Suffrage Movement.* 2nd edition. London: Rivers Oram Press.

Lidtke, Vernon L. (1985) *The Alternative Culture: Socialist Labor in Imperial Germany.* New York, Oxford: Oxford University Press.

Lopez-Morillas, Juan (1981) *The Krausist Movement and Ideological Change in Spain.* Cambridge: Cambridge University Press.

Machotka, O. (1968) T.G. Masaryk as we see him today in Rechcigl (ed.), *Czechoslovakia Past and Present.* pp.1540–6.

MacIntyre, Alasdair (1987) The Idea of an Educated Public in Hirst, Paul (ed.) *Education and Values, The Richard Peters Lectures,* London: University of London, Institute of Education.

Mackinder, H.J. and Sadler, M.E. (1891) *University Extension, Past, Present, and Future.* London: Cassell.

Mann, M. (2001) Globalization and September 11, *New Left Review,* 12, November / December 2001, pp.51–72.

Maróti, Andor (1993) Adult Education in Hungary in *Convergence,* Vol.XXVI, No.3, 1993, pp.27–39.

Marriott, Stuart (1987) Un rôle sociale pour les universités ? Reactions françaises au mouvement d'extension des universités en Angleterre dans les années 1890s in Ueberschlag and Muller (eds) *Education Populaire,* pp.41–67.

Marriott, Stuart and Hake, Barry J. (eds) (1994) *Cultural and Intercultural Experiences in European Adult Education.* Leeds: Leeds Studies in Continuing Education, Cross-Cultural Studies in the Education of Adults, No.3.

Mercier, L. (1987) L'Université Populaire en France: une realité populaire in Ueberschlag and Muller (eds) *Education Populaire,* pp.167–77.

Miaso, Jozef (1981) Education and Social Structures in the Kingdom of Poland in the Second Half of the Nineteenth Century in *History of Education,* Vol.10, No.2, pp.101–9.

Moretti, Franco (1983) *Signs Taken for Wonders Essays in the Sociology of Literary Forms.* London: Verso.

Morton, A.L. (1976) *A People's History of England.* London: Lawrence and Wishart.

Negt, Oskar and Kluge, Alexander (1993) *Public Sphere and Experience Towards an Analysis of the Bourgeois and Proletarian Public Sphere.* Minneapolis: University of Minnesota Press.

Nussbaum, Martha C. (1997) *Cultivating Humanity, A Classical Defense of Reform in Liberal Education*. Cambridge, MA: Harvard University Press.

Paun, Emil (1992) Romania in Jarvis (ed.) *Perspectives in Adult Education*, pp.97–107.

Picavet, Francois (1901) *Congres international d'Enseignement superieur tenu a Paris du 30 juillet au 4 aout 1900*: proces-verbaux sommaires. Paris: Impr. nationale.

Picht, W. (1914) *Toynbee Hall and the English Settlement Movement*. London: G. Bell and Sons.

Pickering, M. (1993) *Auguste Comte, An Intellectual Biography*, Vol.1. Cambridge: Cambridge University Press.

Popper, Karl (1974) *Unended Quest an Intellectual Biography*. Glasgow: Fontana/ Collins.

Prothero, I. (1997) *Radical Artisans in England and France, 1830–1870*. London: Cambridge University Press.

Protopoff (1896) Russia in *University Extension Journal*, Vol.II, No.2, November 1896, p.19.

Rechcigl, Miloslav (ed.) (1968) *Czechoslovakia Past and Present*, Vol.2, The Hague: Published under the auspices of the Czechoslovak Society of Arts and Sciences in America, by Mouton.

Reinfeld, Barbara K. (1991) Masaryk and Havlicek in *East European Quarterly*, Vol.XVV, No.3, September 1988, pp.307–24.

Roberts, J.M. (2001) *Europe 1880–1945* (3rd edition). Harlow: Longman.

Rose, Jonathan (2001) *The Intellectual Life of the British Working Classes*. New Haven and London: Yale University Press.

Ross, Kristen (1988) *The Emergence of Social Space: Rimbaud and the Paris Commune*. Minneapolis: University of Minnesota Press.

Rowbotham, Sheila (1997) *A Century of Women*. London: Viking.

Schama, Simon (1977) *Patriots and Liberators: Revolution in the Netherlands, 1780–1813*. London: Collins.

Schultze, Ernst and Hamdorff, G. (1907) *Archiv fur das Volksbildungswesen aller Kulturvolker*. Hamburg.

Seitter, Wolfgang (1994) Adult Education and Associational Life in Frankfurt am Main and Barcelona: a structural comparison in Marriott and Hake (eds) *Cultural and Intercultural Experiences in European Adult Education*, pp.37–51.

Silver, Harold (1965) *The Concept of Popular Education*. London: MacGibbon & Kee.

Simon, Brian (1960) *Studies in the History of Education 1780–1870*. London: Lawrence and Wishart.

Simon, Frank and Van Damme Dirk (1993) Education and Improvement in a Belgian industrial town (1860–1890). Francois Laurent and the working classes in Ghent in *History of Education*, 1993, Vol.22, No.1, pp.63–84.

Skilling, H. Gordon (1994) *T.G. Masaryk: Against the Current, 1882–1914*. London: Macmillan.

Smith, Mark (2005) Paulo Freire, Infed org. Available at: http://www.inf(ed)org/ thinkers/et–freir.htm. [Accessed 6 June 2006].

Solá, Pere (1996) The Divorce between University and Popular Universities in Pre-Civil War Catalonia, in Hake, Steele and Tiana (eds) *Masters, Missionaries and Militants*, pp.61–80.

Soós, Pál (1988) The Universities and Adult Education in Hungary, in *International Journal of University Adult Education*, Vol.XXVII, No.3, 1988, pp.23–7.

Steele, Tom (1987) From Class Consciousness to Cultural Studies: the WEA in West Yorkshire, 1914–1950, *Studies in the Education of Adults*, Vol.19, No.2, Autumn 1987, pp.109–26.

—— (1992) A Science for Democracy: The Growth of University Extension in Europe 1890–1920 in Marriott and Hake (eds) *Cultural and Intercultural Experiences in European Adult Education*, pp.61–85.

—— (1998) Elisée Reclus and Patrick Geddes: Geographies of the Mind, the Regional Study in the Global Vision. Edinburgh: University of Edinburgh, Centre for Continuing Education, Tom Schuller (ed.) Occasional Paper.

Steele, Tom and Taylor, Richard (1995) *Learning Independence, A Political Outline of Indian Adult Education*. Leicester: NIACE.

Steenberg-Horsens, Andreas (1907) 'Das Volksbildungwesen in Denmark', in Schultze and Harmdorff, *Archiv fur das Volksbildungswesen*.

Stelmaszuk, Zofia Waleria (1994) Helena Radlinska and the School of Adult Education and Social Work at the Free University of Poland in Marriott and Hake (eds) *Cultural and Intercultural Experiences*, pp.224–46.

Stifter, Christian (1996) Knowledge, Authority and Power: The impact of university extension on popular education in Vienna 1890–1910 in Hake, Steele and Tiana (eds) *Masters, Missionaries and Militants*, pp.159–90.

—— (2005) Short historical introduction, Vienna: Österreichisches Volkshochularchiv. Available at: http://www.vhs.or.at/archiv/english.htm, [Accessed 18 November 2005].

Swindells, Julia (1995) 'Are We not Half the Nation?' Women and the 'Radical Tradition' of Adult Education 1867–1919 in Mayo, M. and Thompson, J. (eds) *Adult Learning, Critical Intelligence and Social Change*, Leicester, NIACE, pp.34–46.

Thomas, J.E. and Elsey, B. (1985) *International Biography of Adult Education*. Nottingham: University of Nottingham.

Thompson, A. (1929) Sweden: Popular Lectures in *WAAE International Handbook*, pp.406–11.

Thompson, E.P. (1968) *The Making of the English Working Class*. Harmondsworth, Penguin Books.

301

Tiana-Ferrer, Alejandro (1996) University Extension and Popular Universities in Spain at the Turn of the Century: An educational strategy for social reform in Hake, Steele and Tiana (eds) *Masters, Missionaries and Militants*, pp.13–38.

Torstensson, Magnus (1994) Expectation and a worthy, respectable position in society: means and aims of library work within the early Labour Movement in Sweden. in 60th IFLA General Conference Proceeding, 21–27 August 1994. Available at: http://www.ifla.org/IV/ifla60/60–torm.htm, [Accessed 12 January 2006].

Toth, J. (1999) Folk High Schools in Hungary 1930–1945 a sociological overview in Filla, Gruber and Jug (eds) *Erwachsenenbildung in der Zwischenkriegszeit*, pp.256–67.

Trier, Gerson (1896) A Visitor to the Cambridge Summer School, *UEJ*, December 1896, Vol.II, No.12, pp.37–8.

Trzeciakowski, Lech (1988) The Role of Learned Societies in the Development of Polish Culture During the Period of the Partitions in *East European Quarterly*, Vol.XXII, No.3, September 1988, pp.291–303.

Ueberschlag G. and Muller F. (eds) (1987) *Education Populaire: objectif d'hier et d'aujourd'hui*. Lille: Presses Universitaire de Lille.

Uglow, Jenny (2002) *The Lunar Men the Friends who made the Future*. London: Faber and Faber.

van Gent, Bastiaan (1987) Government and Voluntary Organisations in the Netherlands: Two hundred years of adult education and information in *International Journal of Lifelong Education*, Vol.6, No.4, October–December 1987, pp.279–94.

—— (1991) Toynbee Work in the Netherlands in Friedenthal-Haase, et al. *British-Dutch-German Relationships*, 211–26,

Vergidis, Dimitris (1992) Greece in Jarvis (ed.) *Perspectives in Adult Education and Training*, pp.219–32.

von Koch, G.H. (1907) Volksbildungsarbeit in Schweden in Schultze and Hamdorff, *Archiv*, pp.296–302 (Stuart Marriott's translation and notes).

Wahlin, Vagn (1993) Denmark, Slezvig-Holstein and Grundtvig in the 19th Century in Allchin et al. (eds) *Heritage and Prophecy*, pp.243–70.

Wangermann, Ernst (1969) *From Joseph II to the Jacobin Trials: Government Policy and Public Opinion in the Habsburg Dominions in the Period of the French Revolution*. New York: Oxford University Press.

Waxweiler, Emile (1893) in *The University Extension World* (Chicago, USA) November 1893, p.154.

Webb, R.K. (1960) *Harriet Martineau: A Radical Victorian*. London: Heinemann.

Webster, Nesta H. (1928) *Secret Societies and Subversive Movements*, n.p., Christian Book Club of America.

Weisberger, R. William (1986) The True Harmony Lodge: A Mecca of Masonry and the Enlightenment in Josephinian Vienna in *East European Quarterly*, Vol.XX, No.2, June 1986, pp.129–40.

Wintle, Michael J. (2000) *An Economic and Social History of the Netherlands, 1800–1920: Demographic, Economic, and Social Transition*. Cambridge, UK; New York: Cambridge University Press.

WAAE (1929) *International Handbook of Adult Education*. London: World Association for Adult Education.

Wright, T.R. (1986) *The Religion of Humanity, The Impact of Comtean Positivism on Victorian Britain*. Cambridge: Cambridge University Press.

Yeaxlee, Basil (ed.) (1922) *Settlements, Their Outlook*. London.

Zavala, Iris M. (1971) *Masones Communeros y Carbonarios*. Madrid: Siglo Vientiuno de España Editores.

Zeldin, Theodore (1967) Higher Education in France, 1848–1940, in *Journal of Contemporary History*. Vol.2, No.3, 1967, pp.53–80.

—— (1979) *France 1848–1945, Politics and Anger*. Oxford: Oxford University Press.

Index

Aberdeen, Lady, 161
Abramoff, M.Y., 268
    Sunday Schools in Russia, 268
    The Book for Adults, 268
Academia dei Lincei, 19
Academia del Cimento, 19
Académie des Sciences, 23
Académie Française, 23
Action Française, 120
Adler, Friedrich, 156, 177
agrarian socialist movement (Hungary), 250
Agrupacion Artistica Socialista, 108
Altamira, Rafael, 103, 104, 107
America, 246, 283, 284, 286, 290, 291
    (*see also* USA)
Amsterdam, 229, 230, 232, 235, 236, 238
Anarchism, 104, 110
anarchist, 100, 108–17, 135, 143, 148, 248, 266
anarchists, 94, 106, 108, 110, 111, 112, 113, 117, 145, 148, 226
Andalusia, 100
Andersen, Hans Christian, 67
Anglo-Saxon, 76, 79, 206, 208, 209, 218, 241–6
anticlericalism, 94, 95, 96, 103, 112, 125, 134, 137, 215, 229, 238
anti-Semitism, 162, 246
Anti-Socialist laws, 165, 170
Arbeiterbibliotheken, 173
Arbeiterkreisen, 1
Arbeiterbildung, 62, 170
Arbeiterbildungsvereine, 154, 157, 179
Arbeitsgemeinschaft, 156, 163, 165
Arbeturinstitut, 192

Aristotle, 287
Arosgarden Institute, 194
Association for the Encouragement of Popular Scientific Education, 231
Association for Scientific Courses (ASC) (Poland), 266
Association of Folk Reading Rooms (TCL) (Poland) 262
Association of Rural Youth (*Wici*), 262
Ateneos, 11, 59, 98, 102–7,
Ateneo Scientifico, Literario y Artistico, 105
Athenaeum, 247, 274
Athens, 277, 278
Austria, 36, 37, 156, 158, 174–83, 249, 256
Austrian (Poland), 245, 264, 272, 273
Austro–fascism, 183
Austro-Hungarian Empire, 174, 182, 241

Babaud-Laribière, 134
Bacon, Francis, 6, 7, 8, 21, 46, 80, 171
Balcescu, Nicolae, 273
Balkans, 249, 272–78, 279
Bakhtin, Mikhail, 43
Bakunin, Mikhail, 111
    Bakuninite, 111
Baltic States, 185, 186, 267, 270–2
Banning, Willem, 237
Barcelona, 100, 103, 104, 105, 106, 107, 109, 112, 114, 117
Bartok, Bela, 255
Batavian Republic, 29, 228
Bauman, Zigmund, 267, 289
Bäurle, Theodor, 156
Bazala, Albert, 276
Bebel, Auguste, 64

Belgian Socialist Party, 109, 130
Belgium, 125, 130, 209–25, 227–39, 259, 266
Belgrade, 241, 276
Beowulf, 79
Berlin, 158, 159, 165, 171
Berlin Society of Sciences, 30
Bernstein, Eduard, 172, 173
bibliothèques populaires, 136
Bildung, 12, 72, 150–2, 156, 170, 171, 201, 204, 205, 206
Birmingham Lunar Society, 27, 43
Blumauer, Alois, 34
Boccaccio, 21
Boccaccio, Giovanni, 21
Bohemia, 21, 36, 242–5
Bohemian Society of Sciences, 36
Boletin de la ILE, 103
Bomholt, Julius, 85
Born, Ignatz von, 34
Bourbon Restoration (Spain), 95
Bourgeois, Leon, 126, 127, 128, 129, 137, 140, 141
Bourse de Travail, 146
Brandes, Georg, 85
Brazil, 291
Britain, 187, 192, 197, 209, 216, 217, 221, 229, 236, 239, 280, 290
British, 188, 191, 194, 195, 205, 207
Brentano, 158, 159
Brougham, Henry Peter, Lord, 188
  Practical Observations upon the Education of the People, 188
Bruno, Giordano, 22
Brussels, 109, 130, 212–27, 238
Brussels Exhibition, 224
Bucharest, 274, 275
Budapest, 250–4
Buisson, Frederic, 139, 140
Bukovniks (Slovenia), 276
Bulgaria, 272–3
Bulgarian Learned Society, 272
Bulgarian National Revival, 272

Burns, Robbie, 50
bürgerliche Gesellschaft, 31

Cabinet des Freres Dupuy, 23
Calvinist, 255
Cambridge, 88, 89
Cánovas del Castillo, Antonio, 101
Carlyle, Thomas, 49, 55, 157, 161
carnival, 20
Carpenter, Edward, 61
Casas del Pueblo, 108
Castrén, Zachris, 205
  The State and Liberal   Adult Education, 205
Castro, Fernando de, 98
Catalonia, 101, 105, 111, 117
  Catalan, 106, 107, 109, 115, 117
Cathars, 21
Catholic Action movement, 95
Catholic Country Association, 254
Catholic Workers' Circles, 95
Cavour, Giuseppi, 118
Cederblad, Carl, 194
  Our Nation and Education, 194
Centros Obreros, 112
Cercle d'Enseignement laïque, 115
Chaine d'Union, 138
Charles University, 241
Chartism, 41, 53, 54, 55
Chaucer, Geoffrey, 21
Christian Socialism, 158f, 238
Christiana, 207
Cieszkowski, August, 38
Cobbett, William, 53, 55
Coleridge, Samuel Taylor, 159
Comenius, Jan, 4, 243
Communism, 253, 264, 280
Comte, Auguste, 5, 7, 9, 12, 96, 121, 127–37, 139, 143, 192
  Comtean, 125, 145, 246
Comtean positivism, 85
  A Discourse on the Positive Spirit (1844), 133

A General View of Positivism (1849), 133

The Catechism of Positive Religion (1852), 133

Cours de philosophie positive (1853), 132

Condorcet, Jean Antoine, Marquis de, 56

Congres international d'Enseignement superieur, 231

Congress of People's Universities, 269

Congress of Popular Education, 269

Congresso Pedagogico, 104

Constantinople, 272

Coopération des Idées, 144, 145

Copenhagen, 67, 68, 77, 86–9, 185, 186

Cosmopolitanism, 286

Croce, Benedetto, 228

Czarist, 258, 267, 270

Czechoslovakia, 5, 17, 36, 64, 242–49, 252, 259, 276

'Daltonisation', 236

Danish Association for Folk High Schools, 89

Danish folk high schools, 1, 67–91, 158, 162, 164, 167, 185, 188, 191, 197, 209, 237, 238, 242, 253, 254, 258, 262, 266, 269, 271

Davenport, Alan, 52

Darwin, Charles, 89, 110, 127

Darwinism, 90

Davidsfonds, 213

Denis, Hector, 221, 222, 226

Deherme, Georges, 59, 148–53

Denmark, 11, 14, 67–91, 185, 186–88, 191, 197, 206, 255, 259, 262, 271

de Labra, 103

Desaguliers, 32

Descartes, Renee, 22

Desjardins, Paul, 144

Destrée, Jules, 130, 211, 227

Dewey, John, 78, 113, 116, 291

Dick, James, 117

Diderot, Denis, 70

Diggers and Levellers, 44

Dissenting Academies, 27

Divinis Illius Magistri, 93

Dreyfus affair (1896), 59, 134, 142, 143

Drtina, Franz, 242–5

Dugteren, van, 235, 236

Durkheim, Emile, 128, 131, 152, 153, 246

De la division du travail social, 128

Duruy, Victor, 141

Dvorak, Anton, 246

Dziubinska, Jadwiga, 259–2, 266

Ecole Ferrer de Lausanne, 116

Ecole Normale Superieure, 150

Ecole Pratique des Hautes Etudes, 141

Ecole superieure gantoise pour l'Enseignement du peuple, 218

educación integral, 108, 109

education intégrale, 56, 57, 59, 100, 111

Extension Universitaire, l', 225

Eliot, George, 138

Elgeskog, Justus, 190

Einstein, Alfred, 175, 176

England, 214, 216, 218, 224, 225, 235, 239, 250, 251, 266, 268

English, 194, 195, 196, 197, 201, 206, 207, 209, 214–39

English Revolution, 41, 43, 45, 46, 48

Eötvös, Baron Joseph, 250, 252

Erasmus, Desiderius, 44, 70

Erdberg, Robert von, 156, 159–74

Escuela Moderna, 113, 118, 120, 121

Espinas, Alfred, 142

Estonia, 270

Fabre, Auguste, 143

Fachgruppen, 182

Falangist, 118

Federation Regional Epsilon, 110

Federazione Italiana delle Bibblioteche Popolari, 122

feminism, 64, 137, 206, 232, 235, 246, 286, 289

Fennomania, 197, 201–4

Ferdinand VII, 93

Ferguson, Adam, 25, 51, 72, 100, 130, 131

Astronomy explained upon Sir Isaac Newton's Principles, 25

Ferrer, Francisco, 11, 58, 59, 94, 103–7, 110, 114–17, 123

The Origins and Ideals of the Modern School (1913), 116

Ferry, Jules, 115, 135, 139, 140, 141

Fichte, Johann Gottlieb, 96, 97

Figueras, Jose del perojo y, 99

Finland, 14, 39, 185, 186, 188, 197–205, 254

Finnish folk high schools, 188, 190–7, 198, 203–6

Fischer, Kuano, 99

Flamingant', 213, 215, 218

Flemish popular education, 209–18, 223, 231, 238

'Flying University', 258, 266

Franklin, Benjamin, 25

Freire, Paulo, 290–2

Cultural Action for Freedom, 291

Pedagogy of the Oppressed, 291

Extension de l'Universite Libre, 220

Flitner, Wilhelm, 156, 167

Folk High Schools (Holland), 231, 238

Folk High Schools (Poland), 242, 253–71

Folk House (Holland), 230–2, 238

folkbildning, 86, 187

folkelighed, 71, 76, 263

folkeoplysning, 73

Folkeuniversitetsforeningen, 87

Folkuniversitetsforeninger, 87

Fondation Universitaire de Belleville, 144

Forchhammer, Froken Henni, 86, 87

foredrag, 78

Fourier, Charles, 53, 57, 111, 132, 137, 142

Fourierists, 102, 147

France, Anatole, 115, 144

Francoism, 128

Frankfurt, 161, 165

Frédericq, Paul, 213–16

Free Church (Sweden), 188, 192

Free Lyceum (Szabad Lyceum), 251

Free University of Brussels, 130

Université Libre, 224

Free University for Political and Economic subjects, 273

Free University of Poland, 266

Freemasonry, 3, 10, 12, 30, 94, 107, 125, 128, 134, 135, 136–42, 145

freemasons, 96, 110, 125, 132, 142, 145, 146, 175, 226, 246 (*see also* masons)

Speculative Masons, 34, 154, 229

French Revolution, 95, 127, 134

Friends of Science of Warsaw, 256

Froebel, Gottfried, 99, 113

Gabrys, J., 272

Education of youth abroad and in our country, 272

Galileo, Galilei, 19

Gambetta, Leon, 136, 139

Gandhi, Mahatma, 73, 290

Garibaldi, Giuseppi, 118, 250

Gasset, Ortega y, 99, 101

General Magazine of Arts and Sciences, 25

Germany, 30, 149–74, 235, 256, 259, 266, 273

German philosphical idealism, 76, 200, 246

*Geisteswissenschaft*en, 151

Gesellschaft für Volksbildung, 157

Ghent, 210–18

Gide, Charles, 127, 142, 143, 144

308

Principles of Political Economy (1883), 127
Glasgow, 7, 8, 38, 189
globalisation, 280, 281, 285
Glöckel, Otto, 182
Gothenburg, 195
Gramsci, Antonio, 109, 114, 120–3, 178
Grand Orient, 33, 125, 135, 136, 138
Greece, 277–78
Greef, van der, 221, 226, 227
Groningen, 231, 234, 235
Grundtvig, Nicolae, 10, 11, 62, 63, 67–91, 155, 162, 167, 200, 254, 258, 262, 263, 264, 267, 269, 271, 272, 274, 275
World History, 74
Grundtvigian, 191, 198, 204
Guillotin, Dr., 33
Gusti, Dimitire, 274, 275
Guyau, Jean Marie, 58

Habermas, Jürgen, 1–5, 10, 24, 27, 41–3, 46, 65, 84, 151, 154, 183, 283, 285, 289
Habsburg, 33, 64, 247
Hagman, Sofia, 204
Hamel, van, 231, 232, 234, 235
Haret, Spiru, 274
Hartmann, Ludo Moritz, 158–1, 180, 181
Hartmann, Willem, 229
Havlicek, Karel, 242, 247, 248
Heaford, William, 115
Hegel, George, 96
   Hegelian, 98, 196, 200
Helsinki, 199, 202, 203, 204, 205
Heide, Hermien van der, 237, 238
Herder, Johann Gottfried von, 62, 71, 72, 76
Hermes, Gertud, 163, 164
Hill, Christopher, 43, 44, 45, 46, 47
Hirdman, Gunnar, 193, 194
Hirsch, Arthur, 215, 222, 223

Hjarne, Harald, 90
Hobbes, Thomas, 2, 22,
Hobsbawm, Eric, 3, 12, 258
Holland, 209, 214, 228–38 (*see also* Netherlands)
Holyoake, George, 143
Horthy Regime, 251, 253, 256
Humanus Genis, 136
Humboldt Academy, 165
Hume, David, 7, 8, 9, 22
Hungary, 64, 241–56, 273
Hus, Jan, 247
   Hussites, 21
Hutcheson, Francis, 7, 8, 9, 101
Huygens, Cornelie, 235

Ibáñez, Blasco, 106
Ibarra, Eduardo, 107
Ideal de la Humanidad, 98
independent working class education, 156, 170–4, 239
Institución Libre de Enseñanza (ILE), 101, 102, 103, 104, 109, 113
   Institutionalistas, 102–4
intelligentsia, 241, 256, 257, 266
International Committee for Christian Socialism, 237
International Order of Good Templars (IOGT), 190, 191
Iorga, Nicolae, 275

Jacobin, 42, 48, 49, 50
Jacobinism, 27, 216
Jacobites, 32
Jesuits, 94
Jewish, 149, 160, 181, 255
Jews, 157
Journal des Sçavans, 24
Journal für Freymaurer, 34
Jowett, Benjamin, 100

Kafka, Franz, 245
Kalevala, 199

kansansivistys, 199
kansanvalistus, 199
Kansanvalistusseura (KVS), Society for People's Enlightenment, 201–4
Kant, Immanuel, 2, 7, 287
Kerdijk, Arnold, 234
Key, Ellen, 86
Khun, Bela, 253
Kierkegaard, Soren, 67
Kiev, 269
Knappert, Emilie, 232, 237, 238
Knauf, Heinrich, 172
'Knowledge' Chartism, 10
Knox, John, 50
Kold, Christian, 11, 14, 63, 65, 81, 82, 83, 240, 262
Kolping, Adolph, 154, 155
Korsgaard, Ove, 69, 71, 72, 84, 85, 86
Kosmowska, Irena, 260
Kossuth, Louis, 249
Kraft, Jenny, 236
Krakow, 241, 264–6
Krause, Karl, 96–9
    Krausism, 11, 95–101, 104, 114
Krok, 36
Kropotkin, Peter, 57, 58, 111, 114
Krzywicki, Ludwik, 266

L'Action Maçonique, 137
La Helga General, 114
La Revista Blanca, 113
Labour Party (British), 52
Latin, 80, 88
Laurent, Francois, 210–12
Latvia, 271
Le Salleans, 94
Leclere, Leon, 214, 216, 218–22, 225, 226
    Les Universités Populaires dans Les Pays Anglo-Saxon, 218
Leiden, 230–2, 237, 238
Leeds, 28
Leo XIII, 95, 141

Lernfreiheit, 169
Lesegesellschaften, 154
Ley Moyano, 94
Liebknecht, Wilhelm, 1, 171, 172
libertarian, 108, 110, 112, 115
Liebniz, Gottfried, 30, 243
Liga Internacional para la Educacion Racional de la Infancia, 110
Ligue de L'Avenir, 137
Ligue de l'enseignement (France), 12, 130, 136–9, 146, 250
    Ligue Française de l'Enseignement, 144
Ligue de l'Enseignement (Belgium), 209–153
Lilburne, John, 47
Lister, Joseph, 38
Literary and Philosophical Societies, 28
Lithuania, 272
Lisbon, 109
Littré, Emile, 5, 134, 135, 139
Llorens, Francisco Javier, 100
livoplysning, 68
Locke, John, 22, 70, 71
Lodge of the Nine Sisters, 33,
Loi Ferry (1882), 115
London Corresponding Society, 43, 49, 51
London Working Men's Association, 54
Lorenzo, Anselmo, 111, 114, 117
Louis Napoleon, 137
Ludwiczak, Antonin, 262
Lukacs, George, 252, 253
Lundell, J.L., 194, 195, 196
    The Participation of the Workers in Contemporary Civilisation, 196
Luther, Martin, 70, 78
    Lutheran, 69, 70, 77, 185, 199, 206, 238, 254, 255
Luxemburg, Rosa, 172, 173, 258
Lvov, 241

Mach, Ernst, 158, 159, 175, 176, 177

Macé, Jean, 137, 138
Machado, 96
Madrid, 97, 98, 102, 103, 105, 106, 109, 112
Madrid University, 97
Magyar, 249, 252
Maison du Peuple (Belgium), 109, 209
Mansbridge, Albert, 77, 165
Marists, 94
Martin, Benjamin, 25
Martineau, Harriet, 5, 133
Marx, Karl, 8, 121, 131, 132
    Grundrisse, 282
    Marxism, 12, 13, 86, 121, 143, 148, 149, 156, 158, 175–7, 248
    Marxist, 60, 62, 123, 143, 159, 171–6, 252, 270, 281, 289–1
Masaryk, T.G., 37, 242–49, 252
    Realist' movement, 248
Masaryk Institute, 246
masons, 31, 50, 54, 60, 107, 118, 119, 135–38, 146
    masonic, 50, 54, 60, 95, 103, 115, 118, 125, 126, 134–8, 142–7, 154, 159, 175, 176, 179, 181, 190, 209–15, 238, 247, 250, 266, 277
Massol, Andre, 135
Maurras, Andre, 120
Mazzini, Giuseppi, 122
Matice ceska, 36
Mechanics Institutes, 28, 157, 179
Mehring, Franz, 172, 173
Menzel, Alfred, 164
Mercier, Helene, 232, 235
Mersenne, Marin, 23
Meuron, Agatho, 202
Mickiewicz, Adam, 264, 265
Milan, 118, 119, 122, 123
Mill, John Stuart, 5, 8, 64, 135, 138, 145, 175, 246
    On the Subjection of Women, 246
Milne-Edwards, 127
Milton, John, 44, 47

Montgolfier brothers, 33
Montmor, Habert de, 24
Montoliu, 104
Montpellier, 59, 142
More, Thomas, 44
Morral, Mateo, 117
Morris, William, 60, 61
Moscow, 242, 267
Movements of Landless Rural Workers, 291
Munich, 159
Muarina, Zenta, 271
Mussolini, Benito, 121, 123, 124
mutual improvement societies, 42, 50–3

Napoleon, 36
National Socialist Party (Czech), 248
National Society for Catholic Education, 168
nationalism, 71, 76, 77, 89, 186, 196, 203, 206, 212–16, 228, 241–60, 267, 276, 279
Natorp, Paul, 159
Nazism, 85, 149, 169, 183, 238, 256, 262, 280
Negt and Kluge, 5, 41
Neill, A.S., 116
Neo-Kantians, 100
Netherlands, 28
Neue Richtung (New Direction), 12, 14, 15, 149, 156, 159, 162, 165, 166, 172, 209, 231, 237
New Atlantis, 22
Newton, Sir Isaac, 8, 22,
Nietzsche, Friedrich, 150, 153, 166
Nimes, 59, 142, 143
Nordic, 185, 186, 188, 197, 208, 259, 270
Noreen, Adolf, 194
Norse Mythology, 74
Norway, 14, 67, 79, 89, 185, 186, 187, 188, 206–8
Nussbaum, Martha, 286, 287, 288, 289

Nyrere, Julius, 290
Nyström, Anton, 192, 193, 196, 205, 207

Odessa, 268, 269
Olsson, Oscar, 189, 190
Ottoman, 249, 272, 277
Our House, 232
Owen, Robert, 52, 53, 54
    Owenism, 41, 53, 54
    Owenite, 127
Owenite Halls of Science, 54
Ottäkring, *Volksheim*, 13, 177, 178–2
Oviedo, 105, 106, 107, 108

Paine, Thomas, 24, 48, 49, 52, 55
    The Age of Reason, 24
    The Rights of Man, 24
    Common Sense, 25
Palacky, Frantisek, 242, 244
Paris, 33, 226, 228–1
Paris Commune, 58
Parnassus Literary Society, 277
Peasant Party (Poland), 263
people's universities (Poland), 241, 242, 270–7
Pestalozzi, 113
Petersburg, St., 265, 268, 269
Petzold, Alfons, 181
Piarists, 94
pillarisation, 212, 228, 230, 238
Pius XI, 93
Place, Francis, 52
Poland, 185, 242, 256–66, 270
Polish Socialist party, 258
Popper, Karl, 175–
Popular Cultural Associations (Hungary), 250
popular educational movements (Latin America), 280, 289, 290
Popular Library Movement (Germany), 162

popular universities, 93, 102–4, 105, 106, 108, 119–23, 180, 264, 267 (*see also* people's universities)
Posada, Adolfo, 103, 105
positivism, 97, 99, 109, 120, 121, 127, 134, 136, 142–7, 192, 195 (*see also* Comtean positivism)
positivist, 97, 99, 100, 121, 125, 130–8, 140, 144, 152, 214, 215, 234, 269, 274, 277
Positivist Library, 130
Positivist Society for the popularisation of science, 192
Posnanie, 265
Povlsen, Alfred, 89
Poznan Society of the Friends of Science, 38
Prague, 36, 241–6, 272, 276
Priestley, Joseph, 25, 50, 80
The Proper Object of Education in the Present State of the World, 28
Protestant Association for the Practical Study of Social Problems, 142
Protestantism, *passim*
Protopoff, Prof., 268, 269
Proudhon, Pierre-Joseph, 53, 57, 111, 126, 135, 248
Prussia, 37
Puritan, 26
Purkynê, Jan, 36
Poland, 5, 17, 37

Radical Party (France), 115, 127, 135, 137, 139, 140
Radical Socialist government (France), 126
Radio Popular University, 231
Radlinska, Helena, 260, 266
Raet, Lodewijk de, 216, 217
Rational Schools, Spain (Anarchist), 59, 103, 112
Reclus, Elisée, 57–9, 114, 115, 226, 227

La Nouvelle Geographie Universelle, 226
Reich, Emil, 159, 164, 181
Reid, Thomas, 51, 100
Riedel, J. Bruinwold, 233, 234
Rein, Wilhelm, 158, 159
Religion of Humanity, 131, 134
Remonstrance of Many Thousand Citizens, 47
Renan, Ernest, 141
Renaudot, Theophraste, 23
republicanism, 105, 108, 135
Rerum Novarum, 95
Reventlow brothers, 71
Revista Contemporánea, 99
Rhein-Mainische Verband, 163
Richelieu, Cardinal, 23
Río, Sanz del, 96–9, 101, 128
Rios, Giner de los, 96–105, 113, 114, 123
Risorgimento, 118, 119
Rivera, Primo de, 113
Rochdale Pioneers, 149
Roman Catholicism, *passim*
Romania, 241, 273–5
Rotterdam Toynbee Association, 232
Rousseau, Jean-Jacques, 27, 70, 71, 72, 113, 114, 127, 131
Runeberg, Johan Ludwig, 200
Ruskin, John, 80, 166
Ruskin College, Oxford, 146, 205, 290
Russia, 37, 256, 267–71
    Russian, 257–59, 261, 264, 265, 269–3
Russification, 270

Saint-Simon, 53, 127, 132
    Saint-Simonian, 100, 135
Salamanca, 95, 104, 105
Salesians, 94
Salomon, Alice, 160
Saragossa, 104, 105, 107

Scandinavia, 30, 68, 72, 90, 186, 187, 194, 199, 206
Schaw, William, 31
Schleswig Holstein, 77, 155
Schulze, Ernst, 158
Scotland, 3
Scottish Enlightenment, 7, 32, 130, 188
Scottish Rites, 33
Seailles, Gabriel, 144
Secular Societies, 157
Self-Teaching Handbook, 257
Senden, van, 237
September Revolution (Spain 1866), 98
Seville, 103, 104, 105, 111
Sheffield Constitutional Society, 49
Sheffield Corresponding Society, 49
Sibelius, Jean, 203
    Karelia Suite, 203
Sidney, Philip, 44
Skraeppenborg, Peder Larsen, 81
Slovenia, 276–7
Smiles, Samuel, 53
Smith, Adam, 7, 8, 50, 55, 130, 131, 229
Snellman, J.V., 200, 201, 206
Social Catholicism, 103
Social Democracy, 159, 165, 173, 187, 192
Social Democratic Party (SDP)
    (Austria), 176–82
    (Czech), 248, 251, 255
    (Denmark), 85
    (Finland), 204, 205
    (Germany), 61, 156, 157, 159, 170–4
    (Holland) 237–39
Social Weekly, 234, 235
socialism, 95, 100, 108, 111, 129, 137, 144, 147, 149, 159, 176, 187, 206, 246, 252, 259, 278, 285, 289
socialist, 104, 107–15, 120–9, 137, 142, 148, 149, 156, 157, 164, 170–6, 186, 187, 192, 204, 205, 208–17, 225, 227–30, 235, 238, 250, 257, 265
Socialist Institute, 236

Societé d'Economie Populaire, 149
Sociétés ouvriéres, 210
Sociétés d'instruction populaire, 146
Sociétés républicaines d'instruction, 138
Society for Adult Education (Germany), 157, 166
Society for the Common Benefit (SBF) (Nut), 28, 209, 213, 228–4, 238
Society for the Diffusion of Useful Knowledge (SDUK), 189
Society for the Improvement of the Working Class, 229
Society for Primary Education, 264
Society of Friends of Science of Warsaw, 37
Society of Jesus, 118
Society of the Museum of Transylvania, 252
Sofia, 273
Solarz, Ignacy, 262–4
Solarz, Zofia, 263
solidarism, 126–9, 140, 142, 147
Soliman, Angelo, 35n
Sorbonne, 139, 141, 144, 150
Soriano, Trinidad, 111
Sorø folk high school, 75, 76
Soviet, 242, 251, 253, 270–2
Spain, 11, 93–118
Spencer, Herbert, 100, 110, 113, 246
Spittalfields Mathematical Society, 51
Steiner, Rudolph, 171, 172
Stockholm, 192, 193, 195, 196, 199, 207
'Strength through Joy', 169
Stuart, James, 105, 130
Studenter och Arbetare, 197
studieförbund, 188
Study Circle (Swedish), 188, 189, 190,
Summer University (Debrecen), 253
Sweden, 14, 67, 79, 85, 89, 90, 185–208, 259, 270
Swedish Workers' Educational Association (ABF), 191, 193
Syndicalist, 210

Szabó Ervin, 251
Szechenyi, Count Istvan, 250

Tampere, 198, 204
temperance, 187, 189, 190, 192
Temperance Movement, 188
Thessaloniki, 278
Thompson, E.P., 43, 49, 50
Toledo, 109
Tonisson, Jaan, 270
Tory mobs, 28
Toynbee Hall, 104, 105, 140, 158, 160, 214, 232, 233, 235
Transylvania, 252, 274
Treaty of Württemberg, 70
Trier, Gerson, 88, 89
True Harmony Lodge, 34
Tull, Jethro, 229
Turin, 119, 120, 121, 123, 124
Turku, 199, 200, 202, 203
Türr, Istvan, 250
Tyndale, William, 44

Ujamaa, 290
Ulmanis, Karlis, 271
Unanumo y Jugo, Miguel de, 101, 113
United States of America (USA), 187, 276, 281–4
universita populari (Italy), 122
Universitätsausdehnung, 159
universités populaires, 1, 12, 15, 59, 123–126, 140–7, 209, 210, 213, 217, 235, 236, 265
university extension, 1, 5, 9, 11, 12–17, 67, 86–8, 90, 102–6, 122, 123, 130, 135, 138, 141, 142, 145–7, 157–67, 178–1, 188, 194–7, 203, 206, 207, 209–38, 241–5, 249, 251–4, 264, 265, 267–75
University Extension Assoc. of Copenhagen, 86
University Extension Journal, 88
'University of Tamissaari', 205

University of Vienna, 159, 177, 179
Uppsala, 194, 196
Urania, *Volksheim,*156, 179
USSR, 271

Valencia, 104, 105, 106, 109
Vandervelde, Emile, 130, 209, 215, 227
Vassilieff, Prof. A., 269
Venstre, 180
Vernet, Madelaine, 59
Vico, Giambattista, 22
Victor Emmanuel II, 118
Vienna, 33, 158–9, 176–83, 247, 257, 276
Vienna Circle (*Wiener Kreis*), 177, 178,
Vinogradoff, Prof., 267
Virgin cult, 248
Virumaa, 270
Voionimaa, Vaino, 205
Vold, Mourley, 207
Volders, Jean, 107
Volk, 279
Volksbildstätten, 169
Volksbildung, 156, 157, 159, 160, 161, 162, 165, 178, 182, 199, 203
Volksbildungsarchiv, 162
Volksgemeinschaft, 162
Volksgeist, 76, 200
Volksheim, 1, 13, 158, 161, 177, 178–3
Volkshochschule, 159, 162, 178, 179
Volkshuisen, 210, 230
Volksuniversität, 179
Volksuniversiteiten, 231
Voltaire, 33, 70, 85
Vooruit, 215, 217

Wagner, Charles, 144
Wagner, Richard, 149, 153
Walloon, 209, 213, 217
Warrington Academy, 27
Warsaw, 258, 259, 266
Warsaw Scientific Society, 38

Waxweiler, Emile, 212, 214, 221, 225
Whiggery, 32
Willemsfonds, 213
Williams, Raymond, 3
Winstanley, Gerrard, 45, 46
Wintsch, Jean, 59
Essai d'Institution Ouvriere, 116
Wissenschaft, 97, 151, 152, 172
Wlassics, Jules, 252, 253
Wordsworth, William, 78
Wohlfahrtspflege, 160
Women Question, The, 260
Women's Educational Circle, 258
Woodbrooke, 209, 237, 238
Workers' Educational Assoc. (WEA) (Britain), 156, 161, 163, 164, 167, 174, 190, 192, 205, 236, 239
Workers' Educational Union (Denmark), 85
(Finland), 205
Workers' Institutes, 189, 192, 195, 198
   Stockholm, 86
Workers' International, 109, 210
workers' movements, 98, 104, 105, 108, 125
Workers' Party (Poland), 264
Working Men's College, 141
World Association for Adult Education (WAAE), 83, 155, 164–68, 190, 196, 235, 250, 255, 258, 266, 273
World Citizen, 287
Wright, Viktor Julius von, 204
Wyclif, John 21

yellow unionism, 95
Yugoslavia, 275, 277

Zagreb, 242, 276
Zetkin, Clara, 172
Zilsel, Edgar, 177, 178
Zola, Emile, 115, 144
Zois, Baron Zig, 276

315